THE INTER-BANK BOND MARKET IN THE PEOPLE'S REPUBLIC OF CHINA

AN ASEAN+3 BOND MARKET GUIDE

AUGUST 2020

ASIAN DEVELOPMENT BANK

ADB

Notes:
ADB recognizes "China" as the People's Republic of China and "Hong Kong" as Hong Kong, China.

In this report, international standards for naming conventions—International Organization for Standardization (ISO) 3166 for country codes and ISO 4217 for currency codes—are used to reflect the discussions of the ASEAN+3 Bond Market Forum to promote and support implementation of international standards in financial transactions in the region. ASEAN+3 comprises the Association of Southeast Asian Nations (ASEAN) plus the People's Republic of China, Japan, and the Republic of Korea.

The economies of ASEAN+3 as defined in ISO 3166 include Brunei Darussalam (BN; BRN); Cambodia (KH; KHM); the People's Republic of China (CH; CHN); Hong Kong, China (HK; HKG); Indonesia (ID; IDN); Japan (JP; JPN); the Republic of Korea (KR; KOR); the Lao People's Democratic Republic (LA; LAO); Malaysia (MY; MYS); Myanmar (MM; MMR); the Philippines (PH; PHL); Singapore (SG; SGP); Thailand (TH; THA); and Viet Nam (VN; VNM). The currencies of ASEAN+3 as defined in ISO 4217 include the Brunei dollar (BND), Cambodian riel (KHR), Chinese renminbi (CNY), Hong Kong dollar (HKD), Indonesian rupiah (IDR), Japanese yen (JPY), Korean won (KRW), Lao kip (LAK), Malaysian ringgit (MYR), Myanmar kyat (MMK), Philippine peso (PHP), Singapore dollar (SGD), Thai baht (THB), and Vietnamese dong (VND).

Contents

Tables and Figures

Figures

Foreword

The Asian Development Bank is working closely with the Association of Southeast Asian Nations (ASEAN) and the People's Republic of China, Japan, and the Republic of Korea—collectively known as ASEAN+3—to develop local currency bond markets and facilitate regional bond market integration under the Asian Bond Markets Initiative for development of the region's resilient financial systems.

Thanks to the efforts of member governments, local currency bond markets in ASEAN, the People's Republic of China, and the Republic of Korea have grown rapidly, with the total outstanding amount of bonds reaching more than USD16 trillion at the end of 2019. Despite this remarkable development, intraregional investment in bond markets has remained subdued. As the Asian Development Bank has estimated that developing Asia will need to invest USD26 trillion from 2016 to 2030 (or USD1.7 trillion per year) in infrastructure to support continued growth, it is critical to mobilize the region's vast savings for the enormous investment needs. As an essential platform for such resource mobilization, financial markets in ASEAN+3 need to be more harmonized for better integration. Also, regional efforts should support developing member countries at the early stages of market development.

The ASEAN+3 Bond Market Forum (ABMF) was established with the endorsement of the ASEAN+3 finance ministers in 2010 as a common platform to foster the standardization of market practices and harmonization of regulations relating to cross-border bond transactions in the region. As an initial step, ABMF published the *ASEAN+3 Bond Market Guide* in 2012, which was welcomed as the first official information source offering a comprehensive explanation of the region's bond markets.

Since publication of the *ASEAN+3 Bond Market Guide*, bond markets in the region have continued to develop. ABMF recognizes the need for revisions to the guide to reflect these changes, though it is never an easy task to keep up with rapid changes in the markets. This report is an outcome of the strong support and contributions of ABMF members and experts, particularly from the People's Republic of China. The report should be recognized as a joint product to support bond market development among ASEAN+3 members. It is our hope that the revised *ASEAN+3 Bond Market Guide* will facilitate further development of the region's bond markets, contribute to increased intraregional bond transactions, and promote efficient capital allocation within the region.

Yasuyuki Sawada
Chief Economist and Director General
Economic Research and Regional Cooperation Department
Asian Development Bank

Acknowledgments

The *ASEAN+3 Bond Market Guide* was first published in 2012 as the initial output of Phase 1 of the ASEAN+3 Bond Market Forum (ABMF).[1] Across the region, domestic bond markets, including the bond market in the People's Republic of China (PRC), have experienced tremendous development over the past 8 years. Now in Phase 3, ABMF would like to share, in the public domain, information on these developments by publishing an update on the China bond market, with a particular focus on the Inter-Bank Bond Market.

The ABMF Sub-Forum 1 team—comprising Satoru Yamadera (Principal Financial Sector Specialist, Asian Development Bank [ADB], Economic Research and Regional Cooperation Department); Kosintr Puongsophol (Financial Sector Specialist, ADB, Economic Research and Regional Cooperation Department); and ADB consultants Shigehito Inukai and Matthias Schmidt, together with ABMF International Expert Hirohiko Suzuki—would like to stress the significance and magnitude of the contributions made by ABMF national members and experts from the PRC, including the China Central Depository & Clearing Co., Ltd.; China Foreign Exchange Trade System; and Shanghai Clearing House Co., Ltd.

The ADB team would also like to express its special thanks to the Financial Market Department of the People's Bank of China and to a number of ABMF International Experts, including Citibank N.A., HSBC, and SWIFT, as well as to China International Capital Corporation Limited. These policy bodies, regulatory authorities, and market institutions generously gave their time for market visit meetings, discussions, and follow-up. They also reviewed and provided inputs on the draft *ASEAN+3 Bond Market Guide for the Inter-Bank Bond Market in the People's Republic of China* over the course of ABMF Phase 3.

No part of this report represents the official views or opinions of any institution that participated in this activity as an ABMF member, observer, or expert. The ABMF Sub-Forum 1 team bears sole responsibility for the contents of this report.

August 2020

ASEAN+3 Bond Market Forum

---

[1] ASEAN+3 refers to the 10 members of the Association of Southeast Asian Nations (ASEAN) plus the People's Republic of China, Japan, and the Republic of Korea.

Abbreviations

ABMF	ASEAN+3 Bond Market Forum		NAFMII	National Association of Financial Market Institutional Investors
ABN	asset-backed notes		NCD	negotiable certificate of deposit
ABS	asset-backed securities			
ADB	Asian Development Bank		NDRC	National Development and Reform Commission
AMBIF	ASEAN+3 Multi-Currency Bond Issuance Framework		OTC	over-the-counter
ASEAN	Association of Southeast Asian Nations		PBOC	People's Bank of China
ASEAN+3	Association of Southeast Asian Nations plus the People's Republic of China, Japan, and the Republic of Korea		PDF	portable document format
CBIRC	China Banking and Insurance Regulatory Commission		PFB	policy bank financial bond
CBRC	China Banking Regulatory Commission		PPN	private placement notes
CCDC	China Central Depository & Clearing Co., Ltd. (ChinaBond)		PRC	People's Republic of China
CFETS	China Foreign Exchange Trade System		QFII	Qualified Foreign Institutional Investor
CFFEX	China Financial Futures Exchange		QOII	Qualified Overseas Institutional Investor
CIBM	China Inter-Bank Bond Market		RMB	Chinese renminbi
CIT	corporate income tax		RQFII	Renminbi Qualified Foreign Institutional Investor
CNY	Chinese renminbi (ISO code)		SAFE	State Administration of Foreign Exchange
CP	commercial paper		SCP	super short-term commercial paper
CRA	credit rating agency		SF1	Sub-Forum 1 of ABMF
CSD	central securities depository		SF2	Sub-Forum 2 of ABMF
CSI	China Securities Index Co., Ltd		SHCH	Shanghai Clearing House Co., Ltd.
CSRC	China Securities Regulatory Commission		SMEs	small and medium-sized enterprises
DCM-FANS	Debt Capital Market Filing Analysis Notification System		SOE	state-owned enterprise
DTA	double taxation agreement		SPV	special purpose vehicle
EXIM	Export–Import Bank of China		SRO	self-regulatory organization
FSDC	Financial Stability and Development Commission		USD	United States dollar (ISO code)
IFRS	International Financial Reporting Standards		VAT	value-added tax
MOF	Ministry of Finance		WHT	withholding tax
MTN	medium-term notes			

USD1 = CNY6.9762
(PBOC rate on 31 December 2019)

Overview

A. Overview of Bond Market Segments

The bond market in the People's Republic of China (PRC) is divided into three market segments: (i) the China Inter-Bank Bond Market (CIBM), (ii) the exchange bond market, and (iii) the commercial banks' counter market. Free-trade zone bonds are not so much a separate market segment as a distinct bond type in the CIBM. Considering the scale of these market segments, the CIBM and the exchange bond market are the dominant segments (Table 1.1); the commercial banks' counter market in effect represents a market segment for on-selling debt financing instruments issued and traded in the CIBM to general and retail investors.

Due to the separate legal, regulatory, and institutional frameworks of the respective market segments, each segment is recognized as a market in its own right; at the same time, however, these market segments complement, interconnect with, and complete each other. This bond market guide describes the CIBM as one of the two main market segments in the PRC accessible to foreign investors.

The scale and style of regulation differs between the CIBM and the exchange bond market. The markets have historically adopted different regulatory approaches from one another. For example, under the supervision of the People's Bank of China (PBOC), the National Association of Financial Market Institutional Investors (NAFMII) admits and administers active market participants and intermediaries in the CIBM and facilitates the registration of debt financing instruments issued by nonfinancial enterprises, pursuant to its mandate as the market's self-regulatory organization (SRO). The PBOC admits foreign institutional investors to the CIBM via a number of investment avenues and also approves issuances by financial institutions.
In comparison, in the exchange bond market, the China Securities Regulatory Commission (CSRC) and the Securities Association of China (SAC), as SROs, and the stock exchanges, as listing and trading authorities, cooperate on regulations with each covering different regulatory objectives. Listing and trading in the exchange bond market falls under the unified guidance of CSRC, which resulted in the establishment of similar and consistent rules at the Shanghai Stock Exchange and the Shenzhen Stock Exchange.

In another example of rules and regulations that differ between these markets, bonds issued in the exchange bond market are legally defined as securities under the Securities Law, while many such instruments issued in the CIBM are not regarded as securities and instead are referred to as debt financing instruments. This is due to the legacy of the different regulatory systems in the PRC. Consequently, this bond market guide uses the term debt financing instruments instead of debt securities.

Table 1.1: Major Bond Market Segments in the People's Republic of China

Feature	Inter-Bank Bond Market (over-the-counter market)	Commercial Banks' Counter Market	Exchange Bond Market
Main regulator	People's Bank of China (PBOC)	PBOC	China Securities Regulatory Commission (CSRC)
Self-regulatory organization (SRO)	National Association of Financial Market Institutional Investors (NAFMII)	N.A.	Securities Association of China (general SRO); Shanghai Stock Exchange (SSE) and Shenzhen Stock Exchange (SZSE) (listing and trading authority SROs)
Trading	China Foreign Exchange Trade System (CFETS)	Commercial banks	SSE and SZSE; National Equities Exchange and Quotations
Central securities depository	China Central Depository & Clearing Co., Ltd. (CCDC or ChinaBond); Shanghai Clearing House (SHCH)	Commercial banks	China Securities Depository and Clearing Co., Ltd. (CSDC or Chinaclear)
Available debt securities or debt financing instruments	CCDC only: government bonds (Treasury bonds), local government bonds, central bank bills, enterprise bonds, collective bonds, financial bonds (commercial bank bonds) SHCH only: medium-term notes, commercial paper, super short-term commercial paper, private placement notes, SME collective notes, asset-backed notes, project revenue notes; Panda bonds, green debt financing tools, project income notes, special-drawing-rights-denominated bonds; negotiable certificates of deposit; CCDC and SHCH: policy bank financial bonds, financial bonds (non-bank financial institution bonds), government-backed (agency) bonds; asset-backed securities; repurchase agreements	Government bonds, local government bonds, policy bank financial bonds (applies to both book-entry and certificated bonds)	Government bonds (Treasury bonds), local government bonds, policy bank financial bonds, government-backed (agency) bonds (e.g., railway bonds), enterprise bonds, securities company bonds and short-term notes, corporate bonds and exchangeable corporate bonds, convertible bonds, asset-backed securities, repurchase agreements
Key investors	Institutional investors (e.g., overseas central banks, international financial organizations, sovereign wealth funds, banks, funds, insurance companies, rural credit cooperatives, securities companies, financial companies, enterprises, overseas institutions, QFII and RQFII (since May 2013), QOII (since February 2016)	Individual investors, small enterprise investors	Small and medium-sized institutional investors (e.g., securities companies, insurance companies, funds, financial companies, qualified individual investors, enterprises), QFII and RQFII, individuals (very limited)

N.A. = not applicable, QFII = Qualified Foreign Institutional Investor, QOII = Qualified Overseas Institutional Investor, RQFII = Renminbi Qualified Foreign Institutional Investor, SME = small and medium-sized enterprises.
Source: Deutsche Bank (partly amended by ASEAN+3 Bond Market Forum [ABMF] Sub-Forum 1 team compilation based on ABMF member input).

Regardless of which market they are issued in, the economic nature of these instruments is basically the same. To prevent users and participants in these two main markets from experiencing any disadvantage, increased cooperation between the supervisory authorities for both markets is intended to gradually improve the comparability of their regulatory environments (see also section B.1 in this chapter). The Financial Stability and Development Commission (FSDC), which was established in 2017 to support this purpose, is a reflection of the joint efforts of policy makers in the PRC (see also Chapter IX.A.1).

At the same time, an increase in transactions between these two main markets has also been observed, particularly among professional participants, including both issuers and investors. The technical term used for this type of transaction is cross-market transfer (please see Chapter III.H.1 or Chapter IV.B.1 for a detailed description of this market feature). Qualified Overseas Institutional Investors (QOII) are able to carry out trading in the CIBM as well as in the exchange bond market via securities companies, who are both stock exchange members and designated bond settlement agents in the CIBM.

B.   Introduction to the China Inter-Bank Bond Market

The CIBM is an over-the-counter (OTC) market in which admitted participants agree on trades using the common trading platform provided by the China Foreign Exchange Trade System (CFETS), trade using a market-maker, or conclude trades between themselves via phone or other means. General or individual investors cannot directly participate in this market.

The CIBM started in June 1997, originally as a traditional interbank market between the PBOC and commercial banks, following commencement of the PBOC's open market operation. The origins of some of the institutions and technical terms (see Appendix 5) used in the CIBM today go back to this original purpose of the market. For example, CFETS is also known as the National Interbank Funding Center (and uses Chinamoney as its web handle), which describes its function in the classical interbank market to this day; however, for the purpose of this bond market guide, the role of the National Interbank Funding Center is not directly relevant and, hence, need not be described here in further detail.

The origins of the CIBM also provide context for the ongoing issuance and trading of negotiable certificates of deposit (NCD), which might be considered a bank product or money market instrument in many other jurisdictions and not tradable in the bond market. Since inception, the purpose of the interbank market has gradually expanded, with new instrument types added over time to support the financing of participating public sector entities and banking institutions, as well as the admission of many additional participants beyond the original constituents, resulting in the CIBM—with the emphasis on China Inter-Bank Bond Market—as it appears today.

The CIBM is presently the largest bond market segment in the PRC. Debt instruments issued, traded, and settled in the CIBM consist of mainly public sector bonds, held by the China Central Depository & Clearing Co., Ltd. (CCDC); and supplementary private sector instruments, held by the Shanghai Clearing House Co., Ltd. (SHCH). More than half of the private sector instruments deposited with SHCH at the end of 2019 were money market instruments such as NCD, super short-term commercial paper (SCP), and commercial paper (see section 1 for more details).

The CIBM is considered an institutional market by its participants; general or individual investors are not able to access this market directly. At the same time, access to publicly offered debt financing instruments issued and traded in the CIBM for general or retail investors is possible via the commercial banks' counter market, in which commercial banks on-sell bonds and notes acquired in the CIBM to individual and other investors that cannot participate in the CIBM directly. This practice, in effect, makes the commercial banks' counter market an extension of the CIBM and ensures that issuers continue to issue via public offerings for debt financing instruments to be eligible for the on-selling to general or retail investors. In addition, retail investors can access the NCD market indirectly, via a mobile phone investment in money market fund products, such as those offered by online payment providers.

CIBM participants include banks, other financial institutions (such as fund management companies and insurance companies), and nonfinancial institutions. Issuers, intermediaries, and service providers must be registered with NAFMII—in fact, they must acquire NAFMII membership—to participate in the CIBM, while end-investors need not unless they want to qualify for specific issuances of private placement notes (PPN). The CIBM and its participants are overseen and regulated by the PBOC and administered by NAFMII as the market's SRO. The National Development and Reform Commission (NDRC) sets regulations for and registers the issuance of enterprise bonds as well as the issuance of debt securities abroad by enterprises, while the State Administration of Foreign Exchange (SAFE) governs any applicable currency quotas and the inflow and outflow of foreign exchange in the PRC.[1] The China Banking and Insurance Regulatory Commission (CBIRC) licenses and supervises the actions of banks and insurance companies.

At the end of 2019, the outstanding balance in the CIBM (i.e., debt financing instruments deposited at CCDC and SHCH) represented approximately 86% of the total outstanding balance of bonds and other debt financing instruments deposited at the three securities depositories in the PRC: CCDC, SHCH, and the China Securities Depository and Clearing Co., Ltd. (CSDC) for the exchange bond market (Figure 1.1).

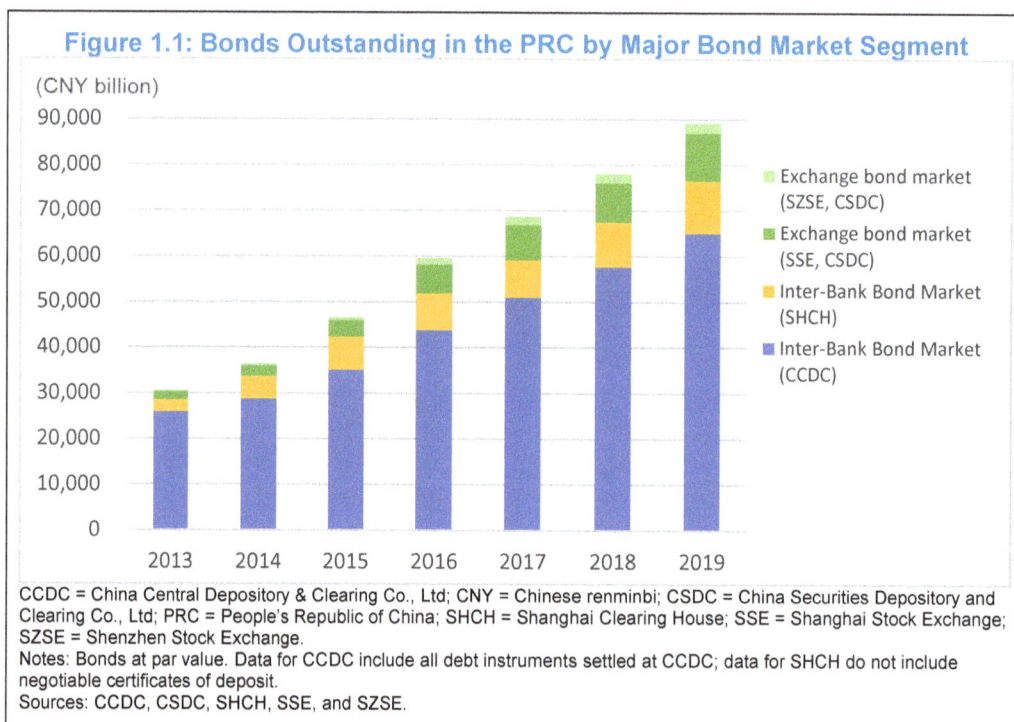

Figure 1.1: Bonds Outstanding in the PRC by Major Bond Market Segment

CCDC = China Central Depository & Clearing Co., Ltd; CNY = Chinese renminbi; CSDC = China Securities Depository and Clearing Co., Ltd; PRC = People's Republic of China; SHCH = Shanghai Clearing House; SSE = Shanghai Stock Exchange; SZSE = Shenzhen Stock Exchange.
Notes: Bonds at par value. Data for CCDC include all debt instruments settled at CCDC; data for SHCH do not include negotiable certificates of deposit.
Sources: CCDC, CSDC, SHCH, SSE, and SZSE.

---

[1] In principle, and for convenience in this bond market guide, bonds that need an application for registration with NDRC for issuance are called enterprise bonds. Other company bonds are distinguished as corporate bonds. Both corporate bonds and enterprise bonds are bonds issued based on the creditworthiness of the issuing companies themselves. "Collective bonds" issued by local enterprises are included among enterprise bonds.

1.   Debt Financing Instrument Issuance in the Inter-Bank Bond Market

At the end of 2019, the issuance amount of debt financing instruments in the CIBM (settled and deposited at CCDC and SHCH) represented approximately 82.8% of the total issuance of bonds and notes settled and deposited at the three securities depositories in the PRC (Figure 1.2a). This proportion has decreased slightly in recent years; for example, the proportion was 84.5% in 2018.

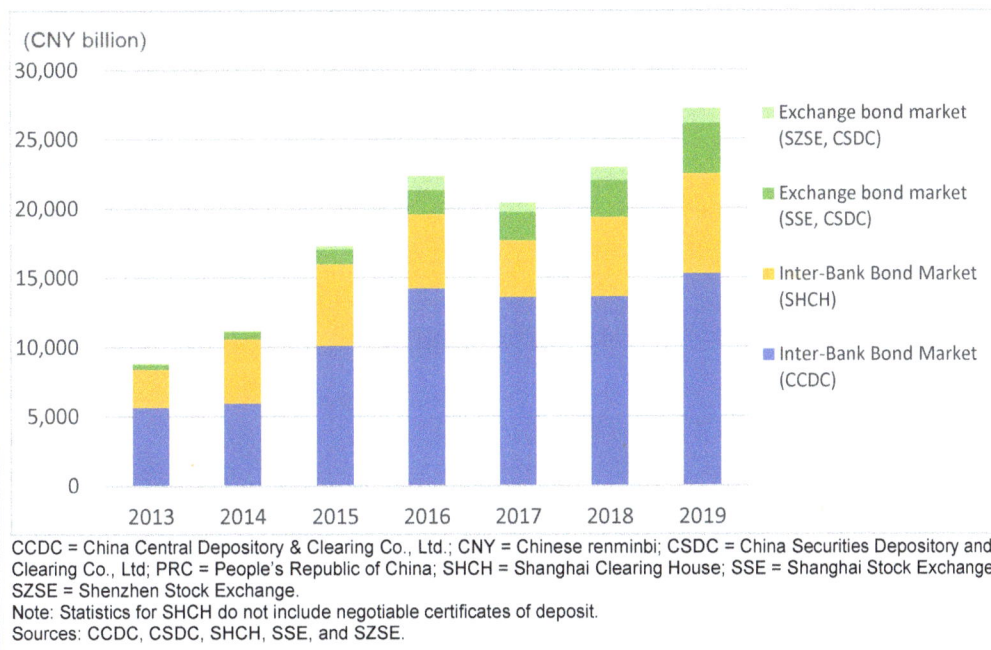

Figure 1.2a: Bond Issuance in the PRC by Major Bond Market Segment

CCDC = China Central Depository & Clearing Co., Ltd.; CNY = Chinese renminbi; CSDC = China Securities Depository and Clearing Co., Ltd; PRC = People's Republic of China; SHCH = Shanghai Clearing House; SSE = Shanghai Stock Exchange; SZSE = Shenzhen Stock Exchange.
Note: Statistics for SHCH do not include negotiable certificates of deposit.
Sources: CCDC, CSDC, SHCH, SSE, and SZSE.

At the same time, if NCD issuances are included in the statistics, the combined issuance numbers in the CIBM show a steady increase (Figure 1.2b).

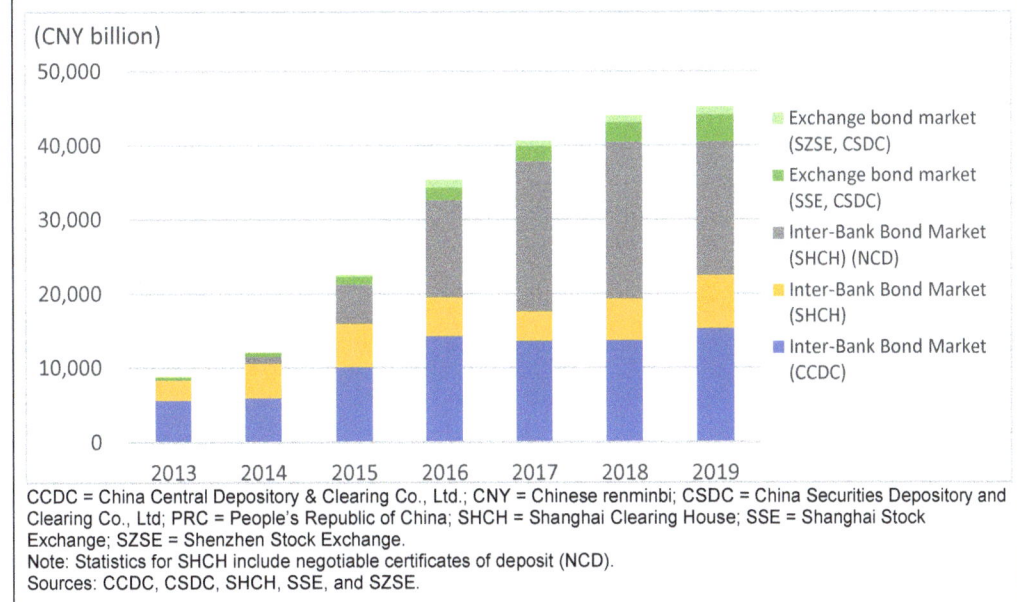

Figure 1.2b: Bond Issuance in the PRC by Major Bond Market Segment— including NCD deposited at SHCH

CCDC = China Central Depository & Clearing Co., Ltd.; CNY = Chinese renminbi; CSDC = China Securities Depository and Clearing Co., Ltd; PRC = People's Republic of China; SHCH = Shanghai Clearing House; SSE = Shanghai Stock Exchange; SZSE = Shenzhen Stock Exchange.
Note: Statistics for SHCH include negotiable certificates of deposit (NCD).
Sources: CCDC, CSDC, SHCH, SSE, and SZSE.

Today, debt financing instruments issued and traded in the CIBM cover a wide range of instruments, including government bonds, local government bonds, policy bank financial bonds (PFBs), government-backed (agency) bonds, central bank bills, enterprise bonds, financial bonds (commercial bank bonds and notes, non-bank financial institution bonds), as well as medium-term notes (MTN), commercial paper and SCP, PPN, and asset-backed notes (ABN) and asset-backed securities (ABS).[2] Panda bonds—debt financing instruments issued by nonresident issuers—are also issued and traded in the CIBM. In addition, NCD represent an important instrument issued and traded in the CIBM, while repurchase agreement (repo) transactions are a common product type.

Given its size and the large variety of debt instruments in the CIBM, the market is serviced by two entities acting as depository and settlement institutions: CCDC and SHCH. Debt financing instruments deposited at CCDC in 2019 represented 37.8% of the total issuance volume in the CIBM that year when NCD issuance is included, while the amount of new issuances deposited with SHCH in 2019, including NCD, represented 62.2% of the total issuance volume in the CIBM in 2019.

Figure 1.3 gives an illustration of the proportion of the types of debt financing instruments that were deposited with CCDC in recent years. Bond issuances in the CIBM being deposited with CCDC largely consist of public sector bonds; in 2019, the proportion of public sector bonds issued in the CIBM and deposited with CCDC was approximately 79.7%.

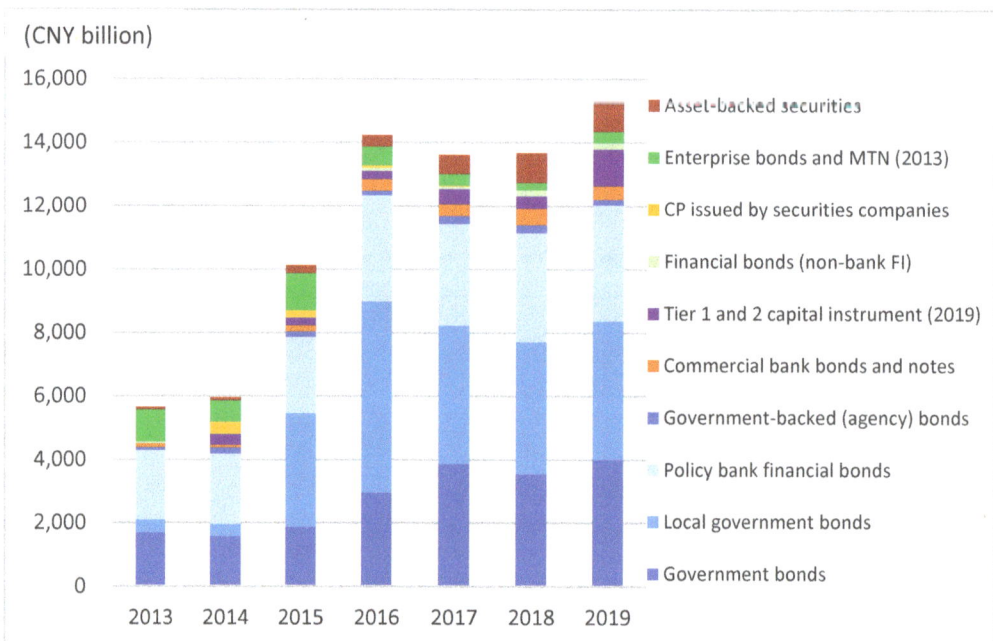

Figure 1.3: Bond Issuance in the CIBM and Deposited with CCDC by Instrument Type

CCDC = China Central Depository & Clearing Co., Ltd; CIBM = China Inter-Bank Bond Market; CNY = Chinese renminbi; CP = commercial paper; FI = financial institutions; MTN = medium-term notes.
Sources: *CCDC Annual Review, 2013* (English). pp.13–14; *CCDC Bond Market Statistical Analysis Report, 2014–2017*; *CCDC Annual Report, 2016–2017, CCDC Bond Market Operation Analysis, 2017; CCDC 2018–2019/12* 统计月报: 2-01 债券发行量(按券种).

---

[2] ABS do not constitute securities under the Securities Law.

Table 1.2 provides further insight into the value of debt financing instruments issued in 2019 and deposited with CCDC by instrument type.

Table 1.2: Debt Financing Instruments Issued in the CIBM and Deposited with CCDC in 2019

Instrument		2019 Total Issuance Amount (CNY billion)	Share
Public sector bonds (79.7%)	Government bonds	4,009.10	26.2%
	Local government bonds	4,362.43	28.5%
	Policy bank financial bonds	3,660.21	23.9%
	Government-backed (agency) bonds	165.00	1.1%
Private sector bonds (21.3%)	Commercial bank bonds and notes	432.95	2.8%
	Tier 1 and Tier 2 capital instruments	1,164.60	7.6%
	Financial bonds (by non-bank FI)	187.45	1.2%
	Commercial paper issued by securities companies	0.00	0.0%
	Enterprise bonds	360.92	2.4%
	Asset-backed securities	963.46	6.3%
CCDC Total		**15,306.12**	**100.0%**

CCDC = China Central Depository & Clearing Co., Ltd; CIBM = China Inter-Bank Bond Market; CNY = Chinese renminbi; FI = financial institution.
Source: *CCDC, 2019/12* 统计月报: 2-01 债券发行量(按券种).

On the other hand, SHCH focuses more on private sector debt financing instruments such as MTN, PPN, commercial paper, SCP, and green debt financing instruments (from 2016 onward) (Figure 1.4).

SHCH also serves as the central depository for NCD traded in the CIBM, but in statistical classifications they are typically treated or shown separately from bonds and other debt financing instruments due to their banking product nature and short-term tenors. Please refer to Chapter III.C.4 for a description of the basic characteristics of the NCD traded in the CIBM.

Figure 1.4: Debt Financing Instrument Issuance in the CIBM and Deposited with SHCH by Type

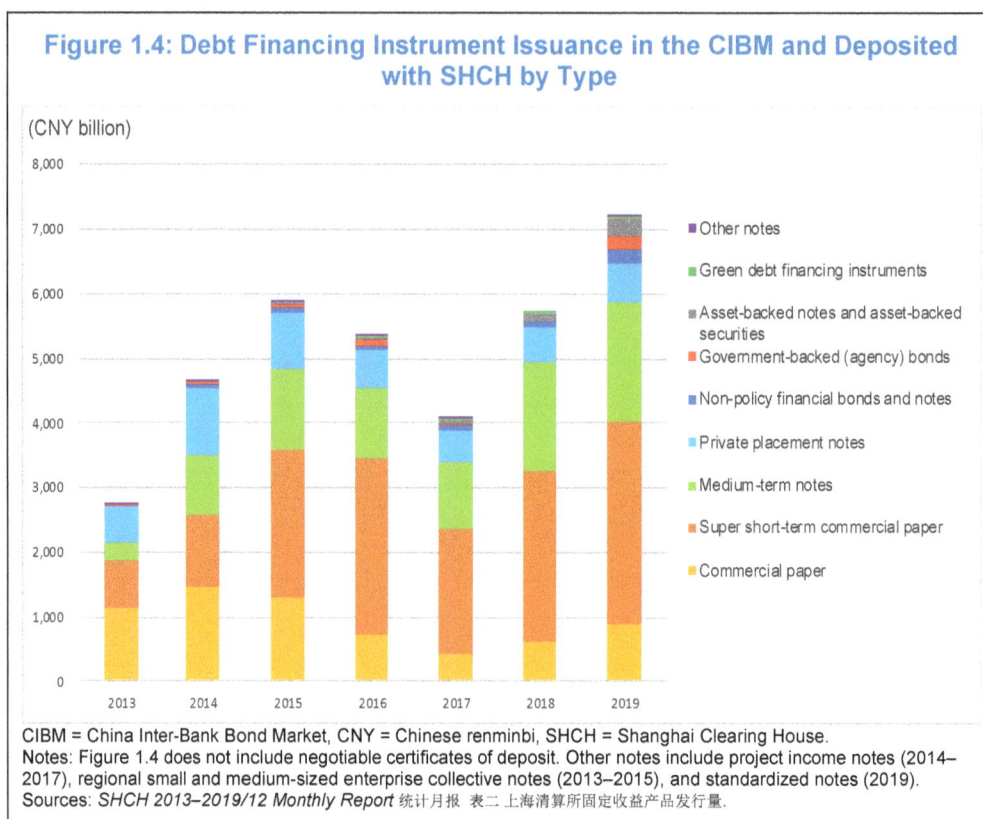

CIBM = China Inter-Bank Bond Market, CNY = Chinese renminbi, SHCH = Shanghai Clearing House.
Notes: Figure 1.4 does not include negotiable certificates of deposit. Other notes include project income notes (2014–2017), regional small and medium-sized enterprise collective notes (2013–2015), and standardized notes (2019).
Sources: SHCH 2013–2019/12 Monthly Report 统计月报 表二 上海清算所固定收益产品发行量.

To give an impression of the significance of the amount of NCD relative to other debt financing instruments in the CIBM, issuance amounts from 2013 to 2019 are shown in Figure 1.5.

Figure 1.5: Debt Financing Instrument and NCD Issuance in the CIBM

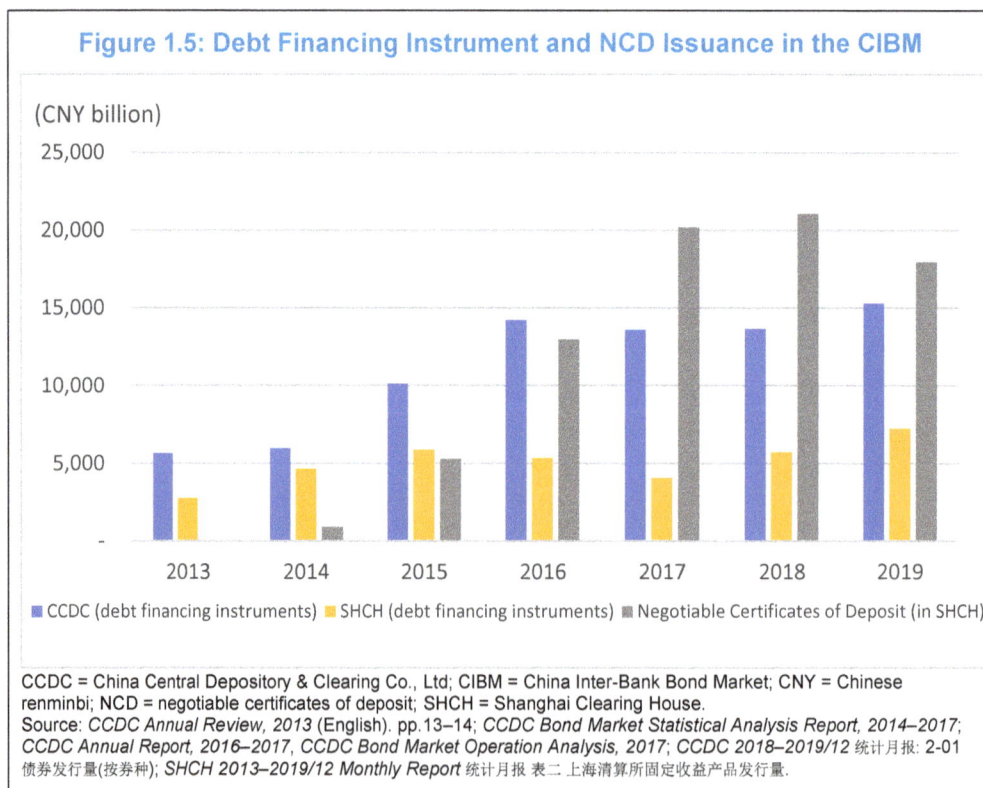

CCDC = China Central Depository & Clearing Co., Ltd; CIBM = China Inter-Bank Bond Market; CNY = Chinese renminbi; NCD = negotiable certificates of deposit; SHCH = Shanghai Clearing House.
Source: CCDC Annual Review, 2013 (English). pp.13–14; CCDC Bond Market Statistical Analysis Report, 2014–2017; CCDC Annual Report, 2016–2017, CCDC Bond Market Operation Analysis, 2017; CCDC 2018–2019/12 统计月报: 2-01 债券发行量(按券种); SHCH 2013–2019/12 Monthly Report 统计月报 表二 上海清算所固定收益产品发行量.

A further breakdown of individual debt financing instrument types issued in the CIBM can be found in Chapter III.D.

2.   Debt Financing Instrument Trading in the Inter-Bank Bond Market

Debt financing instruments and NCD issued in the CIBM are traded on the platform operated by CFETS (please see Chapter IV for more details). At the end of 2019, the total trading and transaction volume in the CIBM reached approximately CNY1,068 trillion and represented approximately 81.3% of the overall bond market trading and transaction volume (Figure 1.6).

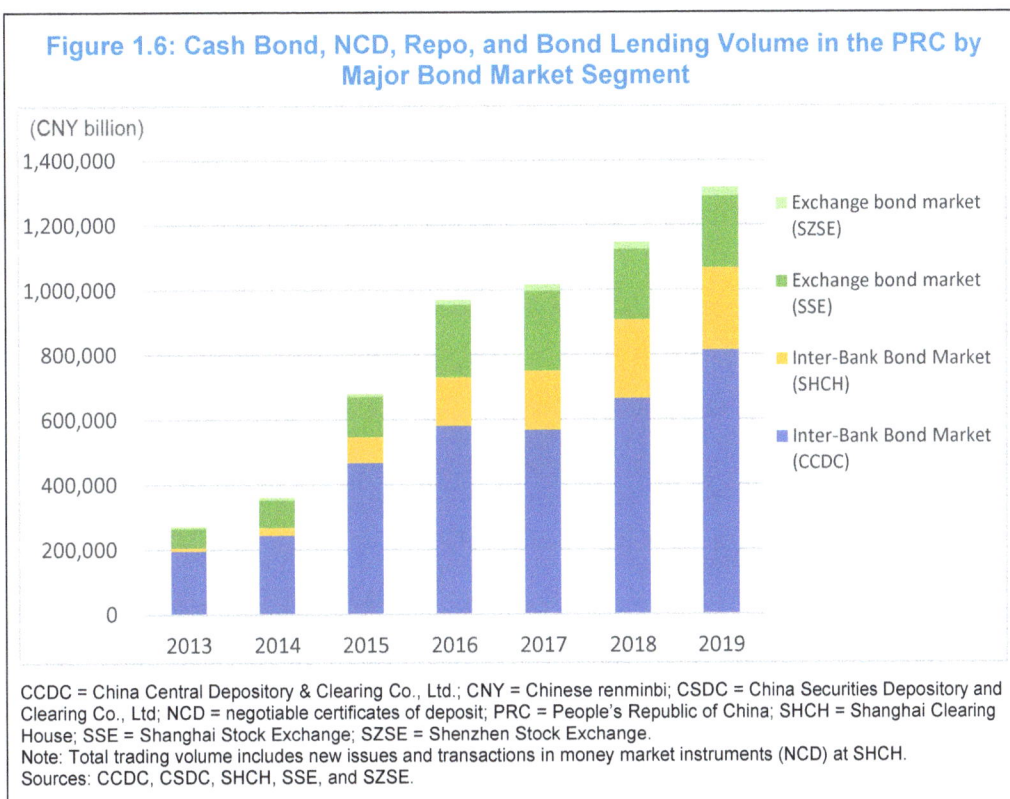

Figure 1.6: Cash Bond, NCD, Repo, and Bond Lending Volume in the PRC by Major Bond Market Segment

CCDC = China Central Depository & Clearing Co., Ltd.; CNY = Chinese renminbi; CSDC = China Securities Depository and Clearing Co., Ltd; NCD = negotiable certificates of deposit; PRC = People's Republic of China; SHCH = Shanghai Clearing House; SSE = Shanghai Stock Exchange; SZSE = Shenzhen Stock Exchange.
Note: Total trading volume includes new issues and transactions in money market instruments (NCD) at SHCH.
Sources: CCDC, CSDC, SHCH, SSE, and SZSE.

3.   Corporate Bonds and Enterprise Bonds

There are three types of nonfinancial corporate bonds in the PRC: (i) enterprise bonds (企业债), (ii) corporate bonds (公司债), and (iii) debt financing instruments of nonfinancial enterprises (非金融企业债务融资工具).

Originally, enterprise bonds (企业债) referred to the bonds issued by central government-related agencies, state-owned enterprises (SOEs), or state-owned holding companies affiliated with NDRC. NDRC is responsible for supervising the issuance of enterprise bonds. For historical reasons, enterprise bonds have always been supervised by NDRC, being a government agency overseeing SOE reform. With the progress of privatization, the delineation between corporate bonds and enterprise bonds has become less strict. In general terms, enterprise bonds are included in corporate bonds and often called corporate bonds.

Enterprise bonds are mainly issued by nonlisted SOEs or government-backed entities and are issued in the CIBM or the exchange bond market, or in both markets. Most enterprise bonds are fungible between the CIBM and exchange bond market. On the other hand, corporate bonds are issued in the exchange bond market and listed on the exchange(s).

In principle, and for convenience in this bond market guide, bonds that need an application for registration with NDRC for issuance are called enterprise bonds; other company bonds are distinguished as corporate bonds. Basically, both corporate bonds and enterprise bonds are bonds issued based on the creditworthiness of the issuer companies themselves.

Please also see Chapter III.B for a description of the types of bonds and notes issued in the CIBM.

4.   Formation of the Private Placement to Designated or Specialized Institutional Investors Concept

On 29 April 2011, NAFMII issued the Rules for Private Placement of Debt Financing Instruments of Non-Financial Enterprises in the Inter-Bank Bond Market (银行间债券市场非金融企业债务融资工具非公开定向发行规则) (2011, No. 6). With these rules, NAFMII introduced new concepts in private placement: "private placement (定向发行)" and "designated institutional investor (特定机构投资人)" or, in short, "private placement investor (定向投资人)."

These concepts are similar to (i) the placement to Qualified Investors (向合格投资者非公开发行), and (ii) the concept of Qualified Institutional Investors (合格投资者中的机构投资者) in the exchange bond market.

The 2011 Rules stipulated that the term "private placement (定向发行)" refers to the issuance of debt financing instruments by nonfinancial enterprises with legal qualifications (i.e., enterprises) to "designated institutional investors (特定机构投资人)" who are designated by the issuer and the lead underwriter in the CIBM, also referred to as "private placement investors (定向投资人)," and includes the transfer of such debt financing instruments within the scope of designated institutional investors (DIIs) only.

The term private placement investors stems from the practice that an issuer and its appointed underwriter had to specifically identify (i.e., target), upon every issuance, a list of institutional investors to which the debt financing instruments could be issued. Hence, debt financing instruments issued via a private placement (非公开定向发行方式发行的债务融资工具) are also known as "nonpublicly placed debt financing instruments (非公开定向债务融资工具)," or simply "private placement instruments (定向工具)."

Private placement investors who invest in private placement instruments should issue a written confirmation letter to NAFMII confirming that they are aware of the investment risk of the private placement instruments, have the ability and willingness to assume the investment risk of the private placement instruments, voluntarily accept the management of investors in the CIBM by NAFMII, and fulfill membership obligations.

In addition to the abovementioned method of designating institutional investors, on 26 November 2015, to standardize the selection procedure of private placement investors (定向投资人), NAFMII subsequently issued the Rules for the Registration and Issuance of Debt Financing Instruments of Non-Financial Enterprises (非金融企业债务融资工具注册发行规则) and the Provisions for the Selection of Specialized Institutional Investors of Private Placement Notes (定向债务融资工具专项机构投资人遴选细则), including a formal definition of "specialized institutional investors (专项机构投资人)" to be selected by NAFMII. At the same time, NAFMII named 120 specialized institutional investors (SIIs) on the List of Specialized Institutional Investors of Private Placement

Notes (定向债务融资工具专项机构投资人名单). Being on this positive list, SIIs need not acknowledge their risk awareness and acceptance of market membership rules to NAFMII for every issuance of a debt financing instrument they are interested to buy. By October 2019, this positive list contained about 180 investors.

As a result, an issuer may choose to offer its debt financing instruments in the CIBM through a private placement to either institutional investors selected by NAFMII or institutional investors who are designated by the issuer and the lead underwriter. The abovementioned concepts also made possible the private placement of Panda bonds to designated or SIIs.

In April 2020, NAFMII announced the latest revisions to its rules on private placements. While there were no changes to the investor concepts mentioned above, the latest rules focused on the streamlining of the registration process and more efficient disclosure practices and introduced a further categorization of issuer types with distinct disclosure obligations for each category. The new rules became effective on 1 July 2020.

5. Repos and Bond Lending Transactions in the Inter-Bank Bond Market

Repo transactions play a significant role in trading in the CIBM. In 2019, repo transactions in the CIBM represented 78.2% of the total market repo volume in the PRC. Due to the intraday repo practices in the market, repo transaction volumes appear as very large numbers (Figure 1.7).

Figure 1.7: Repo and Bond Lending Transaction Volume by Major Bond Market Segment

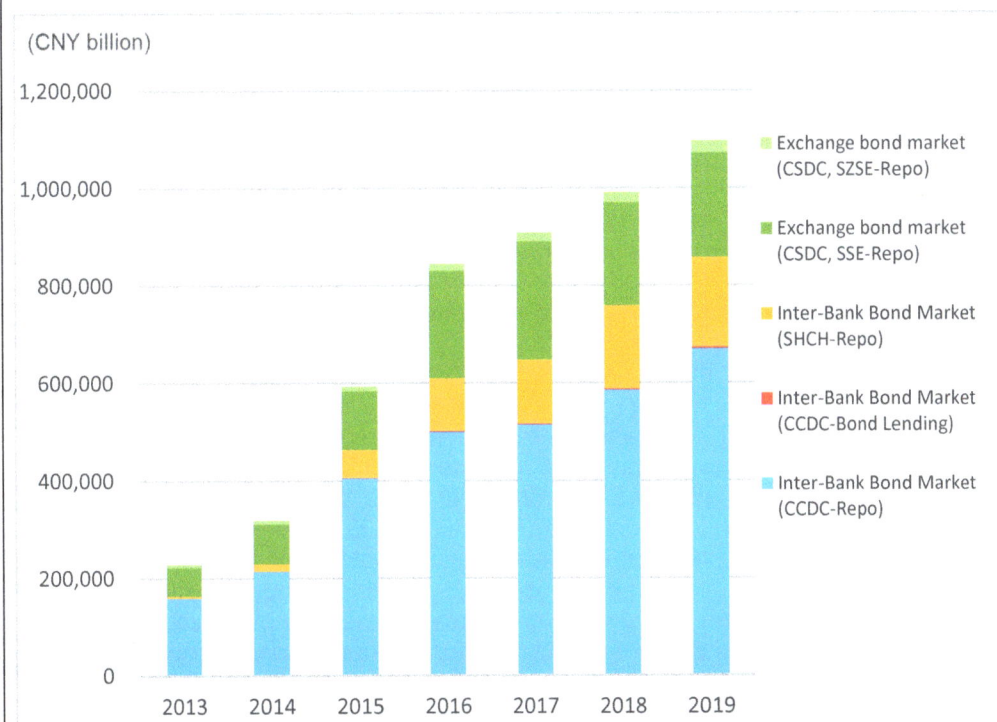

CCDC = China Central Depository & Clearing Co., Ltd; CIBM = China Inter-Bank Bond Market; CNY = Chinese renminbi; CSDC = China Securities Depository & Clearing Co., Ltd; SHCH = Shanghai Clearing House; SSE = Shanghai Stock Exchange; SZSE = Shenzhen Stock Exchange.
Note: Bond lending only applies to CIBM.
Source: *CCDC Bond Market Statistical Analysis Report, 2013–2017; SSE Fact Book 2016, 2017* (data for 2015, 2016); SSE website (data for 2013, 2014, 2017); *SZSE Fact Book, 2013–2017*.

Repo transactions in the CIBM are supervised by the PBOC, while the participants are subject to NAFMII membership and applicable regulations, as well as CFETS trading rules. Please see Chapter IV.G for a comprehensive description of the repo market in the CIBM.

In addition, securities borrowing and lending transactions, which in market practice are referred to as bond lending, may only be carried out in the CIBM. For details on bond lending practices, please refer to Chapter IV.H.

C.   Outline of the Investment Schemes to Open the Capital Market

Since the PRC's accession to the World Trade Organization in 2001, the Government of the PRC has established various concepts for the opening of the domestic bond and capital markets in line with the needs of foreign investors and potential issuers.

Specifically, investors may invest in the PRC's bond market, which is commonly referred to as the "China bond market," through any one of five concepts for which they may be eligible (in their order of introduction): (i) Qualified Foreign Institutional Investor (QFII), (ii) the Pilot Scheme for Three Types of Institutions (三类机构), (iii) Renminbi Qualified Foreign Institutional Investor (RQFII), (iv) the CIBM Direct Scheme, and (v) Bond Connect. In this context, QFII and RQFII are often mentioned together due to their similar eligibility criteria, approval process, and origins in the exchange market.

Please see Table 1.3 for a brief summary of each concept's features. Chapter III.M contains a full description of the features of each of the market access concepts available for investors in the CIBM.

The individual concepts introduced by the government served specific purposes in line with the various stages of development of the bond market. While at its inception in 2002 as the first foreign access method to the PRC capital market, QFII focused on the exchange market and favored equities, other initiatives were established as part of the national policy of the internationalization of the Chinese renminbi—such as the Pilot Scheme for Three Types of Institutions and RQFII—to provide means of effective use of offshore Chinese renminbi (ISO code: CNH) that accumulated outside of the PRC. In the earlier concepts, it had still been necessary for each foreign institutional investor to be approved by the competent authorities and to observe a quota.

The availability of foreign investment access methods was followed by opportunities for nonresident issuers as well as by introducing the issuance of Panda bonds. From 2015, in particular, further policy and regulatory measures to open the China bond market—as part of the broader liberalization of the capital market—have shifted from a framework with inherent limitations to a framework with a focus on enabling investment at the discretion of foreign investors. From February 2016, nonresident financial institutions were able to invest in the CIBM with only a notification to the PBOC. CIBM Direct, as it is now known, has emerged as a highly flexible framework without a need for approval, an investment limit, or repatriation restrictions. The most recent measure, Bond Connect, introduced in July 2017, takes a further step toward the opening of the domestic bond market in the PRC, allowing nonresident investors with established accounts in Hong Kong, China to access the CIBM with a streamlined approval and onboarding process.

Table 1.3: Overview of Market Access Routes into the China Bond Market

Item	QFII	Pilot Scheme for Three Types of Institutions	RQFII	CIBM Direct	Bond Connect (Northbound)
Market	• Exchange Market • CIBM	CIBM	• Exchange Market • CIBM	CIBM	CIBM
Commenced	• 2002 • 2011	2010	2011	2016	2017
Currency	FCY	CNY (CNH)	CNY (CNH)	CNY (CNH), FCY	CNY (CNH)
Approving Authorities	• CSRC, SAFE • CSRC, SAFE, PBOC	PBOC	• CSRC, SAFE • CSRC, SAFE, PBOC	PBOC, SAFE	PBOC
Original Scheme	Allowed foreign institutional investors who meet certain qualifications to invest in equities and bonds in domestic markets within an approved quota of Chinese renminbi raised in the PRC in exchange for foreign currency to be remitted inbound	Allowed three specific types of institutions to participate in the CIBM: (i) foreign central banks or monetary authorities, (ii) CNH settlement banks in Hong Kong, China and Macao, China; and (iii) cross-border CNH settlement participating banks in Hong Kong, China and Macao, China	Allowed foreign institutional investors who meet certain qualifications to invest in equities and bonds in domestic markets within an approved quota allocated to eligible jurisdictions through Chinese renminbi raised outside of the PRC	Allowed foreign investors (QOII) to access the CIBM upon registration with the PBOC Allowed foreign institutions to trade bonds directly through banks holding a Type A license	Allowed CMU account holders (including foreign investors) to access CIBM via HKMA-CMU links to CCDC and SHCH No quota requirement or need for investors to identify the intended investment amount Registration with the PBOC
Original Restrictions	An investment quota (USD) is applied as well as regulations on remittance of principal injection period, asset allocation, and repatriation, including a lock-up period and outward remittance.	Limitations are placed on participating institutions; investment limit remained within the range of CNH holdings of each institution.	An investment quota (CNY) by country and region is applied and allocated among entities; other original restrictions were the same as for QFII.	Investors must invest (within a 9-month period) at least 50% of the investment amount mentioned in their filing form.	Each institution is required to submit an application to PBOC and CFETS via BCCL, a joint venture of HKEX and CFETS.
Size of the Scheme	Final total quota available was USD300 billion (as of January 2019). Final quota allocated to 311 approved QFIIs was USD111.04 billion (as of August 2019). The quota concept was abolished by SAFE on 10 September 2019.	N.A.	Final total approved quota was CNY1,990 billion (as of September 2019). Total quota allocated to 243 approved entities in 20 approved jurisdictions was CNY691.6 billion (as of September 2019). The quota concept was abolished by SAFE on 10 September 2019.	The number of foreign investors via CIBM Direct was 1,087 (as of October 2019).	The number of foreign investors registered through Bond Connect was 1,533 (as of November 2019).

BCCL = Bond Connect Company Limited; CCDC = China Central Depository & Clearing Co., Ltd.; CFETS = China Foreign Exchange Trading System; CIBM = China Inter-Bank Bond Market; CNH = offshore Chinese renminbi; CMU = Central Moneymarkets Unit; CNY = Chinese renminbi; CSRC = China Securities Regulatory Commission; FCY = foreign currency; HKEX = Hong Kong Exchanges Limited; HKMA = Hong Kong Monetary Authority; N.A. = not applicable; PBOC = People's Bank of China; QFII = Qualified Foreign Institutional Investor; QOII = Qualified Overseas Institutional Investor; RQFII = Renminbi Qualified Foreign Institutional Investor; SAFE = State Administration of Foreign Exchange; USD = United States dollar.
Sources: For data on the size of schemes, Bank of China, BNP Paribas, BNY Mellon, Bond Connect Company Limited, Clifford Chance, King & Wood Mallesons, K&L Gate, Linklaters, and Mizuho Securities; for data on QFII, SAFE and the Bank of New York Mellon; for data on RQFII, SAFE, the Bank of New York Mellon, and other publicly available sources; for data on CIBM Direct, China Foreign Exchange Trade System and the PBOC; for data on Bond Connect: BCCL.

D.   Market Opening Milestones in the China Inter-Bank Bond Market since 2005

While the QFII system was introduced in 2002 and its pilot program officially launched in May 2003, bonds that could be invested via QFII were initially limited to listed bonds in the exchange bond market and not the bonds and notes issued and traded in the CIBM. It took until late 2011 before QFII were able to place investments in bonds issued and traded in the CIBM.

However, the initial opening of the CIBM to foreign investors and nonresident issuers began in 2005. This section aims to recall the important milestones in the opening of the CIBM to nonresident participants, including the more prominent developments related to QFII, RQFII, CIBM Direct, Bond Connect, as well as Panda bond issuance.

1.   Initial Opening to Foreign Investors and Nonresident Issuers, 2005–2010

In February 2005, the PBOC, NDRC, and CSRC formulated the Interim Measures for the Administration of CNY-Denominated Bond Issuances by International Development Organizations (国际开发机构人民币债券发行管理暂行办法) (2005, No. 5), which laid the foundation and was the first regulation for what was to become the Panda bond issuance concept. In these interim measures, international development organizations refer to the multilateral, bilateral, and regional international development financial institutions that grant development loans and carry out investments.

In May 2005, with approval from the PBOC, the Pan-Asia Index Fund and China Bond Index Fund of the Asian Bond Fund II were given direct, if limited, access to the CIBM, thus becoming the first foreign entities approved to invest in debt financing instruments in the CIBM.

In August 2010, by issuing the Notice of the PBOC on Issues Concerning the Pilot Program on Investment in the Inter-Bank Bond Market with Renminbi Funds by Three Types of Institution Including Overseas RMB Clearing Banks (中国人民银行关于境外人民币清算行等三类机构运用人民币投资银行间债券市场试点有关事宜的通知) (2010, No. 217), the PBOC launched a pilot scheme allowing certain institutions to trade and settle bonds in the CIBM.[3] The three types of institution (三类机构) were (i) foreign central banks or monetary authorities; (ii) CNH settlement banks in Hong Kong, China, and Macau, China; and (iii) cross-border CNH settlement participating banks in Hong Kong, China and Macau, China. This pilot scheme represented the first CNY-denominated investment concept using offshore Chinese renminbi (CNH) as the source of funds. An investment limit was set as within the range of CNH holdings by each financial institution (i.e., institutions were allowed to use available CNH balances resulting from normal business activities).

In September 2010, to further standardize the behavior of international development institutions when issuing CNY-denominated bonds, the PBOC, MOF, NDRC, and CSRC jointly issued amendments to the earlier (Panda bond) regulations in the form of the Interim Measures for the Administration of CNY-Denominated Bond Issuances by International Development Institutions (国际开发机构人民币债券发行管理暂行办法) (2010, No. 10), which deregulated the outward remittance of Chinese renminbi proceeds from Panda bond issuance by such international development institutions.[4]

---

[3] See http://www.gov.cn/banshi/2010-08/18/content_1682328.htm.
[4] See http://www.fdi.gov.cn/1800000121_23_68477_0_7.html.

2.   Liberalization of the Qualified Foreign Institutional Investor and Renminbi Qualified Foreign Institutional Investor Schemes, 2011–2013

The QFII scheme was introduced in 2002 to allow foreign investors direct access to the domestic securities market for the first time. However, the investment opportunities did not include instruments issued and traded in the CIBM; instead, the focus was on the exchange (bond) market.

On 16 December 2011, the RQFII scheme was introduced, which allowed the use of offshore renminbi (CNH) raised by the subsidiaries of Chinese domestic fund management companies and securities companies in Hong Kong, China to invest in the domestic securities market, including in the CIBM, for the first time. The underlying regulation was officially called Pilot Measures for Domestic Securities Investment by RQFIIs (Fund Management Companies and Securities Companies) (人民币合格境外机构投资者境内证券投资试点办法) (2011-12-16, CSRC Order No. 76). It was jointly issued by CSRC, the PBOC, and SAFE. Under the new pilot scheme, the PBOC allowed RQFII to access the CIBM, if limited to investments in cash bonds only, in addition to bonds in the exchange bond market under CSRC regulations similar to QFII. The RQFII scheme included CNY-denominated investment quotas for a country or region, which were to be granted by SAFE.

Hong Kong, China, being the test pilot region of the scheme, also referred to as the PBOC's pilot CIBM scheme, obtained the first such quota at CNY20 billion. In the first batch, 21 subsidiaries of Chinese fund management and securities companies based in Hong Kong, China were granted RQFII status and a quota to invest in the CIBM via a domestic bond settlement agent (see also Chapter III.M for a description of the function of a bond settlement agent).

In 2012, the PBOC pilot CIBM scheme was extended to insurance companies domiciled in Hong Kong, China; Singapore; and Taipei,China. From 2012 onward, QFII investment in bonds issued and traded in the CIBM was permitted in addition to the exchange bond market.

Effective 1 March 2013, the original RQFII pilot measures were replaced by the 2013 Pilot Measures for Domestic Securities Investment by RQFIIs (人民币合格境外机构投资者境内证券投资试点办法) (2013-03-01, CSRC Order No. 90), jointly released by CSRC, the PBOC, and SAFE, which expanded the scope of the scheme and relaxed earlier investment restrictions such as asset allocation percentages. Through the revised measures, QFIIs were permitted, subject to PBOC approval, to invest in the CIBM within an approved quota. Subsequently, all RQFIIs across jurisdictions were also allowed to invest in the CIBM, subject to PBOC approval.

To aid the implementation of the revised scheme, CSRC issued the Measures for the RQFII Pilot Program (Decree No. 90) on 6 March 2013, which regulated the securities investment activities of RQFIIs in the PRC. According to the measures, to make securities investments in the PRC, an RQFII needed to entrust a domestic commercial bank with asset custody and a domestic securities company with securities trading on behalf of the RQFII.

On 11 March 2013, SAFE released its Circular on Issues Concerning the Pilot Program of Investment in Domestic Securities by RQFII. On 2 May 2013, the PBOC announced the revised Circular on Issues Concerning the Implementation of Pilot Measures for RQFIIs, which revised the requirements on account opening, account management, and asset allocation for the RQFII scheme, and officially allowed all RQFII to access the CIBM.

3.   Further Liberalization of the Qualified Foreign Institutional Investor and Renminbi Qualified Foreign Institutional Investor Schemes, 2016–2019

Since 2016, the QFII and RQFII schemes have evolved significantly in terms of market accessibility, asset allocation, and capital mobility.

On 5 September 2016, SAFE's RQFII rules were further relaxed regarding the quota application and controls, including simplifying the quota application process, easing inward and outward remittances, and shortening the original lockup period. On 23 September 2016, CSRC announced the removal of all asset allocation restrictions. Instead, QFIIs and RQFIIs were allowed to decide asset allocation at their discretion, other than allocating a substantial percentage of assets to cash and cash equivalent products.

At the 2018 Boao Forum for Asia in April 2018, President Xi Jinping announced a "new phase of opening" of the PRC's economy, including liberalizing the financial system and making the PRC more attractive for foreign investments. The following day, Yi Gang, Governor of the PBOC, outlined the implementation measures and timeline in greater detail. Following the speeches, regulators issued a series of implementing rules and policy statements.

On 12 June 2018, the PBOC issued the Regulations on Foreign Exchange Administration for Domestic Securities Investment by QFII and SAFE issued the Circular on the Administration for Domestic Securities Investment by RQFII to further ease restrictions on foreign institutional investors' access to the domestic financial market. Under the new regulations, the quarterly cap of 20% of total domestic assets that a QFII may remit out of the country was removed. A 3-month lockup period for redeeming investment principal was also removed for both QFIIs and RQFIIs. To facilitate the management of foreign exchange risks related to the securities investment of QFIIs and RQFIIs, investors were allowed to place foreign exchange hedges on their domestic investments.

At the end of July 2018, the total QFII investment quota granted to 287 license holders had reached USD100.46 billion. At the end of September 2018, the total RQFII investment quota had reached CNY1,940 billion, as granted across 20 countries and regions, and the actual investment amount used under the quota reached CNY640 billion across 203 entities.

In January 2019, SAFE doubled the investment quota available to QFII from USD150 billion to USD300 billion, and on 10 September 2019, SAFE announced that it had abolished the quota system for both the QFII and RQFII schemes to promote the further opening of the PRC's financial markets.

4.   Introduction of the CIBM Direct Scheme, 2015–2018

In July 2015, the PBOC released a notice allowing foreign central banks or monetary authorities, sovereign wealth funds, and other international financial organizations (as well as RMB clearing banks in Hong Kong, China, and Macau, China) to directly invest in the CIBM without approval requirements and quota limits. Institutions in these categories were permitted to invest through an onshore bond settlement agent, subject to a filing with the PBOC. This marked a significant shift in the process of opening the PRC's capital market, making it much easier for international institutional investors to access the CIBM and paving the way for further liberalization of cross-border investments in the China bond market. The new scheme was called CIBM Direct and introduced the term "Qualified Overseas Institutional Investor," or QOII, to describe its constituents.

CIBM Direct was launched with the promulgation of PBOC Public Notice No. 3 on 17 February 2016, under which the definition of QOII was also widened to include additional foreign institutional participants, including commercial banks, insurance companies, securities firms, fund and asset management companies, as well as pension and endowment funds; the activities of QFIIs and RQFIIs in the CIBM have since been regulated under the designation QOII.

Further to the above notice, in May 2016, the PBOC Shanghai and SAFE published the Foreign Institutional Investor Rules, implementing the actual opening up of the CIBM. The implementing rules rolled out a "registration" approach to all types of foreign investors and removed quota limitations; foreign investors may remit Chinese renminbi or foreign currency for CIBM investments, and the foreign exchange may be made onshore or offshore, without an approval from SAFE. The bond settlement agent may also provide custodian services in the CIBM. New instruments were also made available for hedging purposes—such as bond lending, bond forwards, and forward rate agreements—subject to the completion of the prescribed legal documentation.

Under the CIBM Direct Scheme, QOIIs may also trade bonds directly through banks holding a Type A license, which is defined as a participant who can trade, settle, and provide custody for CIBM instruments both for themselves and on behalf of Type C investors, who must appoint a Type A investor for settlement to carry out bond trading on their behalf. Type B license holders may trade and settle in the CIBM for themselves only, or trade directly with others.

5.   Further Easing of Panda Bond Regulations, 2014–2019

In March 2014, Daimler AG, the German carmaker and nonfinancial enterprise, issued the first corporate Panda bond in the CIBM, as PPN with a maturity of 1 year.

In September 2015, the PBOC eased restrictions on issuers of Panda bonds, permitting that proceeds raised from the issuance of Panda bonds could be used within or outside the PRC.

On 8 September 2018, the PBOC and MOF jointly issued the Interim Measures for the Administration on Bonds Issued by Overseas Issuers on the National Inter-Bank Bond Market (全国银行间债券市场境外机构债券发行管理暂行办法) (PBOC and MOF Notice 2018, No.16) to further clarify the qualifications and registration procedures for foreign institutions to issue Panda bonds in the CIBM using two methods of issuance: (i) public offering and (ii) private placement to DIIs or SIIs, which are also known as private placement investors (see Chapter III.M for a description of these institutional investor types).[5] The interim measures laid out basic provisions on information disclosure, issuance registration, custody, and settlement, as well as Chinese renminbi account opening, foreign exchange, and investor protection.

On 17 January 2019, pursuant to these interim measures, NAFMII published the Guidelines on Debt Financing Instruments of Overseas Non-Financial Enterprises (for Trial Implementation) (境外非金融企业债务融资工具业务指引(试行)), which provided more detail on the registration for issuance process and information disclosure for Panda bonds.[6]

---

[5] For the Chinese version (PDF), see http://www.pbc.gov.cn/tiaofasi/144941/3581332/3730127/index.html. For the English version, see http://www.pbc.gov.cn/en/3688253/3689009/3788480/3789754/index.html.
[6] For the Chinese version, see http://nafmii.org.cn/ggtz/gg/201902/t20190201_75766.html. For the English version, see http://nafmii.org.cn//english/lawsandregulations/selfregulatory_e/201902/t20190201_75773.html.

6.   Debut of Bond Connect, 2017–2018

The latest scheme to open the China bond market to be introduced, Bond Connect, is a new mutual market access scheme that will eventually allow investors from the PRC and overseas to trade in each other's bond markets through connections between the respective financial infrastructure institutions in the PRC and Hong Kong, China.

"Northbound Trading" commenced on 3 July 2017, allowing foreign investors from Hong Kong, China and other regions to invest in the CIBM through mutual access arrangements with respect to trading, custody, and settlement. Proposed "Southbound Trading," under which investors from the PRC can access the Hong Kong bond market, is not expected to be realized anytime soon.

In addition to the QFII and RQFII schemes, Bond Connect (债券通) provides a new avenue for foreign investors to access the China bond market, particularly the CIBM. The scope of eligible foreign investors under Bond Connect is the same as for the CIBM Direct scheme, being QOIIs. Please see Chapter X.A.4 for more details on Bond Connect.

To establish an interconnection mechanism between the domestic bond markets in the PRC and Hong Kong, China through Bond Connect, the PBOC issued the Interim Measures for the Administration of Mutual Bond Market Access between Mainland China and Hong Kong SAR (内地与香港债券市场互联互通合作管理暂行办法) (中国人民银行令 [2017] 第 1 号 / 同日施行) on 21 June 2017.

On 3 July 2017, the state-owned Agricultural Development Bank of China issued CNY16 billion worth of financial bonds in the CIBM, of which CNY1 billion was allocated to foreign investors through Bond Connect. On 26 July 2017, Hungary issued a CNY1 billion 3-year Panda bond in the CIBM, representing the first foreign sovereign CNY-denominated bond allocated to investors via book-building through Bond Connect. Since then, nonfinancial corporate debt financing instruments, Panda bonds, foreign sovereign government bonds denominated in Chinese renminbi, ABS, and other bonds have also been issued through Bond Connect. Since April 2019, even NCD have been issued to foreign investors via Bond Connect.

Legal and Regulatory Framework

A. Legal Tradition

The legal structure of the PRC follows the socialist legal system with Chinese characteristics guided by the Constitution of the PRC. The current version of the constitution was adopted in 1982, with further revisions in 1988, 1993, 1999, and 2004. The constitution was last amended on 11 March 2018. The legal framework is expressed through the Civil Law, commercial laws, and other laws.

B. English Translation

Laws and regulations in the PRC are generally published in Chinese, the official national language. Official publications use the simplified Chinese character set. Simplified Chinese characters, known as *jiǎnhuàzì* (简化字), are standardized Chinese characters prescribed in the Table of General Standard Chinese Characters for use in the PRC. Along with traditional Chinese characters, they are one of the two standard character sets of the contemporary Chinese written language. The Government of the PRC has promoted them for use in printing since the 1950s to encourage literacy. They are officially used in the PRC and Singapore.

In addition, the State Council, relevant ministries, stock exchanges, SROs, and market institutions may provide official or unofficial English translations of the laws, regulations, and directives for which they are responsible. For example, NAFMII carries on its website a selection of the relevant laws and regulations for the CIBM and selected self-regulatory rules and guidelines in English.[8] CFETS also carries on its website a selection of relevant regulations, market rules, and guidelines for the CIBM in English.[9]

Some market institutions provide unofficial English translations of the laws, regulations, and directives under their own purview. These English translations are typically available from an institution's websites, market observers, or the law departments of universities.[10]

The English version of the PBOC website contains a list of selected laws and regulations related to the CIBM and other market segments, which are available for

---

[8] See http://www.nafmii.org.cn/english/lawsandregulations/relevantlaws_e/index.html/ or http://www.nafmii.org.cn/english/lawsandregulations/selfregulatory_e/index.html.

[9] CFETS rules and regulations related to nonresident issuers and investors can be found at http://www.chinamoney.com.cn/english/rarrmrrud/.

[10] As an example of a regulatory institution's website, SHCH posts rules and regulations with relevance for nonresident issuers and investors on its English language website. See http://english.shclearing.com/ccpservices/rules/?xyz=0.8713127992131637. For an example of a university law department's website, see the Peking University Center for Legal Information (北大英华科技有限公司) http://en.pkulaw.cn/.

viewing or download.[11] Laws and regulations on securities and derivatives—including state laws, administrative laws, judicial interpretations, State Council department rules, and the rules of SROs—are available from the CSRC website, if only in Chinese.[12] CSRC has an English website. Hence, some English translations of laws and regulations, in particular those pertaining to the QFII and RQFII regimes, may be available from this site. At the same time, the CSRC website does not contain rules and regulations related to the CIBM. Otherwise, English translations of laws and regulations may be available from other official or private institutions.

While there may be no specific mention on these websites, only the versions of laws, regulations, and other regulatory instruments issued in Chinese are relied upon for matters before the courts. At the same time, translations of laws, regulations, and rules may result in the use of different terminology in English from what was intended in the original Chinese version. This has been observed, particularly when it comes to the description of rules and regulations. As a result, this bond market guide also includes the title of institutions and major laws and regulations in Chinese characters to aid the reader in ensuring that the correct description of the institutions, laws, or regulations in question is provided.

Please also refer to Chapter III.H for additional information on this topic in the context of debt financing instrument issuance documentation and Appendix 5 for a list of Chinese technical terms and their interpretations in English.

C.   Legislative Structure

The legal framework of the China bond market consists of laws, administrative regulations, department rules, business rules, and business agreements (Table 2.1). This structure applies to all bond market segments, including the Inter-Bank Bond Market.

Key legislation is the summary term for those laws aimed at a particular market such as the securities market or capital market. These laws establish and govern securities markets or market segments, including the bond market, its institutions, members, and participants. Laws are prepared by the National People's Congress (NPC) or its Standing Committee; the laws on the bond market regulate and ensure the effective operation of the market.

Administrative regulations are issued by the State Council and contain market management rules. Administrative rules also include local rules promulgated by local governments, as may be applicable, and cover administrative measures on products, market participants, and other market features.

Departmental rules are categorized as administrative rules and promulgated by the ministries and commissions under the State Council, PBOC, and other departments with administrative responsibilities directly under the State Council, including the bond market regulator(s).

Self-regulatory rules are set by SROs such as NAFMII. Industry provisions and business rules are issued by bond market infrastructure or market institutions such as CCDC, CFETS, and SHCH.

Business agreements are the service agreements signed by and between the bond market infrastructure institutions and their customers or account holders.

---

[11] See http://www.pbc.gov.cn/english/130733/index.html.
[12] CSRC. Laws and Regulations. http://www.csrc.gov.cn/pub/csrc_en/laws/rfdm/.

Table 2.1: Bond Market Legislative Structure in the People's Republic of China

	Legislative Structure
First tier	Constitution
Second tier	Laws (prepared by the NPC or the NPC Standing Committee, with supreme legal force)
Third tier	Administrative regulations (issued by the State Council); Local rules, local opinions (promulgated by local governments)
Fourth tier	Departmental rules (prepared by departments of the State Council, inclusive of bond market supervisory organization[s])
Fifth tier	Self-regulatory rules, industry provisions, business rules, and guidelines (issued by NAFMII and bond market infrastructure institutions such as CCDC and SHCH)
Sixth tier	Business agreements (service agreements signed by and between the bond market infrastructure institutions and customers)

CCDC = China Central Depository & Clearing Co., Ltd.; NAFMII = National Association of Financial Market Institutional Investors; NPC = National People's Congress; SHCH = Shanghai Clearing House.
Source: ASEAN+3 Bond Market Forum Sub-Forum 1 team based on CCDC. 2016. *China Bond Market Overview 2015*. Beijing.

In practice, market laws and regulations are the general terms used when referring to laws, administrative regulations, and department rules. Table 2.2 provides significant examples in each of the respective legislative tiers.

Table 2.2: Examples of China Inter-Bank Bond Market Legislation by Legislative Tier

Legislative Tier	Content or Significant Examples
Constitution of the People's Republic of China	Principles, Rights, and Obligations
Laws (key legislation)	• Law of the People's Republic of China on the People's Bank of China, 2003 • Law of the People's Republic of China on Banking and Supervision, 2004 • Law of the People's Republic of China on Funds for Investment in Securities, 2009 • Company Law of the People's Republic of China, 2013 • Securities Law of the People's Republic of China, 2014
Administrative regulations	• Administrative Measures for Debt Financing Instruments of Non-Financial Enterprises in the Inter-Bank Bond Market, 2008, No.1 PBOC (银行间债券市场非金融企业债务融资工具管理办法) • Administrative Measures for the Registration, Depository and Settlement of Bonds in the Inter-Bank Bond Market, 2009, No. 1 PBOC (银行间债券市场债券登记托管结算管理办法) • Regulations on the Administration of Enterprise Bonds, 2011 Revision

continued on next page

Table 2.2 *continued*

	• Interim Regulation on Enterprise Information Disclosure, 2014 • Guidelines for Book Building in Issuance of Enterprise Bonds (Interim), 2014 • Interim Measures for Administration of the Bond Issuance by Overseas Institutions in the National Inter-Bank Bond Market (全国银行间债券市场境外机构债券发行管理暂行办法) (PBOC and MOF Notice 2018, No.16)
Departmental rules	• Administrative Measures for the Cross-Market Transfer of Government Bonds, 2003 • Regulation of the People's Republic of China on Foreign Exchange Administration, 2008 Revision • Regulation on Treasury Bonds of the People's Republic of China, 2011 • Administrative Measures for the Issuance and Transactions of Corporate Bonds, 2015 • Interim Measures for the Administration of Mutual Bond Market Access between Mainland China and Hong Kong SAR, 2017, No. 1 (内地与香港债券市场互联互通合作管理暂行办法)
Self-regulatory rules, industry provisions, business rules and guidelines	• Rules for the Registration and Issuance of Debt Financing Instruments of Non-Financial Enterprises (非金融企业债务融资工具注册发行规则2016版), 19 February 2016 • Rules for Information Disclosure on Debt Financing Instruments of Non-Financial Enterprises in the Inter-Bank Bond Market (银行间债券市场非金融企业债务融资工具信息披露规则), 8 December 2017 • Rules and Procedures for the Registration of Debt Financing Instruments of Non-Financial Enterprises for Private Placement, (非金融企业债务融资工具定向发行注册工作规程) 29 August 2017 • Provisions for the Selection of Specialized Institutional Investors of Private Placement Notes (定向债务融资工具专项机构投资人遴选细则(2018版)) and the List of the Specialized Institutional Investors of Private Placement Notes (2018年度定向债务融资工具专项机构投资人名单), 14 December 2018 • Model Investor Protection Clauses 2019 (投资人保护条款示范文本(2019版)的公告), 10 April 2019 • Guidelines on Debt Financing Instruments of Overseas Non-Financial Enterprises (for Trial Implementation) (境外非金融企业债务融资工具业务指引(试行)), 17 January 2019 • Guidelines for Default and Risk Disposal on Debt Financing Instruments of Non-Financial Enterprises in the Inter-Bank Bond Market (银行间债券市场非金融企业债务融资工具违约及风险处置指南), 27 December 2019 • Meeting Rules and Procedures for Holders of Debt Financing Instruments of Non-Financial Enterprises in the Inter-Bank Bond Market (2019 Revision) (银行间债券市场非金融企业债务融资工具持有人会议规程) (修订稿), 27 December 2019 • Guidelines for Bond Trustee Business of Non-Financial Enterprise Debt Financing Instruments in the Inter-Bank Bond Market (for Trial Implementation) (银行间债券市场非金融企业债务融资工具受托管理人业务指引(试行)), 27 December 2019 • Rules and Procedures for the Registration of Debt Financing Instruments of Non-Financial Enterprises for Public Offering (非金融企业债务融资工具公开发行注册工作规程2020版), effective 1 July 2020

MOF = Ministry of Finance, NAFMII = National Association of Financial Market Institutional Investors, OTC = over-the-counter, PBOC = People's Bank of China, SAR = Special Administrative Region.
Notes: www.lawinfochina.com is a website for English-language resources on Chinese law created and maintained by Chinalawinfo Co., Ltd. and the Legal Information Center of Peking University. Chinalawinfo Co., Ltd. is a legal information and education company established by Peking University through its Legal Information Center. For details, see http://www.lawinfochina.com/search/SearchLaw.aspx.
Sources: ABMF SF1 and information on laws and regulations from www.lawinfochina.com and the NAFMII website.

D.   Inter-Bank Bond Market Regulatory Structure

The CIBM is overseen by the PBOC (as the overall regulatory authority) and administered by NAFMII (as the SRO for the CIBM) under the guidance of the PBOC. The two depositories for the CIBM—the CCDC and the SHCH—issue self-regulatory rules and business rules for its account holders and constituents that are binding.

It is notable that the scale and style of regulation differs between the CIBM and the exchange bond market. Both markets have historically adopted different approaches for setting regulations. For example, in the CIBM, under the mandate and supervision of the PBOC, NAFMII administers much of the market and its participants.

Table 2.3 gives an overview of the supervisory institutions with relevance for the CIBM. Table 2.4 shows the relation between specific debt instrument types, their issuer categories, and each supervisory institution.

Table 2.3: Supervisory Institutions and Instruments under Their Remit

Institution	Subjects
PBOC	Overall supervision for the CIBM, policy bank financial bonds, Panda bonds (issued in the CIBM)
NDRC	Issuances of enterprise bonds and railway bonds
CBIRC	Financial bonds and credit asset-backed securities issued by banking institutions, financial bonds issued by insurance institutions
CSRC	Exchange bond market, National Equities Exchange and Quotations (new Third Board); securities company short-term notes, corporate bonds, convertible bonds, detachable convertible bonds, enterprise asset-backed securities, Panda bonds (issued in the exchange bond market)
SAFE	Panda bonds, QFII and RQFII quotas (until September 2019)

CBIRC = China Banking and Insurance Regulatory Commission, CIBM = China Inter-Bank Bond Market, CSRC = China Securities Regulatory Commission, NDRC = National Development and Reform Commission, PBOC = People's Bank of China, QFII = Qualified Foreign Institutional Investor, RQFII = Renminbi Qualified Foreign Institutional Investor, SAFE = State Administration of Foreign Exchange.
Source: ASEAN+3 Bond Market Forum Sub-Forum 1 team compilation based on China Depository & Clearing Co., Ltd. 2016. *China Bond Market Overview 2015*. Beijing.

Table 2.4: Bond Types, Issuer Categories, and Related Supervisory Institutions

Bond Type	Issuer Category	Institution(s)
Commercial paper of securities companies	Securities companies	CSRC, SAC, NAFMII (for registration)
Debt financing instruments	Medium-term notes, commercial paper, short-term commercial paper, private placement notes, SME collective notes, asset-backed notes	PBOC, NAFMII (for registration)
Enterprise bonds	Enterprises	NDRC, NAFMII (for registration)
Financial bonds	Commercial banks, insurance institutions, non-bank financial institutions	CBIRC, PBOC, NAFMII (for registration)
	Asset management companies	
Panda bonds	Foreign financial institutions, foreign nonfinancial enterprises	MOF, PBOC, SAFE, NAFMII (for registration)
Policy bank financial bonds[a]	Policy banks	PBOC, NAFMII (for registration)

CBIRC = China Banking and Insurance Regulatory Commission, CSRC = China Securities Regulatory Commission, MOF = Ministry of Finance, NAFMII = National Association of Financial Market Institutional Investors, NDRC = National Development and Reform Commission, PBOC = People's Bank of China, SAC = Securities Association of China, SAFE = State Administration of Foreign Exchange, SME = small and medium-sized enterprises.

[a] Policy bank financial bonds may be subsumed in the overall category of financial bonds in statistical and other official publications. Financial bonds are defined as bonds issued by regulated financial institutions (policy banks, commercial banks, insurance institutions, and non-bank financial institutions). However, while policy bank financial bonds are issued both in the Inter-Bank Bond Market and the exchange bond market, other financial bonds, such as those issued by commercial banks and insurance institutions, are only issued in the Inter-Bank Bond Market.

Notes: Table entries relate to the Inter-Bank Bond Market only. Bond types are presented in alphabetical order.

Source: ASEAN+3 Bond Market Forum Sub-Forum 1 team compilation based on Association of Corporate Counsel. 2017. *Capital Markets Global Guide 2016/2017: Debt Capital Markets in China—Regulatory Overview.* Beijing.

1.   Ministry of Finance (中华人民共和国财政部)

The MOF handles fiscal policy, economic regulations, and government expenditure for the state, formulating and implementing policies, rules, and regulations on managing the government's domestic debts and governing treasury bond issuance. The MOF also formulates policies, rules, and regulations on managing the government's external debts. Together with the PBOC, the MOF released the Interim Measures for the Administration on Bonds Issued by Overseas Issuers on the National Inter-Bank Bond Market in September 2018, which regulate the issuance of Panda bonds in the PRC.

As part of its remit to formulate and supervise accounting regulations, the MOF also supervises the accounting firms that help prepare and audit the financial statements of issuers of debt financing instruments in the CIBM.

At the time of compilation of this bond market guide, the website of the MOF was only available in Chinese.

2.   People's Bank of China (中国人民银行)

The PBOC was established on 1 December 1948 through the consolidation of Huabei Bank, Beihai Bank, and Xibei Farmer Bank. In September 1983, the State Council decided to allow the PBOC to function as a central bank. The Law of the People's Republic of China on the People's Bank of China, adopted on 18 March 1995 and amended from time to time, has since legally confirmed the PBOC's central bank status.[13]

The amended Law of the People's Republic of China on the People's Bank of China, adopted on 27 December 2003, provides that the PBOC perform the following major functions:

i.   drafting and enforcing relevant laws, rules, and regulations that are related to fulfilling its functions;

ii.   formulating and implementing monetary policy in accordance with the law;

iii.   issuing the renminbi and administering its circulation;

iv.   regulating financial markets, including the inter-bank lending market, CIBM, foreign exchange market, and gold market;

v.   preventing and mitigating systemic financial risks to safeguard financial stability;

vi.   maintaining the renminbi exchange rate at an adaptive and equilibrium level, and holding and managing the state foreign exchange and gold reserves;

vii.   managing the state treasury as fiscal agent;

viii. making payment and settlement rules in collaboration with relevant departments and ensuring normal operation of the payment and settlement systems;

ix.   providing guidance to anti-money-laundering work in the financial sector and monitoring money-laundering-related suspicious fund movement;

x.   developing a statistical system for the financial industry and being responsible for the consolidation of financial statistics as well as the conduct of economic analysis and forecasts;

xi.   administering credit reporting industry in the PRC and promoting the building up of a credit information system;

xii.   participating in international financial activities in the capacity of the central bank;

xiii. engaging in financial business operations in line with relevant rules; and

xiv.   performing other functions prescribed by the State Council.

In the context of the China bond market, the PBOC regulates and supervises the CIBM and its constituents, and it approves Panda bond issuances by nonresident financial institutions in the CIBM and domestic bond issuances by policy banks. The PBOC appoints and supervises bond settlement agents and market makers. The PBOC's open market operation is also carried out using CIBM infrastructure and practices.

For a list of the significant measures issued by the PBOC and other rules and regulations with direct relevance for the CIBM, please refer to Appendix 3.

---

[13] The Law of the People's Republic of China on the People's Bank of China (中華人民共和國中國人民銀行法).

3. China Banking and Insurance Regulatory Commission (中国银行保险监督管理委员会)

CBIRC is responsible for the licensing and supervision of the activities of banks and insurance companies, and their issuance of financial bonds and ABS.

CBIRC was officially unveiled on 8 April 2018 as a new regulatory authority, combining the functions of the then China Banking Regulatory Commission (CBRC) and the then China Insurance Regulatory Commission (CIRC).

The main responsibilities of CBIRC are to

i. regulate and supervise the banking and insurance sectors in the PRC in accordance with laws and regulations; ensure the legal and stable operation of banking and insurance institutions;

ii. conduct systematic research on reform and opening up as well as on supervisory effectiveness of the banking and insurance sectors; engage in strategic planning for financial reform and development, the drafting of laws and regulations of the banking and insurance sectors, and the establishment of a prudential regulation framework and a financial consumer protection framework; formulate relevant rules and regulations for the banking and insurance sectors, and make recommendations for the formulation and amendment of these rules and regulations;

iii. formulate supervisory rules for prudential regulation and financial consumer protection in accordance with the framework of prudential regulation and financial consumer protection; develop operational rules and supervisory rules for microfinance companies, financing guarantee companies, pawnshops, leasing companies, commercial factoring companies, local asset management companies, and other institutions; and establish a supervisory framework for the business activities of online lending institutions;

iv. license banking and insurance institutions and their business scope in accordance with laws and regulations; review and approve the qualification of senior management of relevant institutions; and formulate codes of conduct for banking and insurance employees;

v. conduct supervision on banking and insurance institutions in terms of corporate governance, risk management, internal control, capital adequacy, solvency, business operation, and information disclosure;

vi. conduct on-site examination and off-site surveillance on banking and insurance institutions, carry out risk and compliance assessment, protect the legitimate rights of financial consumers, and penalize illegal acts and misconducts;

vii. compile and publish statistical reports on the banking and insurance sectors, make due disclosure in accordance with requirements and perform the duty of financial statistical work;

viii. establish risk monitoring, control, assessment, and early warning mechanisms for the banking and insurance sectors; track, analyze, monitor, and forecast the banking and insurance operations;

ix. make recommendations for and oversee the implementation of the contingent risk resolution plans of depository financial institutions and insurance institutions;

x. crack down on illegal financial activities in accordance with laws and regulations, including identifying, punishing, and banning illegal fundraising activities and conducting relevant coordination work;

xi. provide guidance for and monitor the work of local financial regulatory authorities;

xii. engage in the activities of international banking and insurance organizations, including the international regulatory standard-setting work for the banking and insurance sectors; facilitate international cooperation in the banking and insurance sectors;

xiii.   carry out the routine administrative work of the supervisory boards of major banks; and

xiv.   perform other responsibilities assigned by the central government.

In the context of the CIBM, CBIRC licenses commercial banks and some non-bank financial institutions (such as finance companies) that participate in the CIBM, and it approves the issuance of debt financing instruments of commercial banks in the CIBM and the exchange bond market, pursuant to the Law of the People's Republic of China on Commercial Banks, 2015, which is also known as the Commercial Banks Law.

More information on the role and functions of CBIRC following the merger are available on its website.[14]

4.   China Securities Regulatory Commission (中国证券监督管理委员会)

CSRC was established in 1992 to administer the operation of the exchange market and to protect investors' rights and interests in the exchange market, including in the exchange bond market. CSRC is a ministerial-level public institution directly under the State Council. It performs a unified regulatory function, according to the relevant laws and regulations, and with the authority granted by the State Council over the securities and futures market of the PRC and some of its constituents across market segments, it maintains an orderly securities and futures market order, and ensures the legal operation of the capital market.

While CSRC is the key regulatory authority for the exchange bond market, it also fulfills some regulatory functions with regard to the CIBM. In this context, CSRC is responsible for the issuance of commercial paper and ABS by securities companies in the CIBM, as well as the issuance of corporate bonds.

At the same time, CSRC is responsible for the regulations underlying the QFII and RQFII market access schemes and, together with the PBOC, governs their eligibility for and activities in the CIBM.

5.   National Association of Financial Market Institutional Investors (中国银行间市场交易商协会)

NAFMII acts as the SRO for the CIBM under the supervision and guidance of the PBOC. NAFMII issues self-regulatory rules for its members and constituents in the CIBM and their conduct, including regulatory processes on the registration (注册) and issuance of debt financing instruments.

NAFMII was founded on 3 September 2007, based on the approval of the State Council. NAFMII aims to support and drive the development of the OTC financial market in the PRC, which is composed of the CIBM, interbank lending market, foreign exchange market, commercial paper and SCP market, and gold market.

The mandate for NAFMII as an SRO includes the following responsibilities:

i.   formulate self-regulatory rules, business standards, and professional ethics, and supervise their implementation;

ii.   admit and administer the licenses of lead underwriters, underwriters, and credit rating agencies (CRAs) in the CIBM;

---

[14] See https://www.cbirc.gov.cn/en/view/pages/index/index.html.

iii.   protect the legitimate rights and interests of NAFMII members and represent them to raise concerns, proposals, and requests they encounter during their business operations to related authorities and legislatures;

iv.   educate members and enhance their awareness to obey relevant state laws and regulations as well as guidelines, norms, and rules promulgated by NAFMII; supervise and examine member's practices and penalize those who violate the NAFMII constitution and self-regulatory rules in a bid to maintain market order;

v.   mediate disputes between NAFMII members and customers;

vi.   organize continuing education and business training programs for practitioners to improve their business skills and vocational capabilities;

vii.   organize research and exchanges among NAFMII members; initiate and manage the research and development of new products that are demanded by members, suitable to the characteristics of the CIBM and in accordance with relevant state stipulations to promote standardized business operation and business management;

viii.   collect, prepare, and publish relevant market data and information to serve NAFMII members;

ix.   conduct studies on issues related to market development, offer NAFMII members suggestions on business expansion, and provide ideas for market development to relevant supervisory authorities;

x.   carry out other work aimed at fulfilling NAFMII's purpose; and

xi.   undertake other duties and responsibilities bestowed by the Congress of NAFMII and those delegated by the PBOC.

Issuers in the CIBM need to register with NAFMII and also have their nonfinancial enterprise debt financing instruments registered with NAFMII prior to issuance (exceptions apply, see section F for details). Other CIBM market participants and intermediaries—including underwriters, accounting and auditing firms, law firms, and CRAs—should be members of NAFMII. NAFMII issues underwriting and lead underwriting licenses for debt financing instruments of nonfinancial enterprises to qualified financial institutions who must be its members; please see section M for a description of what qualifications are to be met by underwriters. NAFMII also tracks and evaluates the performance of underwriters as well as market makers and issues its findings and corresponding rankings on an annual basis. In addition, NAFMII admits CRAs and administers their licenses in the CIBM, and accepts filings from and administers bond trustees.

Investors need not be NAFMII members by default; however, the two types of PPN institutional investors, DIIs and SIIs, must be members of NAFMII.

For details on the membership, roles, and responsibilities of NAFMII in the context of the issuance, trading, and continuous disclosure on debt financing instruments in the CIBM, as well as governance of the CIBM, please see sections G and H in this chapter.

6.   National Development and Reform Commission (国家发展和改革委员会)

NDRC is the government agency responsible for supervising the issuance of enterprise bonds (企业债券); see also Chapter III.B for more information on the types of bonds issued in the CIBM. For historical reasons, enterprise bonds have always been supervised by NDRC, being a government agency overseeing SOE reform. NDRC also oversees credit ratings for enterprise bonds.

The NDRC's Department of Fiscal and Financial Affairs is responsible for studying and analyzing the capital balance of the whole society; studying fiscal and monetary policies and issues of fiscal and financial system reform, and analyzing the implementation of fiscal and monetary policies and making recommendations in this regard; putting forward development strategies and policy recommendations concerning direct financing; reviewing and approving securities issuance of nonlisted companies; and taking the lead in promoting the development of investment funds and venture funds, as well as the development of relevant systems.[15]

7.   State Administration of Foreign Exchange (国家外汇管理局)

SAFE is an administrative agency tasked with drafting the rules and regulations governing foreign exchange market activities and managing the state foreign exchange reserves for the PBOC. The major functions of SAFE include the following:

i.   study and propose policy suggestions on reform of the foreign exchange administration system, prevention of balance-of-payments risks, and promotion of balance-of-payments equilibrium; study and implement policy measures for the gradual advancement of the convertibility of the Chinese renminbi under the capital account and the cultivation and development of the foreign exchange market; and provide suggestions and a foundation for the PBOC to formulate policy on the Chinese renminbi's exchange rates;

ii.   participate in the drafting of relevant laws, regulations, and departmental rules on foreign exchange administration, releasing standard documents related to carrying out these responsibilities;

iii.   oversee the statistics and monitoring of the balance of payments and external credit and debt, releasing relevant information according to regulations and undertaking related work concerning the monitoring of cross-border capital flows;

iv.   supervise and manage the foreign exchange bond market of the state, undertake supervision and management of the settlement and sale of foreign exchange, cultivate and develop the foreign exchange market;

v.   supervise and check the authenticity and legality of the receipt and payment of foreign exchange under the current account according to law; implement foreign exchange administration under the capital account according to law, and continuously improve management work in line with the convertibility process of the Chinese renminbi under the capital account; and regulate management of overseas and domestic foreign exchange accounts;

vi.   supervise and check foreign exchange according to law and punish behavior that violates the foreign exchange administration;

vii.   undertake operation and management of foreign exchange reserves, gold reserves, and other foreign exchange assets of the state;

viii.   arrange development planning, standards, and criteria for information-technology-based foreign exchange administration, and organize the relevant implementation; supervise information-sharing with the relevant administrative departments according to law;

ix.   take part in relevant international financial activities; and

x.   undertake other matters as assigned by the State Council and the PBOC.

In relation to the CIBM, SAFE had been responsible for allocating and supervising the QFII and RQFII quotas (until September 2019), and it continues to provide approval on the issuance of Panda bonds by nonresident issuers. Please also see section N in this chapter for a detailed description of the QFII and RQFII concepts and the related role of SAFE.

---

[15] See http://en.ndrc.gov.cn/mfod/200812/t20081218_252208.html.

E.   Regulatory Framework for Debt Financing Instruments

The regulatory framework for debt financing instruments in the PRC is very much dependent on the type of bond and the market in which it is intended to be traded. For example, for the purpose of issuing bonds, different provisions apply to different types of bonds with respect to their governing regulatory authority, information disclosure, and credit rating, among others (Table 2.5).

Table 2.5: Overview of Regulatory Framework for Debt Financing Instruments in the Inter-Bank Bond Market

Main regulator	People's Bank of China (PBOC)
Additional regulators	• China Banking and Insurance Regulatory Commission (CBIRC) • China Securities Regulatory Commission (CSRC) • National Development and Reform Commission (NDRC)
Self-regulatory organization	National Association of Financial Market Institutional Investors (NAFMII)
Trading permission	Yes, admission by China Foreign Exchange Trade System (CFETS) to its platform
Fundamental and key legislation, key regulations	• Law of the People's Republic of China on the People's Bank of China, 2003 • Measures for the Administration of Bond Transactions in the National Inter-Bank Bond Market, 2000 • Measures for the Administration of the Issuance of Financial Bonds in the National Inter-Bank Bond Market, 2005
Regulations for cross-transfers between the CIBM and exchange market	• Regulation on Central Government Bonds of the People's Republic of China, 2011 • Regulations on Administration of Enterprise Bonds, 2011
Issuance approval	Yes; by responsible regulatory authority and registration with NAFMII (for debt financing instruments issued by nonfinancial enterprises)
Investor approval	Yes; membership with NAFMII required; regulatory approval necessary for nonresident investors under market access programs (QFII, RQFII, QOII)

CIBM = China Inter-Bank Bond Market, QFII = Qualified Foreign Institutional Investor, QOII = Qualified Overseas Institutional Investor, RQFII = Renminbi Qualified Foreign Institutional Investor.
Source: ASEAN+3 Bond Market Forum Sub-Forum 1 team.

In the CIBM, the issuance of bonds and notes—here referred to as debt financing instruments—requires approval from the PBOC for selected instrument types and registration with NAFMII in cases of issuance of debt financing instruments by nonfinancial enterprises. In addition, bonds and other debt financing instruments to be issued by specific entities require the review and approval of NDRC, while debt issuances by commercial banks, finance companies, and insurance companies require approval from CBIRC. Issuances by securities companies in the CIBM, such as commercial paper, also require the consent of CSRC.

Investment in debt financing instruments issued in the CIBM may be subject to specific approvals, particularly if investors are nonresidents, from the responsible regulatory authorities; please see Chapter III.P for details.

F.   Debt Financing Instrument Issuance Regulatory Processes

There is no universal approval procedure for the issuance of debt financing instruments in the PRC. In principle, the issuer needs to determine the necessary issuance qualifications under prevailing laws and regulations. After approval by or filing with the relevant regulatory authorities, bonds can be issued in the CIBM upon registration with NAFMII. When bonds are intended to be issued in the CIBM, approval from the PBOC may be required for selected instrument types and the bonds need to be registered with NAFMII to be traded on the CFETS platform.

Public offerings of debt securities should meet the conditions prescribed in the Securities Law and the Company Law, as well as administrative regulations formulated by NDRC for enterprise bonds and the provisions in the Commercial Banks Law for financial bonds under the purview of CBIRC. Private placements need to observe relevant regulations and rules for an issuance in the CIBM, including the offer mechanism to specific investor types prescribed by NAFMII.

1.   Regulatory Processes by Issuer Type

Table 2.6 provides an overview of these regulatory processes by corporate issuer type and identifies which regulatory authority or market institution is involved. To make the issuance process by issuer type more comparable across ASEAN+3 markets, the table features common issuer-type distinctions that are evident in regional markets.[16] Not all markets will distinguish all such issuer types or prescribe approvals. Sovereign issuers are typically exempt from corporate issuance approvals but may be subject to different regulatory processes.

Approval required from regulatory authorities, in fact the involvement of regulatory authorities in the issuance process for debt financing instruments, may depend on the nature of the debt financing instrument and the issuer type. The issuance of debt financing instruments by selected domestic financial institutions (e.g., policy banks) is regulated and approved by the PBOC, while commercial banks, finance companies, and insurance companies require approval from CBIRC. These debt financing instruments need not be registered with NAFMII; NAFMII only undertakes the registration for issuances by nonfinancial enterprises. Nonresident financial institutions are required to obtain issuance approval for their Panda bonds from the PBOC. Nonresident issuers approved or registered to issue bonds in the PRC shall complete the applicable foreign exchange registration with SAFE.

---

[16] ASEAN+3 refers to the 10 members of the Association of Southeast Nations (ASEAN) plus the People's Republic of China, Japan, and the Republic of Korea.

Table 2.6: Authorities in the Regulatory Process for the Inter-Bank Bond Market by Issuer Type

Type of Issuer	SAFE	PBOC (supervision of issuances)	NAFMII (registration)	NDRC (approval and registration)	CBIRC or CSRC
Resident issuer					
Resident nonfinancial institution	N.A.	N.A.	X	X[a]	N.A.
Resident financial institution	N.A.	X	N.A.	N.A.	X[b]
Resident issuing FCY-denominated bonds	X	N.A.	N.A.	N.A.	N.A.
Nonresident issuer					
Nonresident nonfinancial institution	X[c]	X	X	N.A.	N.A.
Nonresident financial institution	X[c]	X	N.A.	N.A.	N.A.
Nonresident issuing FCY-denominated	X[c]	X[d]	X	N.A.	N.A.

CBIRC = China Banking and Insurance Regulatory Commission, CSRC = China Securities Regulatory Commission, ГCY= foreign currency, MOГ = Ministry of Гinance, N.A. = not applicable, NAГMII = National Association of Financial Market Institutional Investors, NDRC = National Development and Reform Commission, PBOC = People's Bank of China, SAFE = State Administration of Foreign Exchange.
[a] Approval or registration required from NDRC for enterprise bonds.
[b] Approval required from CBIRC for bonds issued by financial institutions (including non-bank financial institutions, such as finance companies and insurance companies) or CSRC for bonds issued by securities companies.
[c] Approval is not required; a foreign exchange registration with SAFE is required.
[d] Bonds denominated in special drawing rights are approved by the PBOC.
Note: X indicates approval is required.
Source: ASEAN+3 Bond Market Forum Sub-Forum 1 team.

2.   Regulatory Process Overview

The regulatory process map may help with the navigation of the regulatory processes applicable to a bond or note issuance in the CIBM (Figure 2). Debt financing instruments may be issued in the CIBM either through public offering or a private placement.

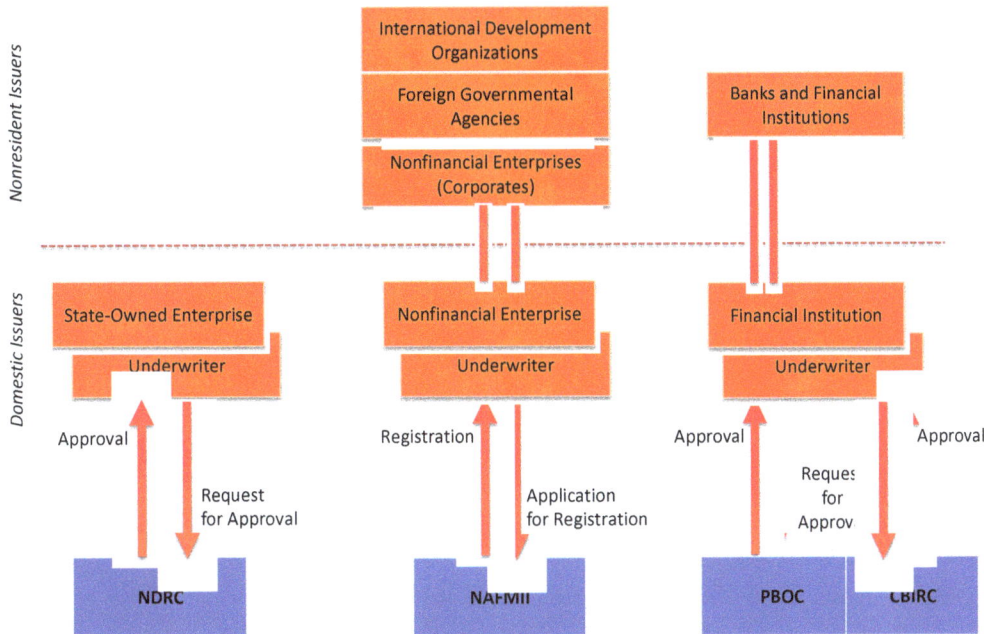

Figure 2: Regulatory Process Map—Debt Financing Instrument Issuance in the Inter-Bank Bond Market

CBIRC = China Banking and Insurance Regulatory Commission, NAFMII = National Association of Financial Market Institutional Investors, NDRC = National Development and Reform Commission, PBOC = People's Bank of China.
Source: ASEAN+3 Bond Market Forum Sub-Forum 1 team.

Individual regulatory processes for the issuance of debt financing instruments in the CIBM, as may be applicable, are explained in the next few sections.

3.   Regulatory Process for Public Offerings

This regulatory process applies to the issuance of debt financing instruments by nonfinancial enterprises.[17] Please see section 7 for detailed information on the issuance process and necessary approvals for financial bonds issued by financial institutions and insurance companies.

The principal regulatory process for the issuance and registration of debt financing instruments in the CIBM is prescribed in a number of NAFMII regulations:

- Rules for the Registration and Issuance of Debt Financing Instruments of Non-Financial Enterprises in the Inter-Bank Market, 2016 (非金融企业债务融资工具注册发行规则 2016 版), commonly referenced as RRI: standardized the NAFMII registration procedures for issuance and explained registration for public offering and private placement and two types of issuances to private placement investors;[18]
- Rules and Procedures for the Registration of Debt Financing Instruments of Non-Financial Enterprises for Public Offering, 2020 (非金融企业债务融资工具公开发行注册

---

[17] Please see Chapter III.A for a definition of debt financing instruments in the CIBM.
[18] NAFMII Announcement (2016, No. 4) is available in Chinese at http://www.nafmii.org.cn/ggtz/gg/201602/t20160219_51278.html; the RRI is available in Chinese at http://www.nafmii.org.cn/ggtz/gg/201602/P020160219637549379178.doc.

工作规程 2020 版), commonly referenced as RPR: covered the Registration Committee, description of the issuer classification management, and filing requirements to NAFMII;[19]

- System of Registration Documents and Forms for Non-Financial Enterprises Publicly Offering Debt Financing Instruments, 2020 (非金融企业债务融资工具公开发行注册文件表格体系 2020 版), commonly referenced as SRP;[20] and,
- Rules for Information Disclosure on Debt Financing Instruments of Non-Financial Enterprises in the Inter-Bank Bond Market, 2017 (银行间债券市场非金融企业债务融资工具信息披露规则 2017 版), commonly referenced as RID: standardized the information disclosure behavior of nonfinancial enterprises in issuing debt financing instruments in the CIBM.[21]

The RPR and SRP were further refined in April 2020 (effective 1 July 2020) to streamline the registration and issuance processes and to optimize disclosure obligations via a new issuer subcategorization and the ability to tailor disclosure to specific products or distribution channels. They also now include provisions related to the use of a bond trustee in the CIBM (see also Chapter III.S for details on bond trustee).

Under Article 3 of the RRI, any prospective issuer who intends to issue debt financing instruments in the CIBM is required to register these debt financing instruments with NAFMII, provided the issuer meets the following criteria for the public offering of corporate bonds (including debt financing instruments issued by enterprises), as stipulated in Article 16 of the Securities Law:

i.   The net assets of the company shall not be less than CNY30 million in the case of a joint stock company and not less than CNY60 million in the case of a limited liability company.
ii.   The aggregate amount of bonds issued does not exceed 40% of the total net assets of the company.
iii. The average distributable profits over the last 3 years are sufficient to cover 1 year's interest payment on the corporate bonds.
iv.   The use of proceeds conforms to the industrial policy of the Government of the PRC.
v.   The interest rate payable on corporate bonds does not exceed the levels set by the State Council.
vi.   The proceeds of newly issued corporate bonds must be used for the purposes approved by the competent authorities and shall not be used to cover losses or for nonproduction expenditures.
vii. Other requirements apply as prescribed by the State Council.

With regard to item ii. above, the aggregate value of the outstanding principal and interest of all its MTN and commercial paper already issued does not exceed 40% of the issuer's net asset value, as also stipulated in Article 4 of the Guidelines on the Issuance of Non-Financial Enterprise Medium-Term Notes in the Inter-Bank Bond Market and Article 4 of the Guidelines on the Issuance of Commercial Paper by Non-Financial Enterprises in the Inter-Bank Bond Market.[22]

The registration with NAFMII only applies to debt financing instruments issued by nonfinancial enterprises (i.e., corporates). NAFMII administers the registration process through a categorization of the issuer and the type of debt financing instrument to be issued. The 2016 RPR contained two categories, which were refined to four categories

---

[19] The RPR is available in Chinese at http://www.nafmii.org.cn/ggtz/gg/202004/t20200416_79936.html.
[20] The SRP is available in Chinese at http://www.nafmii.org.cn/ggtz/gg/202004/t20200416_79936.html.
[21] NAFMII Announcement (2017, No. 32) for the RID is available in Chinese at http://nafmii.org.cn/zlgz/201712/t20171212_66667.html.
[22] Please see Chapter III.A for the definition of medium-term notes.

in the 2020 revision to distinguish between mature and basic-level enterprises differentiated by market recognition, experience in information disclosure, and past issuance activities.[23]

To be classified as a mature enterprise, an issuer would need to meet the following conditions:

i. high market recognition or prominent industry status, sound corporate governance, and production and operations that comply with national macroeconomic and industrial policies;

ii. a stable financial situation with the size, capital structure, and profitability to meet the specific requirements of its industry classification;[24]

iii. an established public information disclosure practice (no less than three separate issuances of debt financing instruments or other debt instruments in the last 36 months and debt financing instrument issuance to the public of not less than CNY10 billion during that period);

iv. no default on or delayed payment of principal and interest within the last 36 months, for both the issuer and parent company, if applicable;

v. no violation of laws and regulations, breaches of NAFMII self-regulations, investigations by competent authorities, or administrative or criminal penalties; and

vi. other conditions set by NAFMII in accordance with investor protection requirements.

A mature enterprise may be classified as a Category I issuer if it can show

i. assets exceeding CNY300 billion, an asset–liability ratio lower than 75%, and a total return-on-assets ratio of more than 3%;

ii. issuance of debt financing instruments in the past 36 months of not less than CNY50 billion; and

iii. it plays a key role in the national economy with assets exceeding CNY800 billion.

A Category II issuer represents any enterprise within the mature category that does not meet the Category I criteria above.

Basic-level enterprises are divided into Category III and Category IV issuers. A Category III enterprise is any that does not fall within the mature category but has a history of registration for public issuance of more than 2 years and has issued debt financing instruments via a public offering in the last 2 years. In contrast, a Category IV issuer is any enterprise that does not fall within the mature category and only has a history of registration for public issuance of less than 2 years and/or has not previously issued debt financing instruments via a public offering.

According to Article 6 of the RPR (2020), any enterprise that has defaulted on a debt financing instrument or made a delayed payment of principal and interest, or where default or delay remain, shall not issue debt financing instruments via a public offering.

A comprehensive description of the issuer categories and their respective registration obligations and considerations can be found in Articles 6–14 of the RPR (2020).

---

[23] "Mature" and "basic-level" enterprises represent the terms in an unofficial English translation of the RPR, which are only available in Chinese; terms used in an official translation by NAFMII or other parties at a later stage may differ.

[24] The appendix of the RPR (2020) contains a table detailing the minimum asset size, maximum assets to liabilities ratio and minimum return on assets percentage prescribed for a mature enterprise (issuer) according to four industry groupings.

Issuers may register for the public offering of a single or multiple debt financing instruments, depending on their categorization. Mature enterprises are able to use the same registration documents for a number of different debt financing instrument types. Basic-level enterprises need to prepare separate registrations for each instrument type they intend to issue.

Registration for a single debt financing instrument type (required for Categories III and IV)

Under provisions in the RPR (2020), a Category IV issuer is required to prepare a registration document and make a registration each for the public offering of SCP, commercial paper, and bonds and notes (except for other types of debt financing instruments specified in the relevant rules or guidelines of NAFMII, which require a separate registration, such as ABS and project revenue notes). Issuers registering for SCP and commercial paper are permitted to form a lead underwriting consortium at the time of registration. Categories I and II issuers may register for a single debt financing instrument type as per their requirements.

Registration for multiple types of debt financing instruments (Categories I and II)

Categories I and II issuers may elect to register multiple types of debt financing instruments in one step and are permitted to not specify the actual type and registered quota for each instrument at the time of registration but only need to specify the type, scale, and terms of each issuance at the time of issuance and form a lead underwriting consortium at the time of registration.

Categories I, II, and III issuers may issue their registered debt financing instruments according to the issuer's own plan while the registration is valid. A lead underwriter and, optionally, a joint lead underwriter for each issuance only need to be designated at the time of issuance. Changes in members of the lead underwriting consortium may be made while the registration is valid, with the issuer submitting a description of the change and a recommendation letter for the newly appointed underwriter from the lead underwriter. The number of members of the lead underwriting syndicate is determined by the planned public offering size.

A Category IV issuer may only publicly issue registered SCP according to its own plan within the validity period of the SCP registration. The validity period for such a registration is 12 months.

In case an issuer no longer fulfills the conditions for its original categorization, the issuer shall amend the registration document in accordance with the rules for the category it now complies with during the review period of its registration; if an existing registration is still valid, any subsequent public offering shall comply with the rules for the original category and any issuance after 12 months of registration acceptance shall be filed with NAFMII in advance; if an existing registration has expired, the issuer shall reregister in accordance with the rules for the new category.

The individual steps of the registration process for a public offering are explained next.

Step 1—Application to the National Association of Financial Market Institutional Investors

An issuer who intends to issue debt financing instruments has to appoint a qualified underwriter who will subsequently submit the relevant registration documents to the Registration Office of the Secretariat of NAFMII. The underwriter needs to be a member of NAFMII. The required activities and obligations of the issuer, lead underwriter, and other intermediaries, as well as the necessary forms for registration documents are outlined in the SRP.

The lead underwriter must monitor the business operation and financial situation of the issuing enterprise during the registration review and throughout the period of validity of the registration, and advise the issuer to make supplementary disclosures on material events and other major events.

Due diligence by the underwriter

Separately, NAFMII requires the lead underwriter to conduct due diligence for the proposed registration. The lead underwriter will compile a due diligence report to be filed with NAFMII. The due diligence should cover, but may not be limited to, the following:

    i.   qualification of the issuance;
    ii.   history of the issuer;
    iii.   ownership structure, the controlling shareholder, and actual controller;
    iv.   corporate governance;
    v.   information disclosure system;
    vi.   business scope and main business status;
    vii.   financial status;
    viii.   credit history; and
    ix.   contingent liabilities and other obligations.

The lead underwriter carries out due diligence via access to the issuer, interviews, participation in meetings, field investigations, information analysis, certifications, and discussions.

As stipulated in the Guidelines on the Issuance of Non-Financial Enterprise Medium-Term Notes in the Inter-Bank Bond Market, the registration documents are to be prepared in line with NAFMII requirements and must include the following:

    i.   registration report for the debt financing instruments to be publicly issued by the issuer (with the resolution of the authoritative body under the constitutional documents of the issuer attached),
    ii.   letter of recommendation from the lead underwriter,
    iii.   the prospectus (募集说明书),
    iv.   other documents that the issuer intends to publicly disclose, and
    v.   any other documents as required by NAFMII.

Documentation to be submitted for registration and official filings with the regulatory authorities need to be in Chinese or are to be translated into Chinese, particularly in the case of a public offering. See also Chapter III.G for more information on the language of documentation and disclosure items.

Any issuer who has made separate registrations for SCP, commercial paper, or MTN may, after an existing registration has expired or the registration quota has been exhausted, submit another registration document for the issuance of the same type of instrument. A Category I or Category II issuer who made a consolidated registration for

SCP, commercial paper, MTN, and other types of debt financing instruments may submit the same kind of registration documents within 3 months before the expiry date of the registration.

The specific use of the proceeds from the debt financing instrument issuance shall be clearly stated in the disclosure document. Any changes made to the use of proceeds before maturity shall be subject to prior disclosure. The corporate credit rating of the issuer should be disclosed in the disclosure document and the credit rating of the debt financing instrument should also be disclosed if the bond contains special terms that may affect the issuer's credit rating.

The issuer shall state the applicable investor protection mechanism(s) in the offering document (发行文件) of the MTN in the event of a deterioration of the financial status of the issuer or other situations that may affect investor interests, as well as details on claim arrangements in case of events of default. The mention of specific measures in the event of a credit rating downgrade of the issuer is not mandated but may be included as one of the situations that may affect investor interests. At present, issuers are only required to disclose a credit rating downgrade once it occurs.

If a downgrade happens after an issuer's registration is accepted (but before bond issuance), the issuer is required to modify their registration documents (i.e., disclosing the relevant adverse events) and submit it to NAFMII for another round of review by the Registration Committee (see also the detailed description in Step 2). The issuer need not redeem the outstanding bonds under such circumstance.

If the credit rating downgrade happens after issuance of the debt financing instruments, the issuer will need to disclose such occurrence as a material event, pursuant to applicable disclosure regulations.

Prospectus (募集说明书)

There is no formal definition of the term prospectus as a key disclosure document in rules and regulations, and the Chinese characters used for the key disclosure document in a public offering do not distinguish between the type of issuance; English translations of the PBOC and NAFMII regulations refer to a prospectus as the key disclosure document for a public offering (other than for Panda bonds). At the same time, market feedback indicates that investors in the CIBM generally consider there to be no material difference between a prospectus and an offering circular and their respective contents.

As stated in the SRP (2020), if an issuer wishes to make a public offering via Bond Connect, a specific disclosure form and supporting documents will need to be submitted with the registration application to NAFMII.

The contents of the prospectus should follow the NAFMII Guidelines for the Prospectus for Debt Financing Instruments of Non-Financial Enterprises in the Inter-Bank Bond Market (银行间债券市场非金融企业债务融资工具募集说明书指引), 2010, and the NAFMII Rules for Information Disclosure on Debt Financing Instruments of Non-Financial Enterprises in the Inter-Bank Bond Market (银行间债券市场非金融企业债务融资工具信息披露规则), 2017. The provisions in the guidelines and rules represent the minimum requirements and information that could have a significant impact on prospective investors' decision-making. The general prospectus requirements include the following:

i.   Information sources and their retrieval date have to be clearly described. Information disclosure shall be fair, sufficient, and impartial.
ii.   Arabic numbers shall be used instead of Chinese numbers. Currency must be quoted in Chinese renminbi unless otherwise stated.
iii.   Clear, accurate, and standardized wording and descriptions are required. Advertisements and praises should be omitted.
iv.   Paper size shall be A4.

The prospectus cover shall be marked with the accurate name of the issuer and name of the debt financing instruments, guarantee (if so applicable), name of the guarantor, name of the underwriter(s), credit rating and the CRA's name, and date of the release of the prospectus.

The table of contents must indicate the titles of each chapter, sections, and the corresponding page numbers. The arrangement of the table of contents should be logical and clear. The issuer shall interpret the specific meanings of matters discussed in the prospectus for investors to clearly understand the investment risks. The interpretation has to be described in the prospectus.

NAFMII's standard disclaimer statements shall be printed on the title page of the prospectus and convey the following:

i.   confirmation that the issuance of the debt financing instruments has been registered with NAFMII;
ii.   registration does not mean that NAFMII makes any judgment on investment values on behalf of investors;
iii.   investors should carefully read the prospectus, relevant information disclosure documents, and conduct an independent analysis on the authenticity, accuracy, and completeness of the information disclosure;
iv.   confirmation that the board of directors or responsible department has approved the prospectus and that all directors have certified the authenticity, accuracy, and absence of any false record or misleading statements or material omissions (board members are subject to individual and joint legal liabilities);
v.   the person in charge of the issuer and the person in charge of the accounting and auditing firms must ensure that the financial statements in the prospectus are true, accurate, and complete;
vi.   the subscription and transfer of the debt financing instruments of the issuer are accomplished legally and the rights and obligations in the prospectus are deemed as voluntarily accepted as per the agreement; and
vii.   the issuer promises to comply with the applicable provisions in laws and regulations and the prospectus to fulfill the obligations to investors.

The issuer shall make a notice on the audited financial statements of the most recent 3 years of the auditor's opinion. The investors should be instructed to read the audit report, related financial statements, and the related business matters in detail carefully.

The issuer shall disclose all risk factors that may have significant adverse effects on business performance, production, and continuing operations, especially in terms of business, marketing, technology, finance, industrial environments, development prospects, financing channels, financial status, and debt solvency, regardless of whether the impact may be directly or indirectly. Risk factors should be described specifically and in full, accurately, and reflect the actual situation and focus on the most recent fiscal year with quantitative analysis (or otherwise with qualitative analysis). The issuer should not only list the types of risk factors but also describe details of the risks and possible consequences in bold letters. The issuer shall warn of the following risks:

    i.   Investment risk
        a. interest rate risk
        b. liquidity risk
        c. repayment risk of the principle and interest
    ii.   Relevant risks of the issuer
        a. financial risk
        b. business risk
        c. management risk
        d. policy risk
    iii. Potential risks of the debt financing product due to special provisions

The issuer must reference risks according to their degree of importance. If the risk has been erased during the most recent accounting period, the issuer should clearly state so.

If a guarantee is provided, the prospectus shall explain the status of the guarantor's credit or collateral, and the significant changes that may occur to the repayment of the principal. The issuer must disclose the following matters related to the guarantee if the debt financing instrument carries an external guarantee:

    i.   Basic information on guarantor
        a. brief information on guarantor
        b. major financial indicators such as net assets, asset–liability ratio, return on net assets, and current ratios
        c. audit
        d. credit status
        e. outstanding amount of guarantee
        f. proportion of balance between accumulated amounts of guarantee and its net assets
    ii.   Main contents of the guarantee agreement or a guarantee letter given in favor of the debt financing instrument
        a. amount of guarantee
        b. length of guarantee
        c. definition of guarantee
        d. scope of guarantee
        e. relationship among investors, issuer, and guarantor with regard to rights and obligations of a guarantee on the debt financing instrument
        f. other matters that may be important

If a mortgage was taken out or a pledge was given, the issuer has to disclose the name, amount (book value and mark-to-market asset value) of the collateral, cover ratio (collateral value versus face value), total principal and interest, handling agent, registration and custody of the collateral, and relevant legal procedures.

As for the actual contents, the prospectus shall disclose the details of the full terms of the issuance, including but not limited to

    i.   name of the debt financing instrument,
    ii.   full name of the issuer,
    iii. business to repay the balance of debt financing instruments,
    iv. amount issued in the current period,
    v.   maturity,
    vi. face value,
    vii. method of determining the issue price or interest rate,

viii.   object of issue,
  ix.   underwriting,
   x.   manner of issuance,
  xi.   date of issue,
 xii.   interest payment dates,
xiii.   subscription period,
xiv.   method of payment,
 xv.   date of redemption,
xvi.   credit rating and name of CRA, and
xvii.   terms and condition of redemption or repurchase (if any).

Debt financing instruments issued by nonfinancial enterprises after 1 July 2020 will need to have an appointed bond trustee, as per NAFMII guidelines. The details of the bond trustee and major provisions from the bond trustee agreement, such as rights and obligations of the bond trustee and disclosure to the meeting of debt financing instrument holders, as well as risk and default resolutions, will need to be included in the issuance documentation (e.g., key disclosure document). The changes were also included in the SRP (2020) to ensure that the key disclosure document would offer greater protection for the parties concerned under the Contract Law.

In the prospectus, the disclosure of basic information on the issuer must include, but may not be limited to

   i.   registered issuer's name;
  ii.   legal representative;
 iii.   paid-in capital;
  iv.   date of founding;
   v.   business (company) registration number;
  vi.   address and post code;
 vii.   phone and fax numbers;
viii.   company history of changes in structures, organization, and capital;
  ix.   major shareholders and real controlling shareholders as well as their percentage of shareholding;
   x.   stakes in other companies (enterprises), including major subsidiaries, holding companies, other joint ventures, and related parties with whom the issuer has significant influence;
  xi.   status of major business units, divisions, and departments of the issuer;
 xii.   directors, supervisors, and executive officers;
xiii.   scope and situation of major business in detail, as well as the objective of business development
xiv.   positioning in the industry, situation of the industry, and competition in the industry;
 xv.   financials and any information that may affect investors' understanding of issuer's financial status, business performance, and cash flows;
xvi.   transactions with affiliates;
xvii.   contingent liabilities; and
xviii.   collateral, pledge, guarantee, and other restrictive arrangements.

The issuer must disclose the credit rating, including but not limited to

   i.   a definition of the credit rating and logo for each rating level,
  ii.   the main risks that are revealed in the rating report,
 iii.   the arrangement for the continuous rating follow-up, and
  iv.   other important matters.

The following relevant credit information in connection with the issuer and its subsidiaries have to be disclosed as well:

i.   main banks,
ii.   whether or not there has been any record of default in the past 3 years,
iii.   records on repayments of debt financing instruments in the past 3 years, and
iv.   other credit information relating to the issuer.

The prospectus should also state the issuance arrangements, which include:

i.   book runner,
ii.   distribution,
iii.   payment and settlement,
iv.   custody arrangement, and
v.   listing and secondary trading (as applicable).

The issuer must also disclose the use of proceeds. If the use of proceeds is for working capital, then specific working capital arrangements shall be disclosed. If the use of proceeds is for long-term investment, then the issuer has to disclose specific projects that the proceeds are intended for. If the use of proceeds is changed, the issuer has to express its intension of changing the use of proceeds and disclose the relevant information in a timely manner in advance. In the SRP (2020), the disclosure requirements on the use of proceeds were further improved.

The issuer has to indicate clearly in the prospectus information about applicable taxes and tax payment methods in regard to the debt financing instrument.

The issuer must disclose the names of the following institutions, their address and legal representative, their telephone and fax numbers, and the relevant personnel handling the debt instrument issuance:

i.   issuer;
ii.   underwriters;
iii.   legal counsel;
iv.   accounting firm;
v.   CRAs;
vi.   guarantor (if any);
vii.   registration, custody, and settlement agencies; and
viii.   other institutions related to the issuance.

With regard to these intermediaries and service providers, the issuer must disclose direct and indirect relationships, such as an equity holding, significant interest, or possible conflicts of interest between the intermediary concerned and its responsible persons, senior management personnel, and the handling personnel.

The following documents shall be construed as part of the prospectus, including but not limited to

i.   audit report (if any);
ii.   supplementary audit opinion (if any); and
iii.   relevant supporting documents (if any), such as a guarantee.

Pursuant to Article 10 of the NAFMII Rules for the Registration and Issuance of Debt Financing Instruments of Non-Financial Enterprises (非金融企业债务融资工具注册发行规则), amended on 6 November 2015, each prospective issuer shall deliver the registration documents to the Registration Office through a qualified underwriter. The registration documents shall include the following:

i.   the registration report for the debt financing instruments to be publicly offered by the issuer (with the resolution of the authoritative body under the constitutional documents of the issuer attached thereto),

ii.   a letter of recommendation from the lead underwriter,

iii.   the prospectus (募集说明书),

iv.   other documents that the issuer intends to publicly disclose, and

v.   any other documents as required by NAFMII.

Both the procedures of registration for a public offering and the registration documents involved in the process shall be publicly disclosed through the Debt Capital Market Filing Analysis Notification System (DCM-FANS) to offer timely information to the public.[25] At the same time, enterprises shall publish any current issue documents through websites accredited by NAFMII per Article 5 of the Rules for Information Disclosure on Debt Financing Instruments of Non-Financial Enterprises in the Inter-Bank Bond Market (银行间债券市场非金融企业债务融资工具信息披露规则), issued and effective on 18 December 2017.

Step 2—Review by the National Association of Financial Market Institutional Investors

After receiving the registration documents, the Registration Office conducts a preliminary review to assess the completeness of the registration documents within 1 working day. The Registration Office may then accept the registration documents or advise the issuer or related intermediaries to explain, supplement, or revise the registration documents.

The preliminary review is done based on a two-person system. The Registration Office enforces a conflict of interest avoidance system for the preliminary review. If an assigned reviewer has a potential or existing conflict of interest that could affect the fairness of the performance of duties, then such a reviewer shall be withdrawn from the review.

The Registration Office appoints two reviewers to conduct the preliminary review separately and concurrently on the registration documents to assess the completeness of disclosure information in the registration documents in accordance with applicable self-regulatory rules and guidelines. The Registration Office designates one of the two reviewers as the lead reviewer who shall be responsible for follow-up communications and feedback. If the reviewers find the information disclosure incomplete, the lead reviewer shall aggregate the opinions from the preliminary review and advise the issuer or intermediary through a letter, referred to as the "Suggestion Letter," to furnish additional information. The Suggestion Letter shall be sent out within 2 working days to a Category I issuer, within 5 working days of receiving the registration documents for a Category II issuer, and 10 working days for a Category III or Category IV issuer. Some specific time frames may apply to different debt instrument types.[26]

The issuer or relevant intermediaries are required to submit any supplements or amended registration documents ("Supplement Documents") to the Registration Office within 10 working days of receiving a Suggestion Letter. A written explanation shall be submitted for failing to meet the above time limit. Where the written explanation is not provided or the delays in providing responses during the phase of registration review (including both the preliminary review and the review at the Registration Committee

---

[25] DCM-FANS is a key system for information disclosure in the CIBM; it includes NAFMII's comments to the issuer during the registration process.

[26] For the issuance of SCP and commercial paper, the Suggestion Letter will be sent out within 5 working days from the receipt of the registration documents. For ABN, project revenue notes, or other special types of instruments, it will be sent out within 10 working days. Where alternative provisions are given by other applicable rules and guidelines of NAFMII, such provisions shall prevail.

meeting) have reached more than 60 working days in total, NAFMII will suggest to the issuer or intermediary to withdraw the registration documents.

If the supplement documents are still considered incomplete, the Registration Office will collate its feedback and issue another Suggestion Letter within 5 working days from the receipt of the supplement documents. If the registration documents are considered complete, the reviewers appointed by the Registration Office will write their preliminary review report and submit the report and the registration documents to the Registration Committee.

Upon being satisfied with the result from the preliminary review, the Registration Office will submit the registration documents to the Registration Committee, which is organized by NAFMII and follows the process stipulated in the RPR. The Registration Committee consists of five participants from within the ranks of the registration specialists, who are selected by the Registration Office on a random basis, with a convener appointed to preside over the meeting. The Registration Committee will evaluate the completeness of the information disclosure in the registration documents.

The Registration Committee meets once a week in principle. The Registration Office delivers the preliminary reviewed registration documents to the registration specialists at least 2 working days in advance. At the Registration Committee meeting, each registration specialist will listen to and discuss the preliminary review report from the Registration Office and pronounce independent opinions on the subjects under review. A registration specialist may issue one of three opinions: "registration acceptance," "conditional registration acceptance or qualified registration acceptance," or "deferred registration acceptance." The Registration Committee will (i) accept if all five registration specialists indicate registration acceptance, (ii) defer if two or more registration specialists indicate a deferred registration acceptance, and (iii) accept with conditions attached if the registration specialists' opinions are between (i) and (iii).

The Registration Office will aggregate all opinions from the registration specialists, send feedback to the issuer or intermediary within 1 working day after the conclusion of the Registration Committee meeting, and proceed with any next steps.

If two or more registration specialists indicate Deferred Registration Acceptance, NAFMII shall defer the acceptance of registration and advise the issuer to withdraw its registration documents. If the Registration Committee judges to defer the registration, the issuer may resubmit the registration documents after 3 months.

If all five registration specialists indicate Registration Acceptance, NAFMII shall accept the registration and send the Notice of Acceptance of Registration to the issuer. For any other combination of opinions, NAFMI shall accept the registration with conditions attached and publish the anonymized specialist opinions through DCM-FANS.

In case of a conditional registration acceptance, the issuer or intermediary has to supplement or revise the registration documents within 10 working days after receiving the Notice of Acceptance of Registration with the opinions from the registration specialists and submit such supplemented or revised documents to the Registration Office. A registration specialist shall be deemed to indicate Registration Acceptance if he or she does not provide a response within 5 working days.

If the Registration Committee accepts the registration, the registration becomes valid for 2 years, or for 1 year in the case of a registration from a Category IV issuer for SCP.

If the issuer experiences any of the following events, then the Registration Office shall resubmit the registration documents as amended by the issuer to the Registration Committee meeting for review:

i.   default on a major debt obligation by failing timely payment;
ii.   material losses that exceed 10% of net assets;
iii.   actual controller of the issuer comes under investigation or is suspected of a violation of law;
iv.   capital reduction, merger, division, dissolution, bankruptcy, or shut down;
v.   qualified opinion, adverse opinion, or disclaimer opinion by the auditor;
vi.   losing de facto control of a major subsidiary (the issuer has more than 35% of assets or net assets or operating revenue or net profit);
vii.   downgrading of credit rating;
viii. difficulty in maintaining operation, dire liquidity, or hard to repay outstanding debts; and
ix.   other circumstances that may have a major impact on the value of the issuer.

If the issuer experiences any of the following events, the Registration Office shall resubmit the registration documents as amended by the issuer to the Registration Committee meeting for review:

i.   default on a major debt obligation by failing to make timely payment;
ii.   material losses that exceed 10% of net assets;
iii.   actual controller of the issuer comes under investigation or is suspected of a violation of law;
iv.   capital reduction, merger, division, dissolution, bankruptcy, or shut down;
v.   qualified opinion, adverse opinion, or disclaimer opinion by the auditor;
vi.   losing de facto control of a major subsidiary (the issuer has more than 35% of assets or net assets or operating revenue or net profit);
vii.   downgrading of credit rating;
viii. difficulty in maintaining operation, dire liquidity, or hard to repay outstanding debts; and
ix.   other circumstances that may have a major impact on the value of the issuer.

The review process of the amended registration documents by the Registration Committee follows the process described above. If a Registration Committee decision leads to a Deferred Registration Acceptance, an existing registration will become invalid, and the issuer may submit a fresh registration application immediately.

The progress of the procedure of the registration for public issuance as well as the related registration documents are publicly disclosed through DCM-FANS to ensure transparent disclosure to the public.

Step 3—Actual Issuance

The issuer must formulate an issuance plan within which the terms, including interest rates and term structure of the various notes, may be flexibly designed. The issuer has to disclose the complete issuance plan for bonds in the CIBM on the date when the first issuance is announced.

Categories I, II, and III issuers registered for issuing SCP, commercial paper, and other product types may do so according to their own plan while the registration is valid. A Category IV issuer may issue its registered SCP according to its own plan within 12 months following registration acceptance; the issuer shall file with NAFMII in advance if it intends to issue after 12 months.

The lead underwriter shall, before the issuance of each installment of registered debt financing instruments, write a supplementary due diligence report that reflects the most updated business and financial status as well as significant changes that have occurred since the commencement of the registration and file it with NAFMII. The lead underwriter needs to file this report and any other supplementary disclosure with NAFMII prior to each actual issuance. NAFMII will formally accept the filing and issue a recommendation letter within 2 working days after accepting the supplementary documents, indicating to the issuer and lead underwriter that they may proceed or that further information may be required. If so required, the issuer and lead underwriter need to submit additional information within 10 working days thereafter or provide an explanation if that period will be exceeded. If no written explanation is received within 30 days, or the total time for feedback and remediation exceeds 30 days, NAFMII will recommend to the issuer that it withdraw the issuance filing.

Once the issuance filing is complete, the issuer shall carry out a public offering within 6 months.

Issuers shall publish current issuance documents through websites accredited by NAFMII. The release documents should include at least the following:

    i.   issuing notices,
    ii.   prospectus (募集说明书),
    iii.   credit rating reports and rating tracking (跟踪评级) arrangements,
    iv.   legal opinions, and
    v.   audited financial statements of the issuer for the last 3 years.

In this context of debt financing instrument issuance, a legal opinion is expected to contain confirmation of the legal status of the issuer, the delegation and approval process for the issuance within the issuing company, legal risks or pending litigation, as well as the eligibility of the agents appointed by the issuer. The legal opinion is issued in Chinese.

4.   Regulatory Process for Issuance by a Nonresident Issuer

At the time of compilation of this bond market guide, issuances of bonds and notes in the PRC by nonresidents were referred to as Panda bonds and represented the only path for nonresident issuers to issue debt financing instruments in the CIBM. The issuance of Panda bonds is regulated by the Interim Measures for the Administration on Bonds Issued by Overseas Issuers on the National Inter-Bank Bond Market jointly promulgated by the PBOC and MOF on 8 September 2018. Specific requirements for the approval of debt financing instruments are divided into issuances by nonresident financial institutions (the interim measures use the term "overseas financial institutions") and other types of nonresident issuers. The interim measures also include other specific requirements for all overseas issuers. Proposed issuances of Panda bonds by nonresident financial institutions are subject to the approval of the PBOC only, whereas issuances by nonresident nonfinancial enterprises need to be registered exclusively with NAFMII.

NAFMII issued the Guidelines on Debt Financing Instruments of Overseas Non-Financial Enterprises (for Trial Implementation) on 17 January 2019, which further clarified details of Panda bond issuance registration and information disclosure for nonfinancial enterprises, including international development organizations and government agencies.

For additional information on Panda bonds, please refer to Chapter III.B.5.

a.   Overseas Financial Institutions

Overseas financial institutions issuing bonds in the CIBM are subject to approval by the PBOC.[27] NAFMII is not involved in the issuance approval for Panda bond issuers that are financial institutions.

Overseas financial institutions shall possess the following qualifications to issue bonds as stipulated in Article 6 of the interim measures:

i.   actual paid-in capital not less than CNY10 billion or an equivalent foreign currency amount;
ii.   sound corporate governance and robust risk management systems;
iii.   stable financial conditions, good credit standing, and profitability for the most recent 3 consecutive years;
iv.   experience in bond offerings and sound debt repayment ability; and
v.   subject to effective regulation by the financial regulatory authorities of the country or region where the issuer is located, and key risk regulatory indicators in compliance with the requirements of such financial regulatory authorities.

According to Article 7 of the interim measures, the documents required to be submitted to the PBOC by an overseas financial institution for approval to issue bonds shall include the following:

i.   an application letter for the issuance of bonds;
ii.   valid resolutions of the issuer's competent decision-making body or other evidencing document(s) approving the proposed issuance;
iii.   an offering circular (募集说明书);[28]
iv.   financial statements and audit reports for the most recent 3 financial years and the latest interim financial statements (if any);
v.   regulatory document(s) evidencing the consent of the financial regulatory authorities of the country or region where the issuer is located on the issuer's operation of relevant financial business shall also be provided by the overseas financial institution issuing bonds;
vi.   a credit rating report and credit tracking assessment arrangements (if available);
vii.   the guarantee document (担保协议), also referred to as deed of guarantee and the guarantor's credit information (担保人资信情况说明) (if applicable); and
viii.   legal opinions issued by a law firm qualified in the issuer's home jurisdiction and by a PRC law firm.

The application and supporting documents to be submitted for registration and official filings with the regulatory authorities need to be in Chinese or have to be translated into Chinese if issued in another language. See also Chapter III.G for more information on language of documentation and disclosure items.

---

[27] Joint Announcement of the People's Bank of China and the Ministry of Finance (2018, No. 16); see http://www.pbc.gov.cn/goutongjiaoliu/113456/113469/3634065/index.html (Chinese version) and http://www.pbc.gov.cn/en/3688253/3689009/3788480/3789754/index.html (English version).
[28] In Article 7, the PBOC uses the translation "offering circular" for 募集说明书, instead of "prospectus." As a matter of CIBM market practice, the word prospectus is not used when discussing Panda bonds. Furthermore, the term prospectus is not used in the NAFMII Panda bond guidelines.

b.   Foreign Government Agencies, International Development Organizations, and Overseas Nonfinancial Enterprises

Foreign government agencies, international development organizations, and nonfinancial enterprises (corporates) domiciled outside the PRC shall submit an application for bond issuance registration to NAFMII. PBOC approval is not necessary.

According to Article 8 of the 2019 NAFMII Guidelines, debt financing instruments issued by overseas nonfinancial enterprises shall be underwritten by financial institution(s) possessing the relevant qualification to act as underwriter(s) for debt financing instruments. The 2019 NAFMII Guidelines also stipulate that these issuers will have to appoint an underwriter that has a branch or affiliate in the country or region where the nonfinancial enterprise is incorporated, or where the principal place of its business is located, to ensure that such underwriter(s) have the capability to perform its duties including conducting due diligence.

Pursuant to Article 9 of the 2019 NAFMII Guidelines, foreign governmental agencies, international development institutions, and overseas financial institutions that are seasoned issuers in overseas markets, or that have (previously) issued bonds in the PRC and complied with the ongoing disclosure obligations for more than 1 year, may apply for the registration of multiple issuances in a series up to a total amount.

According to the NAFMII Guidelines, in an offering of debt financing instruments by a nonresident nonfinancial enterprise, the rules or requirements of the relevant regulatory authorities in the PRC shall apply to the accounting and audit standards under which the financial statements of such issuer are prepared. This may be interpreted as financial accounting, or reporting standards in the market of domicile of the nonresident issuer may be accepted by PRC regulators.

c.   Issuance on a Stand-alone Basis or in Tranches

Nonresident issuers may apply to issue bonds on a stand-alone basis or as multiple issuances in a series up to a total amount.

d.   Foreign Exchange Registration

Nonresident issuers approved or registered to issue bonds in the PRC shall complete the applicable foreign exchange registration with SAFE. The account opening, fund remittances and transfers, cross-border settlements, and information reporting in connection with the proceeds shall be in compliance with the relevant rules of the PBOC and SAFE.

The subsequent steps in the Panda bond issuance procedure and related regulatory process are explained in detail next, using the example of a nonfinancial enterprise.

The registration process for Panda bond issuances of overseas nonfinancial enterprises are further prescribed in the Guidelines on Debt Financing Instruments of Overseas Non-Financial Enterprises (for Trial Implementation) (境外非金融企业债务融资工具业务指引（试行）) published by NAFMII on 17 January 2019.[29]

The nonresident issuer will need to engage an eligible lead underwriter (see also section 4.b) and other intermediaries (see also Chapter III.M for a description of the typical intermediaries in the context of debt financing instrument issuance in the CIBM). The nonresident issuer, lead underwriter, and appointed intermediaries will prepare the registration documents which, upon completion, should be delivered to NAFMII by the lead underwriter.

Table 2.7: Registration Documents Required for a Public Offering and Private Placement of Panda Bonds

	Public Offering	Private Placement
i.	Registration report (attaching its certificate of incorporation, constitutional documents, and the resolutions of its competent decision-making body or other evidencing document[s])	
ii.	Letter of recommendation from each lead underwriter	
iii.	Offering circular	Private placement agreement or a private placement offering memorandum
iv.	Audited financial statements for the most recent 3 financial years and the latest interim financial statements (if any)	Audited financial statements for the most recent 2 financial years and the latest interim financial statements (if any)
v.	Credit rating report (one rating is sufficient) and credit tracking assessment arrangements (if available)	Credit rating report is not mandatory to submit
vi.	Legal opinions issued by a law firm in the People's Republic of China and a law firm qualified in the issuer's home jurisdiction; the legal opinions are expected to contain confirmation of the legal status of the issuer, the delegation and/or approval process for the issuance at the issuer, legal risks or pending litigation, and the eligibility of the agents appointed by the nonresident issuer; the legal opinion of the law firm in the issuer's home jurisdiction should be translated into Chinese	
vii.	Consent letter from the issuer's overseas auditors (if applicable)	
viii.	Underwriting agreement	
ix.	Other documents as required by the National Association of Financial Market Institutional Investors	

Source: National Association of Financial Market Institutional Investors. 2019. Guidelines on Debt Financing Instruments of Overseas Non-Financial Enterprises (for Trial Implementation).

The registration documents for a public offering and a private placement of Panda bonds are detailed in Table 2.7.

There is no formal definition for an offering circular in the rules and regulations for the CIBM, and there is no distinction in the Chinese characters used for the key disclosure document between domestic bonds and Panda bonds issued via a public offering. The English term is based on the use in English translations of the PBOC and NAFMII

---

[29] See http://nafmii.org.cn/ggtz/gg/201902/t20190201_75766.html (Chinese version) and http://www.nafmii.org.cn/english/lawsandregulations/selfregulatory_e/201902/t20190201_75773.html (English version).

regulations as the key disclosure document for a Panda bond offering, as well as the use in market practice. Market practice research found that investors in the CIBM generally consider there to be no material difference between a prospectus and an offering circular. At the same time, in this bond market guide, the term offering circular is used in the context of a public offering of Panda bonds since, according to market participants, it is the term most often used.

NAFMII provides guidance on the minimum information disclosure requirements in an offering circular, which is presently only available in Chinese.[30]

The registration request and supporting documents to be submitted for registration with NAFMII need to be in Chinese or have to be translated into Chinese if issued in another language. See also Chapter III.G for more information on the language of documentation and disclosure items.

Step 2—Acceptance and Prereview of Registration Documents by the National Association of Financial Market Institutional Investors

NAFMII will review the completeness of the registration documents within 1 working day upon receipt of the registration documents. NAFMII will accept the registration documents if all types of required documents are complete. If the required documents are incomplete, it will recommend that the issuer or the relevant intermediary supplement or modify the registration documents.

The NAFMII Registration Office will conduct a prereview of the completeness of the registration documents to be disclosed and give its feedback on the result of the prereview within 10 working days. The issuer or the relevant intermediary should submit supplementary documents within 10 working days of the receipt of NAFMII's feedback.

After receipt of the supplementary documents from the issuer or the relevant intermediary, NAFMII Registration Office staff who conducted the prereview may issue a new feedback letter on the result of the latest prereview if they deem that the information to be disclosed in the supplementary documents remains incomplete, or they may submit the registration documents to the Registration Committee if they deem that the information provided meets the requirements set out in the relevant rules and guidelines.

Step 3—Registration Committee Meeting and Approval by the National Association of Financial Market Institutional Investors

After the completion of prereview, NAFMII staff who conducted the prereview will submit the registration documents to the Registration Committee for review, and the Registration Committee will decide whether to accept the registration for the issuance of the debt financing instrument.

The Registration Committee is composed of five registration experts who are selected randomly by NAFMII from the list of registration experts. Each registration expert will deliver an opinion on the registration documents: either "registration accepted," "registration accepted with conditions," or "registration to be postponed."

If all five experts give the opinion of "registration accepted," NAFMII will accept the registration; if two or more experts give the opinion of "registration to be postponed," NAFMII will postpone the acceptance of the registration; in any circumstance other than those above, NAFMII will conditionally accept the registration, in which case the

---

[30] See http://www.nafmii.org.cn/zlgz/201202/t20120226_1653.html.

issuer will be required to supplement or modify the registration documents, according to the opinions of the Registration Committee, and be subject to another review by the experts who previously indicated "conditional acceptance."

Step 4—Acceptance and Registration by the National Association of Financial Market Institutional Investors

After accepting the registration, NAFMII will deliver a formal Notice on Acceptance of Registration to the nonresident issuer. If it is the first time for the nonresident issuer to complete a registration, NAFMII will hold an informational meeting with the senior management of the nonresident issuer or the representative from the nonresident issuer's domestic subsidiary, as well as the lead underwriter, and deliver the Notice on Acceptance of Registration in person so that NAFMII can be in a better position to understand the details of the nonresident issuer and carry out post-registration supervision of the debt financing instrument.

If this is not the first time that the nonresident issuer completes a registration, NAFMII will deliver the Notice on Acceptance of Registration electronically via its online information service platform instead of holding an informational meeting in person.

After the Notice on Acceptance of Registration is delivered, NAFMII will publish the notice on its official website to make it available to the public.[31]

Step 5—Actual Issuance

After receiving the Notice on Acceptance of Registration, the nonresident issuer may proceed with the issuance of its Panda bond. The nonresident issuer should issue its Panda bond in accordance with the following principles stipulated by NAFMII:

    i.   in the case of SCP and commercial paper, it may issue them at its discretion within a period of 2 years;

    ii. in the case of commercial paper and MTN, it may issue them at its discretion within 12 months after the acceptance of the registration; the issuer should make a prior filing with NAFMII if it intends to issue them after the 12-month period; and

    iii. in the case of ABN, project revenue notes, and perpetual notes, the time of issuance and prior filing shall comply with the corresponding rules issued by NAFMII.

Panda bonds may be issued through a public offering or via a private placement. The book-building procedure for both is consistent with the generally adopted process for domestic bond issuance.

Prior to the issuance, the issuer and the lead underwriter should prepare and disclose the issuance program and submit it to NAFMII for filing.

The nonresident issuer (nonfinancial enterprise) shall submit to NAFMII a written plan on the use of proceeds from the proposed issuance no later than 3 business days prior to the publication of the offering documents for each series of debt financing instruments. The written plan on the use of proceeds is not required to be submitted for the first issuance or issuances that are subject to a pre-issuance filing with NAFMII. The proceeds from the issuance of debt financing instruments may—in accordance with applicable laws, regulations, and regulatory requirements—be used within or outside the PRC.

---

[31] See www.nafmii.org.cn.

The nonresident issuer (nonfinancial enterprise) shall ensure that their use of proceeds is in compliance with the requirements of relevant laws, regulations, and national policies, and strictly in accordance with the use of proceeds disclosed in the offering circular. Nonresident issuers shall also meet all relevant information disclosure obligations. If there is a need to change the use of proceeds during the life of the debt financing instrument, the issuer shall complete relevant procedures and disclose such change at least 5 business days prior to such change. The use of proceeds after such change shall also be in compliance with the requirements of relevant laws, regulations, and national policies.

5.   Regulatory Process for Private Placements

Private placements in the CIBM refer to the issuance of debt financing instruments only to DIIs (特定机构投资人) or SIIs (专项机构投资人). The placement and transfer of private placement bonds and notes is limited to such DIIs or SIIs and is not intended for the public. Private placements must be underwritten by qualified underwriter(s) who meet certain eligibility criteria and requirements, including being a member of NAFMII. The issuer appoints a lead underwriter who may form an underwriting syndicate if necessary.

Registration and issuance of private placements in the CIBM is also self-regulated by NAFMII. The issuer of a private placement in the CIBM has to register the private placement with NAFMII, pursuant to the Rules for Private Placement of Debt Financing Instruments of Non-Financial Enterprises in the Inter-Bank Bond Market (银行间债券市场非金融企业债务融资工具非公开定向发行规则) (2011, No. 6), which are generally referred to as the RPP. The corresponding Registration Documents and Forms for Privately Placed Non-Financial Enterprises Debt Financing Instruments were revised with effect from 1 July 2020 to help streamline the registration process and to accommodate other recent changes such as the introduction of a bond trustee (voluntary for private placements).

Similarly to the changes for public offerings, the new categorization of issuers by NAFMII, announced in April 2020, also became relevant for private placements, with a distinction of disclosure obligations between mature and basic-level enterprises (see section F.3 for details on the new issuer categorization and Chapter III.M for more information on the industry classification of mature enterprises).

Key among the disclosure distinctions is the focus on the use of the private placement agreement (in comparison to a prospectus for a private placement), especially for mature enterprises, to allow for concessions in disclosing the use of proceeds and financial statements.

From 1 July 2020, issuers can also register and issue private placements under a shelf-registration (previously only available for public offerings). Should an issuer wish to conduct a private placement via Bond Connect, the issuer will need to also submit disclosure information specific to Bond Connect in a prescribed format.

Step 1—Application to the National Association of Financial Market Institutional Investors

A prospective issuer shall prepare the registration documents in accordance with NAFMII's requirements and deliver them to the Registration Office through a qualified underwriter. The list of the necessary documents for private placement registration is contained in Attachment 2 of the RPP and includes the items and entity responsible for each document as shown in Table 2.8. NAFMII may specify other documents as required.

Table 2.8: Documentation Requirements for a Private Placement Registration

Documentation Item	Responsible Party
Private placement agreement or private placement offering memorandum 定向发行协议	Issuers, investors, and other parties involved
Submission letter for private placement registration document 非公开定向发行注册材料报送函	Issuer
Resolutions of internal authority bodies 内部有权机构决议	Issuer
Copy of business license or document equivalent to a business license of an enterprise (legal person) 企业法人营业执照（副本）复印件或同等效力文件	Issuer
Audited financial statements for the most recent year 最近一年经审计的财务报表	Issuer
Private placement registration information form 非公开定向发行注册信息表	Lead underwriter
Letter of recommendation for registration of private placement 非公开定向发行注册推荐函	Lead underwriter
Private placement legal opinion(s) 非公开定向发行法律意见书	Law firm
Qualification certificate of relevant institutions and practitioners 相关机构及从业人员资质证明	Accounting firms, law firms, other intermediaries
Instruments Investor Confirmation Letter 定向工具投资人确认函	Investors

Source: National Association of Financial Market Institutional Investors. 2019. Guidelines on Debt Financing Instruments of Overseas Non-Financial Enterprises (for Trial Implementation).

Pursuant to requirements refined by NAFMII in the Registration Documents and Forms for Privately Placed Non-Financial Enterprises Debt Financing Instruments (2020 version), a form-based system that outlines all necessary disclosure subjects, the private placement agreement, which in market practice is also referred to by the English term "private placement offering memorandum," should cover but may not be limited to the following information:

i.   basic situation of the issuer;
ii.   use of proceeds and its appropriateness, and compliance;
iii.   list of investors and terms and conditions of the private placement;
iv.   rights and obligations of the issuer and investors in relation to the private placement;
v.   name, amount, issue period and price, and the way of determining the coupon rate;
vi.   timeline of appropriation of use of proceeds or details of new use if use of proceeds changes before maturity;
vii.   specific standards and the way of information disclosure;
viii.   conditions and range of secondary circulation of the private placement;
ix.   risk factors;
x.   application of law and dispute resolution;
xi.   confidentiality clause; and
xii.   enforceability of private placement agreement.

If the issuer is categorized as a mature enterprise, the private placement agreement for a PPN need not contain specific information on the use of proceeds and other issuance terms. Other issuers will need to disclose information on the use of proceeds and other details depending on the enterprise category they fall into.

All issuers can take advantage of NAFMII's concessions on disclosure when using a private placement agreement and will only need to disclosure the most recent 1 year of audited financial statements, instead of 2 years of financial statements when using any other key disclosure document type. At the same time, the key disclosure document for a private placement may now contain a new chapter in which the issuer may describe specific risks or proposed actions to the investors, allowing them to conduct a more detailed risk assessment.[32]

Debt financing instruments issued by nonfinancial enterprises from 1 July 2020 will also need to have an appointed bond trustee, as per NAFMII guidelines. The details of the bond trustee and major provisions from the bond trustee agreement will need to be included in the issuance documentation such as the key disclosure document.

The registration request and supporting documents to be submitted for registration of a private placement with NAFMII need to be in Chinese or must be translated into Chinese if issued in another language. NAFMII guidelines permit the private placement agreement to be in English if the issuer and investors so agree, but, in market practice, the use of English is typically limited to continuous disclosure as stipulated in the private placement agreement. See also Chapter III.G for more information on the language of documentation and disclosure items.

Step 2—Formality Review by the National Association of Financial Market Institutional Investors and Approval

The Registration Office should receive the qualified private placement registration documents and verify the completeness of the format of the registration materials. The registration of private placements is not subject to a full review by the Registration Committee in NAFMII. NAFMII only conducts a formality check on the private placement registration documents.

The Registration Office may advise the issuer or intermediary to supplement or revise the registration documents, as may be applicable.

If private placement registration documents are complete in format, NAFMII will issue a Notice of Registration Acceptance. The private placement registration is valid for 2 years.

Step 3—Actual Issuance

Any issuer issuing debt financing instruments via a private placement shall make private placement disclosure of the issuance documents pertaining to the current issuance to the private placement investors in a manner recognized by NAFMII. Private placement disclosure refers to disclosure information that will be negotiated and agreed between issuer and the private placement investors, potentially aided by the lead underwriter.

Please also see Chapter III.N for a definition and comprehensive explanation of private placement investors.

---

[32] The key changes in the disclosure requirements and the focus on the private placement agreement are described in the announcement by NAFMII published on 17 April 2020 and are available at http://www.nafmii.org.cn//english/news_e/202004/t20200430_80044.html.

6.   Obligations after Registration and after Issuance

In the CIBM, a number of obligations need to be met by the issuer after the registration by NAFMII of the debt financing instruments issued by nonfinancial enterprises and after the actual issuance of the bonds. Some specific provisions apply to nonresident issuers of Panda bonds.

Enterprises shall publish current issuance documents through websites accredited by NAFMII. The release documents should include at least the following:

i.   issuing notices,
ii.   prospectus (募集说明书),
iii. credit rating reports and rating tracking (跟踪评级) arrangements,
iv.   legal opinions, and
v.   audited financial statements of the enterprise for the last 3 years.

If a debt financing instrument is issued in the first issue, the issuance documents shall be published at least 5 working days before the date of issue, and the issuance documents shall be published at least 3 working days before the date of issue for any subsequent tranches.

a.   Public Offerings

Any issuer that issues debt financing instruments via a public offering shall publish the issuance documents pertaining to the current issue through a platform recognized by NAFMII, specifically,

i.   no later than 3 working days before the issuance date for the first public offering,
ii.   no later than 2 working days before the issuance date for subsequent public offerings, or
iii. no later than 1 working day before the issuance date for any public offering of short-term instruments such as commercial paper.

After the successful issuance of the debt financing instruments, the issuer must disclose the disclosure documents on a new issue through websites recognized by NAFMII such as DCM-FANS. The information on the new issue shall cover

i.   an issuance announcement,
ii.   the prospectus (募集说明书),
iii. the credit rating report and arrangements for follow-up ratings,
iv.   the legal opinion issued by the law firm retained by the issuer, and
v.   issuer's audited financial statements in the most recent 3 years.

According to Article 7 of the Rules for Information Disclosure on Debt Financing Instruments of Non-Financial Enterprises in the Inter-Bank Bond Market, for the new issue announcement, the issuer releases information via the websites recognized by NAFMII no later than the next working day after the date of registration (债权债务登记日) (to the central securities depository [CSD], after actual issuance), including
i.   actual issuance size,
ii.   price,
iii. maturity of the debt instruments, and
iv.   other information of the debt financing instrument.

During the validity period of the registration, where an issuer's current corporate credit rating falls below the rating it held when registering an MTN, the issuer will have to report the event and such registration shall automatically become void; NAFMII will release an announcement regarding such an event.

b.   Private Placements

The issuer must report the completion of the distribution of the private placement to NAFMII in writing through the lead underwriter by the next working day after the day of the completion.

The registration of the debt financing instruments with CCDC and the transfer to the private placement investors (i.e., the actual distribution) must be reported to NAFMII in a timely manner (i.e., within 5 working days of the month following the date of the distribution).

In addition, intermediaries involved in the registration, safekeeping, and settlement services (e.g., the CSDs) for privately placed debt financing instruments shall report to NAFMII holdings and settlement statistics for a given month within 5 working days of the following month.

c.   Financial Bonds

The issuer has to form an underwriting syndicate upon issuing a financial bond. The issuer and the underwriters will need to execute an underwriting agreement and disclose it to the general public. The lead underwriter should submit a due diligence report to the PBOC.

Upon approval of the issuance of financial bonds by the PBOC (see also next section for a description of the regulatory process for financial bonds), the issuer has to disclose the prospectus (募集说明书) and the new issuance announcement within 3 working days prior to the issuance of each financial bond. The new issuance announcement for the financial bond should include at least the following information:

  i.   seniority or preference in repayment and risk factors;
  ii.   the basic situation of the issuer including business conditions for the past 3 years, the basic situation of business development, financial reports and summary of financial indicators for the most recent 3 years, as well as governance and capital structures;
  iii. terms and conditions of the financial bond and use of proceeds;
  iv.   method of underwriting and syndication, rights, and liabilities agreed in the underwriting agreement;
  v.   contact details of parties involved (issuer, underwriters, auditor, legal counsel, rating agency, bond register, and depository); and
  vi.   website where disclosure documents and press release are available for investors to inspect or download.

The information in the new issuance announcement shall not conflict with the corresponding information provided in the prospectus.

The issuer shall submit to the PBOC a written report about the completion of the financial bond issuance within 10 working days after the completion of the issuance of the financial bond. Underwriters have to submit to the PBOC a bond underwriting report within 10 working days after the issuance of a financial bond.

d.   Panda Bonds

Nonresident issuers issuing Panda bonds in the CIBM are also subject to the obligations for information disclosure, among others, contained in the Interim Measures for the Administration on Bonds Issued by Overseas Issuers on the National Inter-Bank Bond Market, which were jointly published by the MOF and PBOC in September 2018. These measures stipulate that, similar to domestic issuers, the nonresident issuer shall ensure that its information disclosure is truthful, accurate, complete, and made in a timely manner without any false records, misleading statements, or material omissions.

In practice, these obligations of the nonresident issuer are carried out or supported by the so-called post-registration manager, typically the lead underwriter of the Panda bond in their capacity as representative in the domestic market for the nonresident issuer, as prescribed in the interim measures.

In addition, nonresident issuers that already need to provide disclosure information in another securities market also have the obligation to publish such information in the CIBM, either simultaneously or as soon as reasonably possible. In practice, the release of continuous disclosure information in English may be possible but must have been specified in the offering circular or the private placement agreement of the Panda bond at the time of offering.

Financial institutions and international development organizations issuing Panda bonds can state the accounting or financial reporting standard according to which their financial information is compiled, but also need to provide information on the salient differences between the standard adopted and the PRC Enterprise Accounting Standards, if the chosen accounting standard is not recognized by the MOF.

In addition, the overseas accounting firm(s) that audits the financial statements of the Panda bond issuer shall file with the MOF no later than 20 business days prior to the submission by the overseas issuer of an application for the issuance of bonds; they must annually file such statements with the MOF during the life of the bonds.

Information disclosed by nonresident issuers for public offerings need to be provide in simplified Chinese or accompanied with a simplified Chinese translation. Information disclosed for private placements may be published according to the provisions agreed between issuer and investors, including on the language. Please also see Chapter III.G for more details on language of issuance documentation and information disclosure.

7.   Issuance Process Specific to a Domestic Financial Institution

Bonds issued in the CIBM by a financial institution—commercial banks, finance companies, or non-bank financial institutions including insurance companies—are referred to as financial bonds. Policy bank financial bonds issued by the three policy banks are treated separately from ordinary financial bonds due to their government-linked nature. For instance, a policy bank wishing to issue debt instruments has to submit to the PBOC an application for issuing bonds on an annual basis. The application should include the volume of issuance, proposed time frame, method of issuance, and other relevant details.

Financial bonds are a distinct asset class in the CIBM, and their issuance is approved by CBIRC—for commercial banks, finance companies, and insurance companies—

and supervised by the PBOC. Pursuant to the Commercial Banks Law and relevant CBIRC regulations, a commercial bank must meet the following conditions for issuing bonds:

i.   a sound corporate governance mechanism,
ii.   core capital adequacy ratio of at least 4%,
iii.   a favorable balance sheet for 3 consecutive years,
iv.   adequate reserves for loan losses,
v.   risk control indicators conforming to the relevant provisions of the regulatory institution,
vi.   no record of a serious violation of any law or regulation during the recent 3 years, and
vii.   other conditions as prescribed by CBIRC.

Upon application by a commercial bank, CBIRC may exempt the commercial bank from one or more of these conditions.

The reply deadlines for the PBOC to examine and approve an application for issuance of financial bonds by the financial institutions it directly supervises are defined in the relevant provisions of the Measures of the People's Bank of China for the Implementation of Administrative Licensing.

The issuer should begin to issue financial bonds within 60 working days after the PBOC approves its issuance and shall complete the issuance within the specified time frame. If the issuer fails to complete the issuance of the financial bonds within the time limit, the former financial bond issuance approval document will become invalid and the issuer is automatically prohibited from continuing the issuance process for financial bonds. If the issuer still needs to issue the financial bonds, it should pursue a new application.

The financial bond may be issued publicly or to particular investors in the CIBM.[33] The financial bond can be issued at the full amount of bonds at one time or divided into a series of separate placements within a prescribed period and in a limited amount each time. If the financial bond is issued in the form of installments, the issuer shall state the issuance arrangement in the prospectus for each installment.

The issuer (excluding policy banks) shall, no later than 5 working days before the issuance of each installment of the financial bond, submit the prescribed application documents (see list below) to the PBOC for archival purposes and disclose the relevant information required by the PBOC. A policy bank shall, no later than 5 working days prior to the issuance of each placement of the financial bond, submit the prescribed application documents to the PBOC for archival purposes and disclose the relevant information as required by the PBOC.

If the financial bond is issued to particular investors, the financial bond may, upon consent of the underwriters, be exempted from credit rating. A financial bond issued to particular investors can only be transferred among the underwriters themselves. If a financial bond is issued to particular investors, the content and form of its information disclosure shall be stipulated as limited to its subscribers.

The issuance of debt financing instruments in the CIBM by commercial banks and other financial institutions licensed and supervised by CBIRC is regulated and approved separately.

---

[33] Issuing to particular investors could be regarded as a kind of private placement in the CIBM; a designated private placement concept exists otherwise only for nonfinancial enterprises placing MTN to SIIs or DIIs.

a.   Application Documents

Financial institutions, excluding policy banks, need to provide the following application documents to the PBOC for approval of issuance of a financial bond:

    i.   application for the issuance of the financial bond,
    ii.   articles of association of the issuer and other constituent documents,
    iii.   approval document of the relevant regulatory authority on the issuance of the financial bond,[34]
    iv.   issuer's most recent 3 years of audited financial statements and audit reports,
    v.   prospectus (募集说明书),
    vi.   announcement or procedures for the issuance of the financial bond,
    vii.   underwriting agreement,
    viii.   issuer's plan on the payment of the bond in the present phase and its special report about the guarantee measures,
    ix.   financial bond credit rating report issued by a credit rating institution as well as the arrangements for the follow-up tracking rating,
    x.   legal opinion issued by the law firm retained by the issuer, and
    xi.   other documents as required by the PBOC.

In the case of a secured bond, the applicant should, apart from the documents above, provide a guarantee agreement and a description of the credit situation of the guarantor.

Policy banks wishing to issue financial bonds will have to submit these application documents to the PBOC:

    i.   application for the issuance of financial bonds,
    ii.   issuer's most recent 3 years of audited financial statements and audit reports,
    iii.   the measures for the issuance of financial bonds,
    iv.   the underwriting agreement, and
    v.   other documents as required by PBOC.

b.   Contents of the Prospectus

For the issuance of financial bonds to the public, the following matters have to be covered in the prospectus (募集说明书):

    i.   prospectus summary;
    ii.   seniority or preference in repayment and risk factors;
    iii.   terms and conditions of the financial bond and use of proceeds;
    iv.   the basic situation of the issuer including business conditions for the past 3 years, basic situation of business development, financial reports, and the summary of financial indicators in the most recent 3 years, as governance and capital structures;
    v.   management discussion and analysis (issuer's management, operation, and financial status analysis);
    vi.   disclosure details of all outstanding bonds including the history of bond issuance activities and use of proceeds;
    vii.   board of directors and senior management;
    viii.   taxation subjects relevant for the financial bonds and related issues;
    ix.   credit rating;

---

[34] As the primary regulator for banks and insurance companies, CBIRC may be required to approve financial bond issuance in principle before the PBOC will consider the application for financial bond issuance in the CIBM.

x. legal opinion issued by the issuer's legal counsel;
xi. contact details of parties involved (issuer, underwriters, auditor, legal counsel, rating agency, bond register, and depository); and
xii. website where disclosure documents and press releases are available for investors to inspect or download.

In case a financial bond is issued to particular investors, a prospectus is still required. Its contents shall not conflict with the information in the public issuance prospectus and should include the following details:

i.   seniority or preference in repayment and risk factors;
ii. the basic situation of the issuer including business conditions for the past 3 years, basic situation of business development, financial reports, summary of financial indicators for the most recent 3 years, as well as governance and capital structures;
iii. terms and conditions of the financial bond and use of proceeds;
iv. underwriting and distribution methods; and
v. contact details of parties involved (issuer, underwriters, auditor, legal counsel, rating agency, bond register, and depository).

8.   Regulatory Process for Foreign-Currency-Denominated Debt Instruments

There is evidence that the issuance of foreign-currency-denominated debt financing instruments in the CIBM is possible. The first USD-denominated MTN in the CIBM was issued in 2009. In September 2016, the World Bank successfully issued its first tranche of special drawing rights (SDR)-denominated bonds in the CIBM (see also Chapter IX.A.9 for more details). In 2017, the Government of the PRC issued USD-denominated government bonds in the CIBM for the first time in 13 years.

Issuance of debt financing instruments in foreign currency by nonfinancial enterprises and international development institutions is expected to follow the regulatory process for Panda bonds since the issuance process is thought to be comparable except for the issuance currency. Sovereign issuers may require specific approval or consent from the MOF or regulatory authorities.

9.   Regulatory Process for Overseas Issuance of Corporate Bonds

Enterprises in the PRC that intend to directly or indirectly issue debt securities abroad, or to list their securities for trading abroad, are subject to approval from NDRC; such is the case of issuances in Hong Kong, China. After the issuance, foreign debt registration with SAFE and the submission of a post-issuance filing to NDRC are required. Overseas issuances of corporate or enterprise bonds are not governed by NAFMII.

Pursuant to the NDRC Circular on Promoting the Reform of the Administrative System on the Issuance by Enterprises of Foreign Debt Filings and Registrations, the issuer must register the bond issuance with NDRC and obtain a certificate from NDRC evidencing such registration.

The issuer undertakes to (i) provide the requisite information on the issuance of the bonds to NDRC within 10 business days after the issue date and (ii) comply with all applicable laws and regulations in connection with the NDRC post-issuance filing.

Any failure to complete the relevant filings under the NDRC circular within the prescribed time frame following the completion of the issuance of the bonds may have adverse consequences for the issuer of and/or the investors in the bonds.

The obligations of an issuer intending to issue debt securities outside of the PRC are contained in a number of regulations:

i.   within 15 business days after the issue date, the issuer will register the bond, or file or cause the bond to be registered or filed, with SAFE pursuant to the Administrative Measures for Foreign Debt Registration and its operating guidelines;

ii.   the issuer will use its best endeavors to complete the foreign debt registration and obtain a registration record from SAFE on or before 100 business days after the relevant issuance date; and

iii. if applicable, as soon as possible upon being required or requested to do so by any relevant governmental authority, the issuer will file the bond or cause for the bond to be filed with SAFE, pursuant to the Circular of the People's Bank of China on Implementing Overall Macro Prudential Management System for Nationwide Cross-Border Financing, and comply with all applicable laws and regulations in relation to the foreign debt registration.

G.   Continuous Disclosure Requirements in the Inter-Bank Bond Market

Continuous disclosure in the CIBM may depend on the type of debt instrument and is subject to the provisions of PBOC regulations, as well as NAFMII rules.

In principle, for debt financing instruments issued via a public offering, in addition to the prescribed disclosure requirements at regular intervals during the tenor of the bond or note, the issuer should report to NAFMII any case of a significant adverse event that may affect its performance or solvency. In contrast, for private placements, the content and frequency of continuous disclosure should be determined between issuer and parties concerned and specified in the issuance documentation.

1.   Public Offerings

According to Article 8 of the NAFMII Rules for Information Disclosure on Debt Financing Instruments of Non-Financial Enterprises in the Inter-Bank Bond Market (银行间债券市场非金融企业债务融资工具信息披露规则), effective 18 December 2017, the enterprise shall continuously disclose the following information during the lifetime of the debt financing instrument:

i.   annual reports and audit reports for the previous year prior to 30 April of each year;

ii.   balance sheet, profit statement, and cash flow statement for the first half of the year prior to 31 August of each year; and

iii. balance sheet, profit statement, and cash flow statement for the first and third quarters of the year prior to 30 April and 31 October of each year.

The first quarter information may not be disclosed earlier than the previous year's disclosure time, and the above information should be disclosed no later than the time when the enterprise has publicly disclosed it on the stock exchange (if listed), in designated media, or on other occasions.

During the lifetime of a debt financing instrument, an enterprise should disclose to the market in a timely manner any significant event that may affect its ability to service its debt. Disclosure information is to be provided in Chinese.

An enterprise that is already a listed company may be exempted from disclosing financial information on a regular basis, subject to disclosure in accordance with the relevant requirements of the regulatory body of its place of listing, and by means of a link to the information page on the website approved by NAFMII or a text indicating its way of disclosure.

The enterprise information disclosure document shall be delivered to NAFMII's Integrated Business and Information Service Platform (交易商协会综合业务和信息服务平台), known as DCM-FANS, in a form consistent with the prescribed content and format. After completing the audit of the information disclosure document format in accordance with these rules, the integrated platform sends the information disclosure documents in accordance with the prescribed format to CCDC, CFETS, SHCH, the Beijing Financial Assets Exchange (CFAE), and other information disclosure service platforms, and publishes the content on the official website in a timely manner. NAFMII authorizes the CFAE to conduct a format review of the information disclosure documents sent to the integrated platform.

2.   Financial Bonds

Financial bond is the term used in the PRC to denote a bond issued by a financial institution, including policy banks, non-bank financial institutions such as finance and leasing companies, and insurance companies.

The issuer shall fulfill its obligation of information disclosure before and during the issuance of the financial bonds. Disclosure information is to be provided in Chinese if a public offering or if not otherwise specified for a private placement. As designated by the PBOC, information disclosure should be conducted through the Chinamoney Network (of CFETS) and the ChinaBond information network operated by CCDC. If the contents of already disclosed information need to be changed or amended, the issuer has to report such changes to the PBOC and will have to announce the changes to the public together with the reasons for such change or amendment.

Upon approval of the issuance of financial bonds by the PBOC, the issuer discloses the prospectus and the new issue announcement within 3 working days prior to the issuance of each financial bond. During the life of a financial bond, the issuer shall disclose the annual report to the investors by 30 April of each year.[35]

The annual report shall include, among other information, the operating conditions of the issuer in the previous year, the financial statements audited by a certified public accountant, and information on any major litigations involving the issuer.

In the case of issuing guaranteed financial bonds, the issuer has to disclose in its annual report a description of the operation of the guarantor in the previous year, the audited financial statements, and information on any material lawsuits in which the guarantor is involved. The issuer also has to disclose the follow-up credit rating process by 31 July of each year as long as the financial bonds exist.

The financial statements should be audited by a certified public accountant, and an audit report should subsequently be issued. Any legal opinion issued during the lifecycle of the debt instrument shall be issued by a practicing solicitor while any credit rating report shall be issued by a CRA that has the ability to rate the bonds and is recognized to provide bond credit rating services in the CIBM.

---

[35] The financial year in the PRC is the same as the calendar year.

The issuer shall announce interest payments 2 working days prior to each interest payment date and 5 working days before the last interest payment and redemption payment.

Where financial bonds are issued to private placement investors, the content and format of information disclosure shall be stipulated in the prospectus and the issuance instructions. The information shall be disclosed to the private placement investors of the financial bond at the agreed intervals.

According to the PBOC Guidelines on National Inter-Bank Bond Market Management, financial institutions issuing financial bonds should report their market activities to the PBOC branch at or nearest their domicile either quarterly or periodically.

3.   Nonfinancial Enterprise Bonds Issued via a Private Placement

With regard to information disclosure for the private placement of bonds and notes, the issuer and investor(s) should agree on a specific disclosure standard in the private placement agreement, potentially aided by the lead underwriter; this includes the language of the disclosure (see also Chapter III.G for details). The issuer may announce only basic information of the private placement, such as the issue size, maturity, and transferability through a website approved by NAFMII.

The issuer has to inform investors of the details of coupon payments and redemption payments 5 days prior to the payment date.

Other specific reporting requirements may apply and differ depending on the instrument type. In principle, NAFMII issues specific rules for each instrument other than government bonds and financial bonds.

H.   Self-Regulatory Organizations in the Inter-Bank Bond Market

An SRO is an organization that exercises some degree of regulatory authority over an industry or profession. In the PRC, an SRO is the organization authorized by the State Council to exercise control over a certain aspect of the industry and support market growth in the financial, securities, foreign exchange, and capital markets. NAFMII is the sole SRO in the CIBM.

National Association of Financial Market Institutional Investors

NAFMII was founded on 3 September 2007 with the approval of the State Council. NAFMII aims to support and drive the development of the China OTC financial market, which comprises the CIBM, interbank lending market, foreign exchange market, commercial paper market (which is often subsumed into the CIBM), and gold market.

Issuers of debt financing instruments and relevant intermediaries shall be members of NAFMII. Membership is not mandatory for investors unless they would like to invest in PPN in the CIBM. Other market participants are not subject to prescribed membership of NAFMII. As an SRO, NAFMII adopts a registration mechanism for the admission of debt financing instruments issued by nonfinancial enterprises to the CIBM. In addition, NAFMII admits and administers the licenses of lead underwriters, underwriters, as well as CRAs active in the CIBM (see subsection b).

Table 2.9: NAFMII Membership by Category and Details

Category	Member Institutions	Chinese Designation	Number of Members[a]
Banking or financial institutions 银行类金融机构 (1,517)	Rural financial institutions (e.g., credit cooperatives and credit unions)	信用合作社, 信用联社等农村金融机构	384
	Foreign banks	外资银行	49
	Rural commercial banks	农村商业银行	921
	City commercial banks	城市商业银行	142
	Policy banks	政策性银行	3
	National banks	全国性银行	18
Non-bank financial Institutions 非银行类金融机构 (572)	Other non-bank financial institutions	其他非银行类金融机构	24
	Asset management companies	资产管理公司	82
	Futures companies	期货公司	37
	Trust companies	信托公司	62
	Finance companies	财务公司	111
	Fund management companies	基金管理公司	110
	Securities companies	证券公司	108
	Insurance companies	保险公司	33
	Currency brokerage companies	货币经纪公司	5
Credit enhancement agencies 信用增进机构 (20)	Credit enhancement agencies (e.g., guarantee companies, credit re-guarantee companies, and credit enhancement companies)	信用增进机构 (担保股份有限公司/信用再担保股份有限公司)	20
Issuer members 发行人会员 (3,736)	Issuer members	发行人会员	3,736
Intermediary institutions 中介机构 (906)	Other intermediaries	其他中介机构	43
	General accounting firms	一般会计师事务所	38
	Law offices	律师事务所	656
	Rating agencies	评级机构	12
	Gold Coin Market members	金币市场类会员	117
	Securities accounting firms	证券从业会计师事务所	40
Special members 特别会员 (60)	Special members (e.g., asset management companies, Hong Kong, China branches or affiliates of banks	特别会员 (资产管理有限公司/银行香港分行/银行(香港)有限公司他)	60
Other - intermediary platforms 其他 - 中介平台 (5)	CCDC	中央国债登记结算有限责任公司	1
	CFETS	中国外汇交易中心	1
	Shanghai Gold Exchange	上海黄金交易所	1
	Beijing Financial Assets Exchange Co., Ltd.	北京金融资产交易所有限公司	1
	Interbank Market Clearing House Co., Ltd.	银行间市场清算所股份有限公司	1
Other institutions 其他机构 (2)	National Social Security Fund Council	全国社会保障基金理事会	1
	China Gold Coin Corporation	中国金币总公司	1
Institutional members (6,818)	Subtotal: Institutional members		6,818
Individual member (11)	Individual member (person)	个人会员（人）	11
Total			**6,829**

CCDC = China Central Depository & Clearing Co., Ltd.; CFETS = China Foreign Exchange Trade System; NAFMII = National Association of Financial Market Institutional Investors.
[a] Number of institutions as of 10 September 2019.
Source: National Association of Financial Market Institutional Investors. http://www.nafmii.org.cn/hygl/hyfl/.

a.   NAFMII Members and Participants

As the SRO for the CIBM, the membership of NAFMII includes policy banks, commercial banks, credit cooperative banks, insurance companies, securities companies, fund management companies, trust and investment companies, finance companies affiliated with corporations, CRAs, accounting firms, as well as companies in nonfinancial sectors (Table 2.9).

Institutions wishing to participate in the CIBM as an intermediary or service provider will need to become a NAFMII member to ensure their commitment to compliance with the market rules and regulations.

Admission and member management procedures for institutional members and their employees, as well as self-regulatory principles governing membership, are contained in the Membership Rules of the National Association of Financial Market Institutional Investors, last adopted by the NAFMII Governing Council on 29 August 2017.[36] There are separate membership rules for the few individual members of NAFMII.

In 2011, NAFMII introduced the separate category "debt financing instruments underwriting business members (债务融资工具承销业务相关会员)" for member institutions engaged in debt financing instruments underwriting for nonfinancial enterprises. In 2016, NAFMII established a market-oriented evaluation mechanism for them.

b.   Licensing of Intermediaries and Service Providers

Under the mandate given by the PBOC, NAFMII issues licenses to and admits lead underwriters, underwriters, and CRAs to the CIBM (see section I for details). It also administers the ongoing licensing criteria for these intermediaries and service providers and tracks their performance.

c.   Issuance of Self-Regulatory Rules

Under the mandate given by the PBOC, NAFMII is able to define, issue, and implement self-regulatory rules, business standards, and codes of conduct for the CIBM constituents and their activities in the market. These rules and standards range from eligibility to participate and membership (see also section J) in the CIBM to the registration of debt financing instruments issued by nonfinancial enterprises and the stipulation of trading practices and conventions.

A few notable examples of the NAFMII rules are shown. A complete list of relevant rules and regulations issued by NAFMII for the CIBM can be found in Appendix 3.

- Self-Regulatory Rules for Bond Transactions in the Inter-Bank Bond Market (银行间债券市场债券交易自律规则) (2013 Revision)
- Guidelines for the Due Diligence for Debt Financing Instruments of Non-Financial Enterprises in the Inter-Bank Bond Market (银行间债券市场非金融企业债务融资工具尽职调查指引)
- Code of Conduct for Underwriting Staff of Debt Financing Instruments of Non-Financial Enterprises in the Inter-Bank Bond Market (银行间债券市场非金融企业债务融资工具承销人员行为守则)

---

[36] For the full text of the membership rules, please see
http://www.nafmii.org.cn//english/lawsandregulations/selfregulatory_e/201801/t20180110_67082.html.

- Market Self-Disciplinary Rules Relating to Debt Financing Instruments of Non-Financial Enterprises (非金融企业债务融资工具市场自律处分规则)

d.   Enforcement of Self-Regulatory Rules

NAFMII conducts member inspections and reviews the mandated periodical reporting against set benchmarks. For any member (or its employees) who has violated the self-regulatory rules, NAFMII may, depending on the severity of the violation, communicate its concern, circulate a notice of criticism, send a warning or serious warning, or issue a public reprimand. It may also, based on the specific circumstances, order the member to make corrections or offer an apology, restrict its relevant businesses, suspend its membership rights, or revoke its membership. Where a violation of law or regulations is suspected, NAFMII may refer the case to the competent authorities for further action.[37]

I.   Licensing and Admission of Inter-Bank Bond Market Participants

Market participants in the CIBM are licensed by their relevant regulatory authority according to the nature of their business (e.g., commercial banks and insurance companies are licensed by CBIRC and securities companies are licensed by CSRC). Any entity wishing to participate in the CIBM as an intermediary will need to be admitted as a member of NAFMII to ensure a commitment to and the enforceability of the rules for the CIBM issued by NAFMII in its capacity as the SRO for the OTC bond market under a mandate from the PBOC.

NAFMII also issues underwriting licenses for debt financing instruments of nonfinancial enterprises and tracks and evaluates the performance of underwriters, lead underwriters, and market makers, the results of which may have an impact on licensing and admission to the CIBM.

NAFMII also issues licenses to and admits CRAs servicing the CIBM, stipulates their admission criteria, and tracks their performance. Pursuant to PBOC policies admitting foreign-owned CRAs to the CIBM, NAFMII issued the Rules for Credit Rating Agencies' Registration and Participation in Market-Based Evaluation in the Inter-Bank Bond Market in March 2019; the rules are presently only available in Chinese and list the requirements for admission and licensing documentation.

The PBOC appoints market makers for the CIBM as well as bond settlement agents as service providers to investors, including foreign investors.

Please also see Chapter III.M for more information on licensing individual market participants.

J.   Membership Rules of the Inter-Bank Bond Market

Membership in NAFMII is subject to the NAFMII Membership Rules (see also section H), as the underlying self-regulatory rules issued by NAFMII. The membership rules are supplemented by the Guidelines for NAFMII Membership as Institutional Members, which detail eligibility criteria and the application and admission process for new members, as well as other matters.

---

[37] Adopted by SF1 from Article 22 of NAFMII Membership Rules, 2017.

The guidelines are formulated with a view to facilitating market participants to join NAFMII as members and are in accordance with the constitution of NAFMII and the relevant rules and regulations.

According to the guidelines, the prerequisites for membership are that an institution wishes to join NAFMII and accept its self-regulatory management; that it will uphold the constitution of NAFMII; that it is a legal person domiciled in the PRC and intends to engage in relevant businesses in the CIBM; and that it meets other qualifications that NAFMII may set.

If the applicant is a nonfinancial enterprise wishing to issue debt financing instruments in the CIBM, such an issuer shall also meet the following conditions:

    i.   production and management are in conformity with national macro-control policy, industrial policy, environmental protection policy, and relevant laws and regulations; and
    ii.   no major violation of laws or regulations for the preceding 3 years and no administrative punishment by national administrative authorities have occurred.

To facilitate the admission process, the applicant will have to submit the following documents to NAFMII:

    i.   application form (affiliated institutions also need to submit written documents of permit or authorization);
    ii.   constitution of the corporation;
    iii.   copies of business license duplicate or practice license duplicate;
    iv.   introduction to the corporation's profile and resumes of major persons in charge;
    v.   briefings on relevant businesses engaged in the CIBM, including but not limited to the following contents: primary market business, secondary market business, derivative products business, business qualifications obtained and business development briefings, innovative business progress, and description of capability of analysis and research;
    vi.   relevant business regulations, business procedures, and risk control system;
    vii. proof of no major violations of laws and regulations;
    viii. audit report of the preceding year; and
    ix.   membership registration form.

The above materials should be affixed with the official seal and paging seal of the corporation.

The completed membership application form and supporting documents should be emailed to the Members and Laws Affairs Department of NAFMII, where the materials will be reviewed to confirm whether they meet the requirements of NAFMII. After such confirmation and notification by NAFMII, the applicant should submit paper versions of all materials to the Secretariat of NAFMII.

Applications that meet the requirements will be forwarded to the Secretary General Office for deliberation. Once a decision has been reached, NAFMII will send the Notice of NAFMII Membership Record to the applicant upon payment of membership fees, confirming that they are now a member of NAFMII, while updating the member list on the NAFMII website at the same time.

K.   Rules Related to Disclosure and Trading of Debt Financing Instruments

This section references applicable rules for activities in the CIBM as formulated by NAFMII and CFETS for their constituents. Disclosure rules apply primarily to the issuers of debt financing instruments and the intermediaries servicing them, while trading participants are required to comply with the trading rules.

The primary provisions for disclosure requirements are contained in the Rules for Information Disclosure on Debt Financing Instruments of Non-Financial Enterprises in the Inter-Bank Bond Market (银行间债券市场非金融企业债务融资工具信息披露规则), issued by NAFMII and last revised on 18 December 2017, pursuant to the Measures for the Administration of Listed Corporation Information Disclosure and other regulations issued by the PBOC. In addition, initial disclosure and follow-up disclosure requirements are contained in the specific issuance and registration rules and guidelines for individual types of instruments.

A detailed description of the actual disclosure provisions for debt financing instruments in the CIBM may be found in section G in this chapter, and a list of relevant regulations and rules is available in the appendix. For more details on the role and functions of NAFMII as an SRO, please see section H.

NAFMII also published the Self-Regulatory Rules for Bond Transactions in the Inter-Bank Bond Market (银行间债券市场债券交易自律规则) in 2009, which were revised in 2013 and contain the basic principles for trading participants to adhere to in the CIBM. The rules contain risk management and control principles and describe a code of conduct. In the rules, NAFMII actively encourages trading participants to look out for suspicious transactions or unethical behavior and report those to NAFMII for further investigation. These NAFMII rules are also binding for indirect participants, such as corporates, who route their orders through the CFAE for execution on CFETS.

In addition, CFETS, as the central trading platform for the CIBM, formulates and publishes its own trading rules and other rules pertaining to the transactions executed on its platform. The Rules for Bond Transactions of the National Inter-Bank Market were last revised in 2016 and were issued pursuant to the Provisions on the Administration of National Inter-Bank Bond Market Makers (PBOC Document 2007, No. 1) and other relevant rules and regulations issued by the PBOC.

For further details on the actual trading of debt financing instruments in the CIBM, related practices, and the underlying trading market infrastructure, please refer to the individual sections in Chapter IV.

L.   Market Entry Requirements (Nonresidents)

1.   Nonresident Issuers

Nonresident issuers with business operations in the PRC (e.g., the head offices or treasury centers of international corporations) have the opportunity to raise funds in the China bond market using the Panda bond concept. This issuance concept is the only avenue for nonresidents to issue debt financing instruments or debt securities in the PRC. The issuance of Panda bonds is subject to the review and consent of the MOF, as well as necessary approvals by the relevant regulatory authorities. The approvals required differ with the nature of the nonresident institutions planning to issue Panda bonds.

The PBOC is setting a high standard for issuers in the Panda bond market through their regulations, particularly for nonresident financial institutions, for which it approves issuances. The regulations even state that sovereign and supranational international agencies must have experience in debt offerings and issuers must have a proven debt repayment ability.

The use of proceeds from a Panda bond issuance outside the PRC is possible. If a nonresident issuer plans to remit the proceeds from a Panda bond issuance outbound, approval from the PBOC and SAFE will be required.

Please also see Chapter III.B for a description of Panda bonds and Chapter III.E for information on issuance methods. Section E in this chapter contains a detailed description of the Panda bond issuance regulatory process for nonresident issuers.

2.   Foreign Investors

The PRC capital market overall, and the bond market in particular, has become more open and accessible for nonresident or foreign investors in recent years. As a major development in the context of the free flow of capital and the liberalization of the Chinese renminbi, nonresidents may enter the domestic capital market, including the CIBM, via one of the approved investment channels for foreign investors: (i) the QFII scheme, (ii) the RQFII scheme, (iii) CIBM Direct, and (iv) Bond Connect. Section N in this chapter provides a detailed explanation of these investment avenues. Please also see Table 1.3 in Chapter I for a practical comparison of these investment channels for foreign investors.

M.   Market Exit Requirements (Nonresidents)

1.   Nonresident Issuers

In the past, if a nonresident issuer wanted to remit foreign exchange from abroad for use as bond principal and interest payments, the issuer was required to get the approval of SAFE. To transfer offshore Chinese renminbi held by the issuer outside the PRC for bond principal and interest payments in Chinese renminbi in the PRC, the issuer was required to submit an approval request to the PBOC for filing. In May 2010, the rules were liberalized and more issuers were allowed, with the restriction on outbound remittance of proceeds being lifted. There are no specific requirements for nonresident issuers following the redemption of a Panda bond.

2.   Foreign Investors—Repatriation of Qualified Foreign Institutional Investor Quota or Investment

QFIIs who wish to exit the China bond market, including the CIBM, or who wish to repatriate all or part of their quota or investment amount, may do so while observing specific provisions in the QFII regulations. See also section N in this chapter for a full description of the QFII concept.

On 12 June 2018, the PBOC and SAFE issued the Regulations on Foreign Exchange Administration for Domestic Securities Investment by QFII and the Circular on the Administration for Domestic Securities Investment by RQFII to facilitate the repatriation of capital and management of foreign exchange risks associated with the securities investments of QFIIs and RQFIIs.

Under these new regulations, the monthly repatriation limit of 20% of a QFII's assets was removed, as was the requirement for a 3-month capital lockup period for redeeming the investment principal for both QFIIs and RQFIIs, allowing a QFII to repatriate the principal and profits of its securities investment in the PRC at any time based on its needs. Under the previous rules, a QFII could only repatriate the principal and profits of its securities investments by installment after the lapse of a 3-month lockup period. In September 2019, SAFE announced the immediate abolition of the quota system for both the QFII and RQFII schemes; however, there was no direct impact on the repatriation of investments by foreign investors since any repatriation limitations had already been removed.

In the case of liquidation, including product liquidation, the QFII custodian may handle the outward remittance of relevant funds and/or close the account for the QFII in accordance with the investor's written application or instruction, special audit report on returns on investment issued by a certified public accountant in the PRC, and relevant tax clearance or tax filing certificates.

Please also refer to the SAFE website for QFII and RQFII rules about injection and repatriation of quota or investment amounts.[38]

N.   Regulations and Limitations Relevant for Nonresidents

The applicable regulations and possible limitations for nonresidents in relation to the CIBM are provided below in detail and grouped according to the key topics of interest for nonresidents.

1.   CIBM Direct

CIBM Direct was introduced in July 2015, initially to a limited number of participants (e.g., foreign central banks, supranational financial institutions, and sovereign wealth funds). It allowed eligible institutions to access the CIBM under a registration concept with the PBOC instead of requiring preapproval. No quota has been required for CIBM Direct participants since its inception.

In February 2016, the PBOC announced that a wider range of foreign institutional investors—including commercial banks, insurance companies, securities firms, and asset managers—would be able to access the CIBM through CIBM Direct. The announcement also introduced the official term "Qualified Overseas Institutional Investor," or QOII, which summarized the constituents of CIBM Direct. QFIIs and RQFIIs were also included in the list of eligible QOIIs. The changes were implemented in May 2016 and featured the ability to remit funding in Chinese renminbi or foreign currency and execute necessary foreign exchange transactions overseas or with the bond settlement agent (custodian) in the CIBM. A lockup period for investment capital was not introduced.

Registration with the PBOC should be done with the prescribed registration form and mention the intended investment amount. A QOII must invest (within a 9-month period) at least 50% of the investment amount mentioned in the registration form.

Chapter I.D contains a detailed description of the implementation and development milestones of CIBM Direct and other market access schemes for foreign investors. Please also see section 8 for more information on applicable intermediary limitations in the context of CIBM Direct.

---

[38] For Announcement No. 1 of the State Administration of Foreign Exchange (12 June 2018), see http://www.safe.gov.cn/en/2018/0612/1453.html. For Regulations on Foreign Exchange Administration for Domestic Securities Investments by Qualified Foreign Institutional Investors (10 June 2018), an English version in PDF is available at http://www.safe.gov.cn/en/file/file/20180913/6d2d8858afe04753916f 7f1c3f39840f.pdf?n=Regulations%20on%20Foreign%20Exchange%20Administration%20for%20Domestic% 20Securities%20Investments%20by%20Qualified%20Foreign%20Institutional%20Investors.

2.   Qualified Foreign Institutional Investor Scheme

The QFII scheme is a transitional arrangement that allows institutional investors who meet certain qualifications to invest in a defined scope of securities products in the domestic capital market in the PRC. The QFII scheme was introduced in 2002 as one of the first efforts to internationalize the Chinese renminbi. It allowed global institutional investors to directly invest in the CNY-denominated capital market on a selective basis. Once licensed by CSRC, foreign institutional investors were permitted to buy, within a quota approved by SAFE, CNY-denominated debt financing instruments in the CIBM.

Based on CSRC Decree No. 36, promulgated in 2006, a QFII was able to invest in the following financial instruments denominated in Chinese renminbi within the approved investment quota:

i.   stocks, bonds, and warrants traded in or transferred in stock exchanges;
ii.   fixed-income products traded in the CIBM;
iii. securities investment funds;
iv.   stock index futures; and
v.   other financial instruments permitted by CSRC.

A QFII had to meet certain eligibility criteria and remit the approved quota amount in foreign currency, then convert the amount into Chinese renminbi.

The first QFII license was awarded in July 2003. Since then, more than 310 QFIIs—including commercial banks, trust companies, insurers, asset managers, securities firms, sovereign wealth funds, pension funds, and endowment funds—have been approved via this avenue into the PRC's domestic securities market, with a total investment quota of USD111.04 billion at the end of September 2019 (Table 2.10). The current list of QFIIs can be downloaded from the website of CSRC.[39]

Limitations on the asset allocation of QFII were relaxed in September 2016, with only a limitation on cash and cash equivalent holdings remaining. On 12 June 2018, the Government of the PRC stated that it would ease restrictions on foreign institutional investors in a step to further open its financial markets. The 20% cap on the amount of capital that users of the QFII program were able to remit out of the country at any time had already been removed.

In September 2019, SAFE subsequently stated that it had abolished the quota system for the QFII and RQFII schemes in the latest move to open up Chinese financial markets. SAFE also mentioned that restrictions limiting entry to the two schemes to specific countries and regions would be removed as well. However, new investors will still have to apply and meet regulatory requirements to gain entry to the two investment schemes.

---

[39] The current list of QFIIs can be downloaded from the CSRC website at
http://www.csrc.gov.cn/pub/csrc_en/OpeningUp/RelatedLists/QFIIs/.

Table 2.10: QFII Quotas Granted by Economy or Region

No.	QFII Quota Granted to Economy or Region	Allocated Quota		Number of Approved QFIIs[b]
		(USD billion)[b]	(CNY billion)[a]	
1	Hong Kong, China	25.51	179.33	77
2	United Kingdom	11.40	80.13	27
3	Taipei,China	10.86	76.34	37
4	United States	9.44	66.36	48
5	Singapore	7.92	55.67	23
6	Republic of Korea	7.75	54.48	19
7	Macau, China	5.00	35.14	1
8	France	3.68	25.86	7
9	United Arab Emirates	3.50	24.60	1
10	Japan	3.48	24.46	16
11	Switzerland	3.17	22.28	8
12	Canada	3.06	21.51	10
13	Australia	2.60	18.27	4
14	Norway	2.50	17.57	1
15	Malaysia	2.06	14.48	3
16	Kuwait	2.00	14.04	1
17	Germany	1.42	10.03	4
18	Portugal	1.20	8.43	2
19	Qatar	1.00	7.02	1
20	Sweden	0.89	6.25	4
21	Netherlands	0.76	5.34	4
22	Luxembourg	0.40	2.88	4
22	Thailand	0.40	2.88	2
24	Belgium	0.21	1.47	1
25	Brunei	0.20	1.44	1
25	Ireland	0.20	1.44	1
27	South Africa	0.15	1.05	1
28	Lithuania	0.10	0.72	1
28	Spain	0.10	0.72	1
30	Italy	0.08	0.57	1
	Total	**111.04**	**780.59**	**311**

CNY = Chinese renminbi, QFII = Qualified Foreign Institutional Investor.
[a] USD1 = CNY6.9762 as of 31 December 2019.
[b] As per data published by the Bank of New York Mellon.
Note: Data as of 30 September 2019.
Sources: ASEAN+3 Bond Market Forum Sub-Forum 1 team compilation from information collected from publicly available sources including the State Administration of Foreign Exchange (www.safe.gov.cn) and Bank of New York Mellon (https://www.bnymellon.com/apac/en/rqfii/index.jsp).

Section 4 of this chapter contains a tabulated list of QFII and RQFII milestones, while Chapter I.D contains a detailed description of the implementation and development milestones of the QFII scheme and other market access schemes for foreign investors. Please also see section 8 of this chapter for more information on applicable intermediary limitations in the context of the QFII scheme.

a.   Supervising Institutions

A number of regulatory authorities act as supervising institutions for the QFII scheme as well as for the RQFII scheme (Table 2.11).

Table 2.11: Supervising Institutions for the QFII and RQFII Schemes

Supervising Institution	Supervisory Activities
PBOC	Manage the opening of CNY-denominated bank accounts by QFIIs and RQFIIs; monitor and manage the capital inflows and outflows of QFIIs and RQFIIs
CSRC	Conduct supervision and administration of the securities investments of QFIIs and RQFIIs; review applications filed by QFIIs and RQFIIs for the business qualification of securities investment; make a decision within 60 days upon receipt of completed application materials
SAFE	Set and monitor investment quotas for QFII and RQFII schemes; manage the overall investment quotas for QFIIs and RQFIIs (until September 2019); monitor and manage the capital inflows and outflows of investments by RQFIIs and as a result of the issuance of Panda bonds

CNY = Chinese renminbi, CSRC = China Securities Regulatory Commission, PBOC = People's Bank of China, QFII = Qualified Foreign Institutional Investor, RQFII = Renminbi Qualified Foreign Institutional Investor, SAFE = State Administration of Foreign Exchange.
Source: ASEAN+3 Bond Market Forum Sub-Forum 1 team from publicly available sources.

b.   Qualified Foreign Institutional Investor Application Process

The application process to obtain a QFII license and corresponding quota has been significantly simplified in recent years. The necessary steps are outlined below:

 i.   appoint a designated QFII custodian;
 ii.   submit a QFII application to CSRC via the designated QFII custodian;
 iii.   obtain a QFII license from CSRC;
 iv.   apply to open special Chinese renminbi and foreign exchange accounts with the designated QFII custodian;
 v.   appoint up to three dedicated QFII brokers;
 vi.   open securities account(s) in CCDC or SHCH via the designated QFII custodian, depending on the number of brokers appointed;
 vii.   remit funds (quota amount) in foreign currency; foreign exchange transactions are required to be done via the designated QFII custodian;
 viii.   finalize agreements among QFIIs, the designated QFII custodian, and designated broker(s); and
 ix.   commence investments.

Further details on the eligibility criteria for QFIIs, as well as the application and approval process for a QFII license and quota, to the extent still applicable, are available from the SAFE website.[40]

3.   Renminbi Qualified Foreign Institutional Investor Scheme

Established in 2011, the RQFII scheme is a policy initiative that allows foreign investors who held an RQFII quota to invest directly in the PRC's equity and bond markets using offshore Chinese renminbi.[41] The quota requirement was abolished by SAFE on 10 September 2019.[42] The introduction of the RQFII scheme relaxed existing restrictions on currency settlement, added permissible asset classes, and expanded investor eligibility.

As pilot institutions, subsidiaries in Hong Kong, China of PRC-based firms and securities companies were able to use Chinese renminbi raised from business activities in Hong Kong, China to conduct securities investment business in the China (bond) market within the approved investment quota. Until 10 September 2019, the RQFII quota for a single investor was limited to CNY20 billion.

Limitations on the asset allocation of RQFIIs were relaxed in September 2016, with only a limitation on cash and cash equivalent holdings remaining. Effective June 2018, any cap on the repatriation amounts for RQFIIs was also removed, and RQFIIs were granted the ability to place foreign exchange hedges in relation to their debt financing instrument holdings. Chapter I.D contains a detailed description of the implementation and development milestones of the RQFII scheme and other market access schemes for foreign investors.

As of September 2019, when the quota requirement was abolished, the Government of the PRC had granted a total investment quota amounting to CNY1,990 billion to investors in 20 economies and regions. At the same time, CSRC had granted 243 individual RQFII licenses, with a total allocated quota of CNY691.6 billion.

Please also see section 6 of this chapter for more information on applicable intermediary limitations in the context of the RQFII scheme.

a.   Renminbi Qualified Foreign Institutional Investor Quota Development

Table 2.12 gives a representation of the pace of approval and allocation of the original quotas under the RQFII scheme since its inception in 2011. As of September 2019, 243 individual RQFII licenses had been issued.[43]

---

[40] See http://www.safe.gov.cn/en/.

[41] On 16 December 2011, the PBOC, CSRC, and SAFE jointly issued the Measures for Pilots of Domestic Securities Investment by Qualified Foreign Institutional Investors of Fund Management Companies and Securities Companies to allow fund management companies to meet certain qualifications.

[42] See https://www.safe.gov.cn/en/2019/0910/1552.html / https://www.safe.gov.cn/en/2019/0910/1553.html.

[43] The current list of RQFIIs can be downloaded from the CSRC website at http://www.csrc.gov.cn/pub/csrc_en/OpeningUp/RelatedLists/meRQFII/.

Table 2.12: RQFII Quotas Granted by Economy and Region

No.	Month and Year Granted	RQFII Quota Granted to Economy or Region	Investment Quota (CNY billion)	Allocated Quota (CNY billion)	Number of Approved RQFIIs
1	December 2011 July 2017	Hong Kong, China (originally CNY270 billion)	500	344.94	109
2	October 2013	United Kingdom	80	48.46	22
2	October 2013	France	80	24.02	9
2	October 2013 November 2015	Singapore (originally CNY50 billion)	100	78.27	33
5	July 2014	Republic of Korea	120	72.90	35
5	July 2014	Germany	80	10.58	3
7	November 2014	Canada	50	8.65	3
7	November 2014	Australia	50	32.02	3
7	November 2014	Qatar	30	0.00	0
10	January 2015	Switzerland	50	9.58	2
11	April 2015	Luxembourg	50	15.15	7
12	May 2015	Chile	50	0.00	0
13	June 2015	Hungary	50	0.00	0
14	November 2015	Malaysia	50	1.57	1
15	December 2015	Thailand	50	2.07	3
15	December 2015	United Arab Emirates	50	0.00	0
17	June 2016	United States	250	32.52	8
18	December 2016	Ireland	50	1.86	3
19	May 2018	Japan	200	9.01	2
20	June 2019	Netherlands	50	0.00	0
		Total	**1,990**	**691.60**	**243**

CNY = Chinese renminbi, RQFII = Renminbi Qualified Foreign Institutional Investor.
Note: Data as of 30 September 2019.
Sources: ASEAN+3 Bond Market Forum Sub-Forum 1 team compilation from information collected from publicly available sources including the State Administration of Foreign Exchange (www.safe.gov.cn) and Bank of New York Mellon (https://www.bnymellon.com/apac/en/rqfii/index.jsp).

b.   Renminbi Qualified Foreign Institutional Investor Application Process

The application process to obtain an RQFII license and corresponding quota has been significantly simplified in recent years. The actual steps necessary are comparable to those for a QFII (see section 3 of this chapter), with the exception that there is no need to open a foreign-currency-denominated account.

4.   Qualified Foreign Institutional Investor and Renminbi Qualified Foreign Institutional Investor Milestones

Table 2.13 provides an overview of the milestones in the QFII and RQFII schemes, and of the participation of nonresident issuers in relation to the general efforts of the Government of the PRC in opening its markets and internationalizing the Chinese renminbi.

Table 2.13: Milestones Related to Nonresident Issuer and Investor Participation

Date	Description
10 September 2019	SAFE announces the immediate abolition of the investment quota for QFIIs and RQFIIs.
January 2019	SAFE increases the overall investment quota for QFIIs from USD150 billion to USD300 billion.
8 September 2018	The PBOC and MOF jointly issue regulations clarifying qualifications and filing procedures for Panda Bond issuance in the CIBM via public offering or private placement.
8 August 2018	CSRC announces the further opening of the exchange market, with entry requirements for QFIIs and RQFIIs to be relaxed, standardized, and harmonized, and their investment scope expanded.
12 June 2018	The PBOC and SAFE jointly issue regulations to facilitate the repatriation of capital and the management of foreign exchange risks for securities investment by QFIIs and RQFIIs.
3 July 2017	Bond Connect debuts.
March 2017	The first Panda bond is issued by a country located along the Belt and Road Initiative and is listed on the SSE.
23 September 2016	CSRC verbally advises and removes asset allocation restrictions on QFIIs and RQFIIs; QFIIs and RQFIIs are now allowed to decide asset allocation at their discretion.
5 September 2016	SAFE further relaxes the RQFII rules on quota application and control, resulting in a simplified quota application process, easier inward and outward remittances, and a shorter lockup period.
May 2016	The CIBM Direct scheme is launched, which allows foreign institutional investors direct access to the CIBM using a registration approach and bond settlement agent concept.
February 2016	Authorities announce foreign institutional investors will be given quota-free access to the CIBM, which will be known as the CIBM Direct scheme.
September 2015	The PBOC eases restrictions on issuers of Panda bonds, allowing proceeds to be used within and outside the PRC.
July 2015	The PBOC introduces the CIBM Direct scheme for foreign central banks, supranational financial institutions, and sovereign wealth funds without a quota and with registration.

continued on next page

Table 2.13 *continued*

June 2015	The PBOC permits banks carrying out offshore Chinese renminbi business to engage in bond repurchase agreements in the CIBM
1 October 2014	A single identification code is assigned to QFIIs, RQFIIs, and RMB Special Deposit Accounts for securities trading to record investors' identity and securities assets.
2 May 2013	The PBOC announces new rules on account opening, account management, and asset allocation for the RQFII scheme; RQFIIs are permitted access to the CIBM.
March 2013	The scope of the RQFII scheme is expanded by CSRC, SAFE, and the PBOC to relax investment restrictions, the 1-year lockup period, and monthly repatriation frequency.
December 2012	QFII regulations on foreign exchange are revised, including the quota limit and monthly remittances.
December 2011	The RQFII pilot program is launched.
December 2010	The PBOC, MOF, NDRC, and CSRC amend Panda bond regulations and expand the scope of qualified issuers and use of Chinese renminbi proceeds, including outbound remittances.
29 September 2009	QFII regulations on foreign exchange are revised, including the upper quota limit and capital transfer.
24 August 2006	CSRC, the PBOC, and SAFE jointly formalize QFII rules and lower QFII qualifications.
18 February 2005	The first Panda bond regulation is issued by the PBOC, MOF, NDRC, and CSRC.
May 2003	The QFII pilot program is launched; bonds are limited to listed bonds in the exchange bond market.
5 November 2002	The QFII scheme is introduced by CSRC and the PBOC to allow foreign capital to access financial markets in the PRC.

CIBM = China Inter-Bank Bond Market, CSRC = China Securities Regulatory Commission, MOF = Ministry of Finance, NDRC = National Development and Reform Commission, PBOC = People's Bank of China, PRC = People's Republic of China, QFII = Qualified Foreign Institutional Investor, RQFII = Renminbi Qualified Foreign Institutional Investor, SAFE = State Administration of Foreign Exchange, SSE = Shanghai Stock Exchange.
Sources: News releases and other material from BNP Paribas, Citibank N.A., Deutsche Bank, HSBC, Mizuho Securities, SSE, Standard Chartered Bank, and other publicly available sources.

Information on individual milestones can be found in the respective chapters and sections of this bond market guide. To see the development of the QFII quota since the inception of the QFII scheme, please refer to Table 2.8 in this chapter. For individual allocations of RQFII quotas by market or region, please refer to Table 2.10 in this chapter.

5.   Bond Connect

Bond Connect was launched in July 2017 and introduced by Prime Minister Li Keqiang as a way to accelerate the process of opening the CIBM. Bond Connect is a mutual market access scheme that eventually will allow investors from the PRC and overseas to trade in each other's bond markets through connections between the relevant financial infrastructure institutions in the PRC and Hong Kong, China.

Northbound Trading commenced on 3 July 2017, allowing foreign investors from Hong Kong, China and other regions to invest in the CIBM through mutual access arrangements with respect to trading, custody, and settlement. Southbound Trading, where investors from the PRC can access the Hong Kong bond market, may be explored at a later stage.

Apart from the CIBM Direct scheme, Bond Connect is another channel that allows foreign investors to participate in the CIBM. Compared to the CIBM Direct scheme, Bond Connect utilizes the international practice of an omnibus account structure, under which nonresident investors no longer need to open accounts with the domestic infrastructures and sign additional agreements with settlement agents.

Bond Connect also utilizes the Cross-Border Interbank Payment System as the domestic payment system for cash settlement, supporting two types of delivery-versus-payment settlement. At the same time, Bond Connect has the arrangement of a see-through structure, which still allows regulators to identify the end investors accessing the CIBM.

Overseas investors qualified to enter the CIBM can choose to access the market via CIBM Direct and Bond Connect simultaneously.

6.   Foreign Exchange Controls

The Chinese renminbi is the currency of the PRC. While the official currency code for the Chinese renminbi is CNY, the currency is most often abbreviated or referred to as RMB, including in official publications.

The Chinese renminbi is freely convertible from and into other currencies, but it may not be used outside of the PRC. Instead, the PRC offers the use of offshore Chinese renminbi, which is referred to as CNH, to be held in accounts and transacted outside the PRC, but not in its domestic market.

Commercial banks and other financial institutions in Hong Kong, China; the PRC; and in designated Chinese renminbi offshore centers, which are known officially as "offshore RMB centers," are able to facilitate the exchange from onshore to offshore Chinese renminbi and vice versa.

Foreign exchange transactions, with the exception of the initial remittance of QFII or RQFII investment amounts, are required to observe the real demand principle; that is, the customer must prove to the executing financial institution that an underlying transaction or commitment exists to support a foreign exchange transaction.

In the context of the investment in debt financing instruments, the custodian of the investor will normally keep records for both the debt financing instruments and foreign exchange transactions to fulfill this requirement. Violations may attract heavy fines.

7.   Bank Accounts in Domestic or Foreign Currency

Under CIBM Direct, approved nonresident investors are able to open cash accounts in Chinese renminbi and foreign currency with their bond settlement agent (custodian) without further approval from the PBOC or SAFE.

Under the provision of the QFII and RQFII schemes, nonresident investors can open a foreign currency account for their funding currency as well as a Chinese renminbi account for the settlement of foreign exchange and securities transactions.

The CNY-denominated account is referred to as a "Special CNY Account" since it is opened for a particular purpose. Transactions were originally limited to foreign exchange and securities trades, as well as the placement of funds to maximize returns.

The latest regulations promulgated in June 2018 allow QFIIs and RQFIIs to hedge exchange rate risk by entering into CNY–foreign currency derivative transactions using their Special CNY Account.

While the opening of CNY-denominated accounts by foreign institutions is subject to regulations issued by the PBOC, the opening of a Special CNY Account itself is not subject to the approval of the PBOC.

According to SAFE regulations, a QFII or RQFII shall open a foreign exchange account with its custodian for its own funds, client funds, or open-ended funds based on the information filed with or approved by SAFE on the investment amount.[44]

8.   Intermediary Limitations

A number of intermediary limitations or prescriptions exist for each of the investment avenues available to nonresident investors in the CIBM.

a.   CIBM Direct

Under the CIBM Direct Scheme, foreign institutions may trade bonds directly through securities companies or banks. If the foreign investor wishes to use a bank, this institution will have to have a so-called Type A license, which means it can trade, settle, and provide custody for CIBM instruments both for itself and on behalf of institutional investors, including foreign investors.

b.   Qualified Foreign Institutional Investor and Renminbi Qualified Foreign Institutional Investor

When investing in the PRC's capital market, including the exchange bond market, QFIIs and RQFIIs are required to appoint one designated QFII custodian and (up to) three RQFII custodians as well as three designated brokers for all their transactions. QFIIs may only appoint one custodian, while RQFIIs may appoint up to three custodian banks.

c.   Bond Connect

Nonresident investors that access the CIBM via Bond Connect are required to establish a trading relationship with at least one Onshore Participating Dealer, being the official term used for a trading participant in CFETS to execute the nonresident investors' trade orders. This requirement exists regardless of which order routing platform the investors use.

By definition of the Bond Connect concept, the Central Moneymarkets Unit (CMU) of the Hong Kong Monetary Authority, which is the central depository for debt instruments in Hong Kong, China, acts as the depository participant (custodian) on behalf of the nonresident investor.

9.   Foreign Ownership Limitations

In contrast to equities, there are no foreign ownership limitations when acquiring or holding debt financing instruments in the CIBM.

---

[44] See http://www.safe.gov.cn/en/2018/0612/1453.html.

10. Borrowing and Lending

Nonresident investors are not permitted to formally borrow or lend money through their Special CNY Account. This excludes treasury transactions such as the placement of funds from the account in return for the payment of interest.

At the same time, QOIIs, QFIIs, and RQFIIs are able to participate in bond lending transactions, while foreign central banks, international financial organizations, sovereign wealth funds, foreign RMB clearing banks, and participating banks are allowed to participate in bond repo transactions, despite bond lending representing a loan of assets and the nature of the repo being in pledged form (see also Chapter IV.G for more information on repo transactions in the CIBM and Chapter IV.H for information on bond lending practices in the CIBM).

O.   Regulations on Credit Rating Agencies

This section covers the regulations and requirements applicable to CRAs operating in the PRC. For the actual credit rating requirements in the China bond market and the application of such credit ratings in the issuance process of bonds, please refer to Chapter III.O.

In the CIBM, the credit rating business is examined and supervised by the PBOC. As such, it is mainly responsible for drafting relevant rules and regulations governing the credit rating system, and drawing up development strategies and policies. CSRC supervises credit ratings in the exchange bond market, while the NDRC oversees credit ratings for enterprise bonds. In the CIMB, CRAs will need to be admitted as members of NAFMII to provide services to market participants.

The PBOC is also responsible for the examination and publication of the rating results, including legal rating activities by the CRAs as well as any potential illegal activities, such as a breach of rating procedures, unfair competition, and inappropriate pricing based on awarded credit rating levels.

At the time of the compilation of this bond market guide, 11 accredited CRAs were active in the China bond market providing rating services based on local and international methodologies, models, and criteria (Table 2.14).

In addition, NAFMII established a company called China Bond Rating, which is a CRA funded by NAFMII on behalf of all its members (i.e., institutional investors in the CIBM) and focuses on investor-paid rating or the so-called unsolicited rating model.[45] In the case of an investor-paid rating, institutional investors should check the veracity of a credit rating awarded to an issuer and/or their issued bonds and notes. They may request that the issuer and/or their bonds and notes be rated again for comparison against either the original result or the investor's internal assessment.

On 16 July 2017, the PRC began to allow wholly foreign-owned financial services firms to provide credit rating services and begin the licensing process for credit investigation. In March 2018, NAFMII published the Rules for Credit Rating Agencies' Registration and Participation in Market-Based Evaluation in the Inter-Bank Bond Market.[46] The NAFMII CRA rules also specified the required documentation.[47] NAFMII

---

[45] Reference to the information on China Bond Rating Co., Ltd. (中债资信评估有限责任公司) is available at https://www.chinaratings.com.cn/AboutUs/Profile/Overview/.

[46] The rules are available on the NAFMII website in Chinese, at http://www.nafmii.org.cn/zlgz/201803/t20180327_68266.html.

[47] This information has been partly adopted from International Capital Market Association. 2018. *Development in China's Interbank Bond Markets*. Zurich.

is responsible for the licensing and admission of CRAs to the CIBM (see section I in this chapter for details).

Subsequently, in September 2018, the PBOC and CSRC jointly released Announcement No. 14, officially entitled Enhance Unified Management of Credit Rating and Facilitate Connectivity of the Bond Market, which stipulated the gradual unification of the CIBM and exchange bond market credit rating business qualifications.[48] It was aimed at strengthening the sharing of information on the supervision of CRAs, promoting improvement of the internal system of CRAs, unifying rating standards, and improving the quality of credit ratings.

Table 2.14: Credit Rating Agencies Active in the China Bond Market

Credit Rating Agency	CIBM	Exchange Market
China Chengxin Securities Rating (CCXR) 中诚信证券评估有限公司		O
China Chengxin International Credit Rating (CCXI) 中诚信国际信用评级有限责任公司	O	
United Credit Ratings 联合信用评级有限公司		O
China Lianhe Credit Rating 联合资信评估有限公司	O	
Dagong Global Credit Rating 大公国际资信评估有限公司	O	O
Shanghai Brilliance Credit Rating & Investors Service 上海新世纪资信评估投资服务有限公司	O	O
CSCI Pengyuan Credit Rating 中证鹏元资信评估股份有限公司	O	O
Golden Credit Rating 东方金诚国际信用评估有限公司	O	O
China Bond Rating 中债资信评估有限责任公司	O	
S&P Global (China) Ratings 标普信用评级(中国)有限公司	O	
Fitch (China) Bohua Credit Ratings Ltd 惠誉博华	O	

Note: All information as of 1 June 2020.
Source: National Association of Financial Market Institutional Investors.

In January 2019, for the first time, a CRA fully owned by a foreign entity, S&P Global (China) Ratings Co., Ltd., was accredited in the CIBM. In May 2020, Fitch (China) Bohua Credit Ratings Ltd., a wholly owned subsidiary of Fitch Ratings, was given approval to operate in the CIBM by the PBOC and a license issued by NAFMII to conduct bond rating activities. According to news reports, other global CRAs have submitted applications to the PBOC and are awaiting approval.[49] NAFMII also

---

[48] See http://www.pbc.gov.cn/english/130721/3628161/index.html.
[49] This section has been adapted from an article in the *Nikkei Asian Review* on 28 January 2019, as well as an article on the Reuters website at https://www.reuters.com/article/china-pboc-ratings/china-grants-fitch-ratings-approval-for-domestic-ratings-business-idUSB9N2CC01J.

announced the launch of a market-oriented registration and evaluation process for new CRAs in the CIBM in April 2020, with a window until 31 July 2020.[50]

P.   Regulations on Bond Pricing Agencies

This section explains the regulations and requirements applicable to securities pricing agencies operating in the PRC. Information on the pricing or, in this context, the valuation of bonds in the CIBM can be found in Chapter III.K.

At the time of the compilation of this bond market guide, there were no specific regulatory authorities or rules concerning bond valuation and pricing services in the PRC.

---

[50] See http://www.nafmii.org.cn//english/news_e/202004/t20200417_79943.html.

III

Inter-Bank Bond Market Characteristics

The China bond market consists of a number of market segments that are defined by separate regulatory frameworks, participants, and market practices. This chapter details market characteristics that can be observed in the CIBM.

A. Definition of Securities and Debt Financing Instruments

The legal and regulatory framework does not contain a universal definition of securities. Instead, individual concepts of securities or corresponding instruments may differ by competent authority. A number of relevant instances of securities or such instruments are shown in this section for practical reference.

1. Definitions in the Company Law and Relevance of Securities Law

The definition and prescriptions for the issuance of corporate bonds are contained in the Company Law. Companies may decide to issue corporate bonds by following the protocol specified in the law, subject to the approval of the management of the company.

In the Company Law, "corporate bonds" are defined as valuable securities issued by a company according to legally prescribed procedures and pursuant to company covenants to repay the principal and interest within a certain period of time. However, the term "corporate bonds" is typically associated with bonds issued and traded in the exchange bond market (see also section 3). Instead, the term "enterprise bonds" is used in the CIBM. At the same time, enterprise bonds (企业债) refer to bonds that are issued by a nonfinancial company, with a maturity of more than 1 year; the issuers of enterprise bonds are mainly state-owned companies. The bonds are regulated and approved by the NDRC.

Originally, enterprise bonds (企业债) referred to the bonds issued by central government agencies, SOEs, and state-owned holding companies affiliated with the NDRC. With the progress of privatization, the delineation between corporate bonds and enterprise bonds has become less strict.

The Securities Law does not apply to the CIBM, only to the exchange bond market. In the case of the issuance of ABS (资产支持证券) in the CIBM, even though the term "securities" is used in their description, they are recognized as a type of debt financing instrument in the CIBM.

As the market regulatory authority, the PBOC issues the applicable instrument definitions (see also next section).

2.   Debt Financing Instruments in People's Bank of China Regulations

In their decrees, measures, and regulations, the PBOC and NAFMII use the term "debt financing instrument," which refers to any marketable debt instrument issued in the CIBM and includes commercial paper, SCP, MTN, collective bonds issued by regional enterprises, SME collective notes, PPN, ABN issued by nonfinancial enterprises, project revenue notes, standardized notes, and green debt financing instruments.

The term securities is not used in the context of the CIBM except in the case of ABS. The issuers are typically referred to as enterprises.

The PBOC laid the foundation for many of these instrument types with the promulgation of PBOC Decree No. 1 in 2008, which made effective the Rules for the Registration and Issuance of Debt Financing Instruments of Non-Financial Enterprises.

Pursuant to the Measures for the Administration of the Issuance of Financial Bonds in the National Inter-Bank Bond Market, "financial bond" refers to negotiable financing instruments issued in the CIBM by a financial institution legally established in the territory of the PRC for the purpose of guaranteeing the payment of the principal plus interest as agreed to between the parties concerned, including CNY-denominated financial bonds, as well as financial bonds denominated in foreign currency.

The PBOC Guidelines on the Issuance of Non-Financial Enterprises Medium-Term Notes in the Inter-Bank Bond Market define "medium-term notes" as any debt financing instruments issued in phases in the CIBM.

3.   Terms Used in China Central Depository & Clearing Co., Ltd. Rules

The Table of Terms in the CCDC Account Business Guidelines identifies CCDC as the general registration and depository organization for Treasury bonds authorized by the MOF and the general registration and depository organization for enterprise bonds designated by the NDRC.[51] While the guidelines do not include a separate definition of bonds for the CIBM, they do refer to bond accounts.

According to the CCDC glossary in English, corporate bonds (公司债) refer to bonds that are issued by a nonfinancial company and have a maturity of more than 1 year. The issuers of corporate bonds are mainly listed companies. The bonds are regulated and approved by CSRC and typically listed on the exchange bond market.

4.   References in Shanghai Clearing House Co., Ltd. Rules and Documentation

In the English translation of its Rules on Registration, Custody, Clearing and Settlement of Bonds, provided for reference only on its website, SHCH makes reference to bonds and nonfinancial corporate debt financing instruments, but it does not include a separate or distinct definition of either term.[52] Instead, reference is made to the underlying measures and rules for the CIBM issued by the PBOC. Investor accounts in SHCH are also referred to as bond accounts.

In its service agreements, "financial products" is used as a summary term for the instruments registered, cleared, settled, and safekept at SHCH.

---

[51] See http://www.chinabond.com.cn/cb/eng/zqsc/ywgz/zyjsgs/sczrjkxh/20160122/147364086.shtml.
[52] See http://english.shclearing.com/csd/rules/201705/t20170510_258331.html?xyz=0.2628135304999244.

B.   Types of Bonds and Notes

Bonds and notes issued in the China bond market include many different instruments issued by a variety of issuers and catering to a number of different investor types. Not all debt instruments may be found in every market segment. In the CIBM, the main bond classes include government bonds, financial bonds, and enterprise bonds.

1.   Government Bonds

Government bonds consist of debt securities issued by the central government and those issued by local governments. Issuers include the MOF, local governments, and public organizations of the central or local governments (Table 3.1). If issued and traded in the CIBM, government and government-like bonds are also subsumed under the general term debt financing instruments.

Table 3.1: Government and Related Bonds Deposited by Market Segment
(CNY billion)

Debt Instrument	CIBM	Commercial Banks' Counter Market	Exchange Bond Market	Other
Government bonds 政府债券	35,351.84	822.38	1,047.08	1.59
Central government bond (Treasury bonds) 记账式国债	14,697.00	20.96	586.71	1.44
(Electronic) Savings bonds 储蓄国债(电子式)	0.00	798.49	0.00	0.00
Local government bonds 地方政府债	20,654.84	2.93	460.37	0.15
Central bank bills	22.00	0.00	0.00	0.00
Government-backed (agency) bonds 政府支持机构债券	1,625.84	0.00	43.29	3.37
Policy bank financial bonds 政策性银行债	15,622.46	32.24	0.00	40.00
China Development Bank 国家开发银行	8,632.37	31.70	0.00	40.00
Export–Import Bank of China 中国进出口银行	2,735.03	0.08	0.00	0.00
Agricultural Development Bank of China 中国农业发展银行	4,255.05	0.46	0.00	0.00
Total	52,622.14	854.62	1,090.37	44.97

CIBM = China Inter-Bank Bond Market, CNY = Chinese renminbi.
Note: Data as of December 2019.
Source: ASEAN+3 Bond Market Forum Sub-Forum 1 team adapted from ChinaBond. 2019. *December Monthly Bulletin of Statistics: 3-04 Bond Depository Balance* (登录中国债券信息网:统计月报: 3-04 各市场债券托管量).

a.   Treasury Bonds

Treasury bonds are national debt instruments issued in Chinese renminbi by the MOF on behalf of the central government. There are two types of Treasury bonds: book-entry Treasury bonds and savings bonds.

Book-entry Treasury bonds are mainly available to institutional investors in two varieties: coupon bonds and discount bonds; the discount bonds are traded only in the CIBM. Coupon bond tenors include 1, 2, 3, 5, 7, 10, 20, 30, and 50 years. There were no 20-year bonds outstanding at the time of the compilation of this bond market guide. The times to maturity for discount bonds are 91, 182, and 273 days (see also section C).

Book-entry Treasury bonds are issued by tender through the CCDC platform for new issues and are listed or registered and traded in both the CIBM and the exchange market, with the CCDC generally acting as depository. Central government bond positions are fungible between the two markets.

b.   (Electronic) Savings Bonds

In 2006, electronic savings bonds were launched in the China bond market, adding a new instrument for the government to cover its budget deficit and fund public projects. The government had set up a computer system linking large commercial banks to allow individuals to purchase, manage, and redeem the savings bonds electronically. In turn, these banks enable individual investors to hold accounts to purchase electronic savings bonds. While this instrument is not a product for the CIBM as such, it does get included in the statistics on government bonds.

Savings bonds are (i) issued by the MOF, (ii) sold exclusively to individuals in the commercial banks' counter market at fixed coupons that are exempt from tax on interest, and (iii) not tradable in either the CIBM or the exchange market.

c.   Local Government Bonds

Local government bonds are issued by local governments that generate fiscal revenue. Local government financing platforms (地方政府融资平台) established to fund various projects, such as municipal construction and public utilities, are no longer able to issue bonds. The funds raised by local governments are generally used for transportation, communications, housing, education, hospitals, sewage systems, and other local public infrastructure. Local government bonds are classified into general bonds and project bonds.

Local government bonds are issued by tender or as a target issue through the CCDC platform for new issues and traded in both the CIBM and exchange market, with the bonds generally deposited with CCDC. Local government bond positions are fungible between the two markets.

The maturity of general local government bonds may be 1, 3, 5, 7, 10, or 20 years, and the prevailing maturities for project bonds are 3, 5, 7, and 10 years. Other maturities, such as 1–2 years or longer than 10 years, are possible depending on the nature of the project. The most recent long-term local government bonds have a 20-year maturity.

According to the MOF, as of the end of September 2018, the outstanding amount of local government bonds was CNY18.26 trillion, among which the general bonds balance amounted to CNY10.88 trillion and the special bonds balance amounted to CNY7.38 trillion. The aggregate amount was smaller than the overall limit of CNY21.0 trillion set by the MOF and approved by the National People's Congress.[53]

At the end of September 2018, local government bonds had an average remaining tenor of 4.6 years, with an average of 4.5 years for general bonds

---

[53] See http://yss.mof.gov.cn/zhuantilanmu/dfzgl/sjtj/201810/t20181017_3048969.html.

and 4.7 years for special bonds. The average interest rate stood at 3.50%, with an average of 3.49% for general bonds and 3.51% for special bonds.

In the past, local government bonds were issued by tender or as a target issue. However, local government bonds issued with a target issuance method cannot be listed on the exchanges. To further improve the issuance method of local government bonds and improve the efficiency of local government bond issuance, the MOF decided to implement a system of public underwriting for local government bonds. Consequently, the MOF formulated the Regulations on the Public Offering and Issuance of Local Government Bonds (Caiwan No. 68) (地方政府债券公开承销发行业务规程) and announced the new procedure on 30 July 2018 (see also section E.1 in this chapter for more details).[54]

2.   Government-Backed (Agency) Bonds

a.   Railway Bonds

China Railway Corporation (formerly part of the Ministry of Railways) issues railway bonds upon approval by the NDRC. Railway bonds are issued through the CCDC or SHCH platform for new issues, deposited with CCDC or SHCH, and traded in the CIBM.

b.   Central Huijin Bonds

Central Huijin Investment Ltd. is a domestic investment subsidiary of the PRC's sovereign wealth fund, the China Investment Corporation. The bonds are issued upon approval by the NDRC. They are issued through the CCDC or SHCH platform for new issues, deposited with CCDC or SHCH, and traded in the CIBM.

3.   Financial Bonds

Financial bonds are bonds issued by regulated financial institutions such as policy banks, commercial banks, and non-bank financial institutions.

The Law of the People's Bank of China (中華人民共和國中國人民銀行法), the Provisions Governing the Issuance of Financial Bonds in the National Inter-Bank Bond Market and its Related Measures (全国银行间债券市场金融债券 发行管理操作规程), and the Measures for the Administration of the Issuance of Financial Bonds in the National Inter-Bank Bond Market (全国银行间债券市场金融债券发行管理办法) define "financial bonds" as negotiable financing instruments issued in the CIBM by a financial institution legally established in the territory of the PRC for the purpose of guaranteeing the payment of the principal plus interest as agreed to between the parties concerned.

Financial institutions include policy banks, commercial banks, finance companies of enterprise groups, non-bank financial institutions, and other institutions.

The PBOC approves and supervises the issuance of financial bonds; without approval from the PBOC, no financial institution may issue any bond.

---

[54] See http://www.mof.gov.cn/zhengwuxinxi/caijingshidian/zgcjb/201808/t20180822_2995070.html and http://gks.mof.gov.cn/guozaiguanli/difangzhengfuzhaiquan/201808/t20180815_2988486.html.

a.   Policy Bank Financial Bonds

PFBs are issued by the policy banks and at one time comprised the largest outstanding amount among onshore bond types with high liquidity. From 2014 to 2017, the PFB market was slightly larger than the government bond market. However, since July 2018, the value of outstanding PFBs has been less than that of government bonds and local government bonds combined.

There are three policy banks in the PRC; each was established in 1994:

i.   **China Development Bank.** The China Development Bank bond issuance represents the largest portion among the three types of PFBs; it is the world's biggest development finance institution.

ii.   **Agricultural Development Bank of China.** The Agricultural Development Bank of China provides policy financial support to the agriculture sector.

iii.   **Export–Import Bank of China.** Export–Import Bank of China supports the PRC's foreign trade and investment.

The three policy banks are fully owned by the central government and, hence, are considered equal to sovereign (Treasury) bonds. They are rated accordingly by all international rating agencies.

Policy banks have to submit to the PBOC an application of issuing bonds on an annual basis. The application should include the proposed volume of issuance, time frame, method of issuance, and other relevant details. PFBs are issued through the CCDC or SHCH platform for new issues, generally deposited with CCDC or SHCH, and traded in the CIBM.

In statistical and other official publications, PFBs are often subsumed into the overall category of financial bonds, which are defined as bonds issued by regulated financial institutions (e.g., policy banks, commercial banks, insurance institutions, and non-bank financial institutions). However, financial bonds other than those issued by policy banks are only issued and traded in the CIBM.

Even PFBs are mainly traded in the CIBM. In the exchange bond market, the number of listed and traded PFBs is relatively small. In contrast to central and local government bonds, PFBs listed and traded in the exchange bond market cannot be traded in the CIBM and vice versa, thus separating the two platforms. As a consequence, PFB positions are not fungible between the CIBM and the exchange bond market.

b.   Commercial Bank Bonds

Commercial bank bonds are issued by commercial banks that are established in the domestic market and include straight bonds (general financial bonds); subordinate bonds; Tier-2 capital instruments including hybrid capital bonds; SME loan bonds; as well as special financial bonds for agriculture, rural areas, and farm-related sectors. Most recently, perpetual bonds were added as another newly developed commercial bank bond type. In January 2019, the Bank of China became the first domestic bank to issue a perpetual bond, raising CNY40 billion.

Commercial bank bonds are issued through the CCDC platform for new issues, generally deposited with CCDC, and traded in the CIBM.

c.   Non-Bank Financial Bonds

Issuers of these bonds are non-bank financial institutions established in the domestic market and include insurance companies, finance or leasing companies, and auto-finance companies. Insurance companies may issue senior and subordinated bonds. Among these issuers, the issuance of bonds by insurance companies is subject to approval from the CBIRC. Non-bank financial bonds are issued through the CCDC platform for new issues, generally deposited with CCDC, and traded in the CIBM.

Non-bank financial bonds issuers also include asset management firms and securities companies. For these two types of issuers, the bonds are issued through the SHCH platform for new issues, deposited with SHCH, and traded in the CIBM.

4.   Enterprise Bonds

Enterprise bonds, a categorization used for debt instruments not issued by financial institutions, are issued by a number of enterprises or agencies funded or owned by the government. Although similar in nature, the term enterprise bond represents a distinct asset class from corporate bonds, which are issued and traded only in the exchange bond market. Enterprise bonds also include collective bonds issued by local enterprises, project revenue bonds, and extendable bonds. The issuer of nonfinancial enterprise debt instruments in the CIBM has to register the issuance with NAFMII.

There are two main types of nonfinancial corporate bonds in the PRC: enterprise bonds and listed company bonds (also known as corporate bonds). Enterprise bonds are mainly issued by nonlisted SOEs or government-backed entities. NDRC is responsible for supervising the issuance of enterprise bonds, including collective bonds. For historical reasons, enterprise bonds have always been supervised by the NDRC as the government agency overseeing SOE reform.

SOEs started issuing enterprise bonds in the early 1980s as an alternative to bank loans. After the launch of the CIBM in 1997, enterprise bond issuance began. In 2005, the PRC's exchange bond market started, which presented issuing entities with an opportunity to sell their bonds in either market. Today, almost all enterprise bonds are fungible between the CIBM and the exchange bond market.[55] As a result, many enterprise bonds became both exchange-listed and NAFMII-registered—the market term for such practice is "dual-listed."[56] At the end of 2017, about one-third of enterprise bonds were originally issued and traded in the exchange bond market, with two-thirds originally registered in the CIBM.[57]

a.   Enterprise Bonds

Enterprise bonds are the bonds issued by enterprises that are solely funded by or owned by the central government or a local government and/or an agency, or by listed or nonlisted companies controlled by the state. The issuance of enterprise bonds is subject to NDRC approval or registration.

---

[55] Per Standard Chartered Bank, government bonds, local government bonds, and enterprise bonds—but not PFBs and corporate bonds—are fungible between the exchange market and the CIBM.
[56] W. Wang et al. 2015. *One Bond, Two Prices: The Demand Effect of Yield-Chasing Retail Investors*. Booth School of Business Working Paper. Chicago; and H. Chen et al. 2018. *Pledgeability and Asset Prices: Evidence from the Chinese Corporate Bond Markets*. Booth School of Business Working Paper. Chicago.
[57] M. Amstad and Z. He. 2018. Chinese Bond Market and Interbank Market. In M. Amstad, S. Guofeng, and W. Xiong, eds. *The Handbook on China's Financial System*.

There are four types of enterprise bonds: central enterprise bonds, local enterprise bonds, local enterprise collective bonds, and project revenue bonds. Enterprise bonds are uniformly issued into both the CIBM and exchange markets through the CCDC platform for new issues, generally deposited with CCDC, and traded in the CIBM and exchange bond market. However, in 2018 and 2019, there was no record of issuances of local enterprise collective bonds in the PRC.

The issuance of enterprise bonds by a finance company of an enterprise group is also subject to the eligibility criteria set by, and requires the approval of the PBOC.

b.   Local Enterprise Bonds

One important component of enterprise bonds are local enterprise bonds, also referred to as municipal corporate bonds (城投债), which represented 87.8% of enterprise bonds outstanding at the end of 2019 (Table 3.2). Municipal corporate bonds are bonds issued by local-government-related financing vehicles, which are SOEs to support local infrastructure investment, both at the provincial and city levels. Notably, municipal corporate bonds' credit status is the same as other regular corporate bonds.

**Table 3.2: Enterprise Bonds Depository Balance by Market Type
at the End of 2019**
(CNY billion)

Type of Enterprise Bond		CIBM	Exchange Bond Market	Other	Total	Share
Central enterprise bond (中央企业债券)		269.5	91.0	2.7	363.2	12.2%
Local enterprise bond (地方企业债券)	Common bond (普通企业债)	1,818.7	687.6	0.2	2,506.5	84.2%
	Collective bond (集合企业债)	9.1	1.4	0.0	10.6	0.4%
	Project revenue bond (项目收益债)	93.8	4.1	0.0	97.9	3.3%
	Subtotal	1,921.7	693.1	0.2	2,615.0	87.8%
Total outstanding (企业债券托管量)		**2,191.1**	**784.1**	**2.9**	**2,978.2**	**100.0%**

CIBM = China Inter-Bank Bond Market, CNY = Chinese renminbi.
Source: China Central Depository & Clearing Co., Ltd. 2019. *December Monthly Bulletin of Statistic: 3-04 Bond Depository Balance (by market type)*.

When issuing local enterprise bonds, local enterprises must submit the enterprise bond declaration materials directly to the provincial development and reform departments. The provincial development and reform departments will transfer those materials to NDRC within 5 working days of receipt. The review and approval procedure will be completed within 30 working days (or within 60 working days in complicated circumstances) from the date the bond declaration materials are received by NDRC.[58] For further reading, an Enterprise Bond Issuance Approval Guide (企业债券发行核准办事指南) is available in Chinese.[59]

---

[58] Information provided by Zhong Lun Law Firm.
[59] See http://services.ndrc.gov.cn:8080/ecdomain/portal/portlets/bjweb/newpage/guide/guidService.jsp?idseq=7a75a98d77ce45a79f946fda60db2811.

Local enterprise bonds are fungible between the CIBM and the exchange bond market.

c.   Project Revenue Bonds

Project revenue bonds are enterprise bonds that use the proceeds to finance and implement specified projects and the repayment of principal and interest comes mostly or entirely from the operational earnings after the completion of the project. The project developer or its actual controller is the issuer. Project revenue bonds are fungible between the CIBM and the exchange bond market.

d.   SME Collective Notes

Responding to market demand, NAFMII launched the SME collective notes program in November 2009 to provide a long-term funding channel for SMEs. SME collective notes (区域集优中小企业集合票据) are debt financing instruments issued by (between two and ten) licensed enterprises in the CIBM under one product design, a common title, one credit enhancement option, and one issuance and registration option, where principal and interest are repaid within an agreed period. SME collective notes are not fungible between the CIBM and the exchange bond market. SME collective notes are settled at SHCH.

Since the issuers are a group of SMEs, the SME collective notes are regarded as a type of enterprise-issued debt financing instrument. The arrangement of the issuance by a group of SMEs is organized by the initiator. Each issuing enterprise has its own liabilities corresponding to their participation in the respective issuance amount, but all SMEs use the common bond name, collect proceeds from the issuance, and make payments collectively. The typical maturity for SME collective notes is 3–5 years.

Following the first default on SME collective notes in 2014, their issuances have been inactive since 2015 (Table 3.3).

Table 3.3: SME Collective Notes Issuance and Outstanding Deposits at SHCH
(CNY billion)

SME Collective Notes	2013	2014	2015	2016	2017	2018	2019
Issuance Amount	6.1	0.4	0.4	0.0	0.0	0.0	0.0
Amount Outstanding	9.9	8.8	5.6	0.6	0.4	0.0	0.0
Change in Deposited Amount at SHCH	–	(1.1)	(3.2)	(5.1)	(0.2)	(0.4)	0.0

– = data not available, () = negative, CNY = Chinese renminbi, SHCH = Shanghai Clearing House, SME = small and medium-sized enterprise.
Source: SHCH Monthly Reports, 2014–2019 (web) (统计月报 表二 上海清算所固定收益产品发行量 ／ 表四上海清算所固定收益产品托管量).

e.   Extendable Bonds

Extendable bonds are issued in the CIBM by nonfinancial enterprises. They do not have a fixed maturity and the issuer has the option to extend the maturity or redeem the bonds. Because the issuer is a nonfinancial enterprise, extendable bonds are regarded as a type of enterprise bond.

f.   Medium-Term Notes

In the China bond market, the term MTN does not necessarily represent a particular instrument type issued under a program but is used as a general description for publicly offered debt financing instruments issued by nonfinancial enterprises and denominated in Chinese renminbi and with a maturity of more than 1 year; tenors are usually 3–5 years and can be up to 10 years. MTNs are debt financing instruments that can be issued in tranches following a successful registration with NAFMII.

The PBOC introduced the MTN concept in the CIBM in April 2008, offering less stringent issuance conditions and processes for the financing activities of domestic enterprises and to facilitate domestic bond market development.

An MTN is tradable and transferable among institutional investors in the CIBM. MTN are not fungible between the CIBM and the exchange bond market.

5.   Panda Bonds

A Panda bond is not a specific instrument but represents the official term used to denote a CNY-denominated bond issued by a nonresident entity in the PRC. Panda bonds can be issued in both the CIBM and the exchange bond market. Panda bonds can also be issued through a public offering or as a private placement. In features and tenor, Panda bonds follow the practices for corporate bonds in the China bond market.

The PBOC has established the Panda bond market in the CIBM as a dedicated issuing market among prime credit issuers. Its regulations require the issuer to have a track record of offering debt instruments in other markets and a proven ability to repay such debt.

In 2010, the PBOC, the MOF, NDRC, and CSRC jointly issued amendments to the so-called Panda bond regulations, which were known officially as the Interim Measures for Administration of Issuing Renminbi Bonds by International Development Institutions (No. 10). These regulations expanded the scope of qualified issuers and the use of Chinese renminbi proceeds, resulting in a significant liberalization of CNY-denominated remittances out of the PRC resulting from Panda bond issuance.

In September 2018, to further promote the opening of the bond market and regulate issuances from overseas institutions, with the approval of the State Council, the PBOC and MOF jointly issued the Interim Measures for the Administration on Bonds Issued by Overseas Issuers on the National Inter-Bank Bond Market (全国银行间债券市场境外机构债券发行管理暂行办法) (No.16), which are known as the 2018 Interim Measures; at the same time, the 2010 measures mentioned above were formally repealed.

The 2018 Interim Measures further clarified the qualifications and filing procedures for nonresident institutions to issue Panda bonds and laid out provisions on information disclosure, issuance filing, custody, and settlement, as well as on CNY-denominated account opening, fund exchange, and investor protection.

The release of the 2018 Interim Measures improved the institutional arrangements for nonresident institutions to issue Panda bonds in the CIBM, aligned domestic institutional rules with international standards, and helped further the internationalization of the China bond market. The 2018 Interim Measures also clarified that issuers from Hong Kong, China; Macau, China; and Taipei,China are considered overseas institutions for the purpose of Panda bond issuance.

NAFMII subsequently issued the Guidelines on Debt Financing Instruments of Overseas Non-Financial Enterprises (for Trial Implementation) in January 2019 to further prescribe the registration process and other details including information disclosure for such issuances. In these guidelines, issuance requirements for Panda bonds privately placed to DIIs are less stringent in comparison to public offerings in the PRC with regard to the selection of language and the contents of disclosure information; for example, the issuer and DIIs can agree on specific criteria, such as the usage of English in documentation, concise disclosure without using a bond prospectus, and the use of accounting standards applied in the issuer's jurisdiction.

The 2019 NAFMII Guidelines state that "in an offering of debt financing instruments by an overseas nonfinancial enterprise, the rules or requirements of the relevant regulatory authorities in the PRC shall apply to the accounting standards and audit standards under which the financial statements of such issuer are prepared." This may be interpreted as saying that financial accounting and reporting standards can be accepted by regulators as evidence in the market of the domicile of the nonresident issuer. The 2018 Interim Measures clarify that the accounting standard will need to have been recognized by the MOF or the Panda bond issuer will need to formally disclose any significant differences between the accounting standard used and that of the PRC.

An overseas parent company providing an unconditional and irrevocable joint liability guarantee to its wholly-owned financing vehicle issuing Panda bonds in the PRC shall comply with the information disclosure requirements stipulated by NAFMII.

According to the PBOC, between January 2005 and the end of November 2019, foreign institutions issued 137 Panda bonds with an aggregate value of CNY249 billion.

6.   Asset-Backed Securities and Asset-Backed Notes

ABS are bonds backed by a financial asset pool with a number of assets bundled together by the issuer. Cash flows generated by the assets in the pool are to be used for the payment of principal and interest of the issued ABS.[60]

Currently, three types of asset securitization exist in the PRC: enterprise ABS, credit ABS, and ABN. Enterprise ABS are supervised by CSRC, issued in the exchange bond market, and registered at and deposited with CSDC. The asset securitization types issued in the CIBM are explained below.

ABN (非金融企业资产支持票据) are one type of nonfinancial enterprise debt financing instrument supervised by NAFMII, while ABS are not.

a.   Credit Asset-Backed Securities

According to the Administrative Measures for the Pilot Management of Credit Asset Securitization (信贷资产证券化试点管理办法) issued by the PBOC and (then) CBRC on 20 April 2005, and the Administrative Measures for the Pilot Management of Credit Asset Securitization of Financial Institutions (金融机构信贷资产证券化试点监督管理办法) issued on 7 November 2005, ABS refer to income securities in which a banking financial institution acts as the initiator, entrusting credit assets to a trustee, following which the ABS are issued by the trustee, who will also pay income to the investors with cash generated from the underlying assets.

---

[60] This section has been adapted in part from CCDC. 2016. *Overview of China's Bond Market.* Beijing.

Credit ABS (信贷资产支持证券) are mainly supervised by the CBIRC and the PBOC, and mainly traded on the asset-backed commercial paper platform in the CIBM; trust companies play a role as trustee institutions in the course of the securitization of credit assets.

Credit ABS are issued by a special purpose trust and trustee institution (trust company), representing the shares of beneficial rights under a special purpose trust. Subject to the trust property, the trustee institution shall pay income from the ABS to the investor. Credit ABS are mainly issued and traded in the CIBM, but can also be issued and traded across markets. The securities are registered at and deposited with CCDC.

b.   Asset-Backed Notes

ABN are issued under the Guidelines on Asset-Backed Notes of Non-Financial Enterprises (非金融企业资产支持票据指引), which were issued by NAFMII in 2012 and revised in 2017. The guidelines were issued to implement the government's policy intention to actively and steadily reduce corporate leverage, taking measures to revitalize existing assets and standardize and promote the implementation of asset securitization by enterprises.

An ABN is considered a debt financing instrument in the CIBM. The note is supported by the predictable cash flow generated by a specific asset of a corporate issuer and it includes an agreement to repay the principal and interest within a certain period. ABN are usually sold by large enterprises, non-banking financial institutions, or multiple SMEs to the trustees. The trustees will use these assets to support the issuance of commercial notes with tenors of 3–7 years to CIBM investors.

In the context of ABN, nonfinancial enterprises are referred to as "initiating institutions" or "sponsors" that use structured methods to issue a financing tool through an issuing vehicle to achieve financing. The cash flows generated by the underlying assets are used as income support. The issuing vehicle may be a special purpose trust, a special purpose company, another special purpose vehicle approved by NAFMII, or it may be an initiator itself. The ABN are registered at and deposited with SHCH.

With the publication of the revised Rules and Procedures for the Registration of Debt Financing Instruments of Non-Financial Enterprises for Public Offering in April 2020 (effective 1 July 2020), the public offering and issuance under a shelf-registration was also extended to ABN.

C.   Money Market Instruments

Money market instruments are short-term debt instruments, typically issued by the government and the PBOC. They may also be issued by the private sector in the form of commercial paper or SCP, which are instruments specific to the CIBM. Money market instruments generally have maturities of 1 year or less; in the United States (US), commercial paper typically has a tenor of no more than 270 days and in international markets, no more than 365 days; in the China bond market, commercial paper may be issued with a maturity of up to 1 year.

1.   **Instruments Issued by the Government**

a.   Discount Central Government Bonds

Book-entry discount central government bonds are issued by tender through the CCDC Bond Issuance System with maturities of 91 days, 183 days, and 273 days.[61] They are traded in both the CIBM and the exchange market, and are generally deposited with CCDC.

2.   **Central Bank Bills Issued by the People's Bank of China**

Central bank bills are short-term collateralized debt obligations issued by the PBOC to commercial banks acting as primary dealers.

Central bank bills represent a monetary policy tool other than, for example, reverse repo (see also section 6 in this chapter) for the PBOC in its open market operation to adjust the monetary base, manage the money supply, or reduce commercial banks' loanable excess funds and reserves. The PBOC conducts its open market operation via the CIBM. Consequently, central bank bills are the most actively traded instrument in the CIBM.

The term to maturity for central bank bills is usually less than 1 year but may sometimes be extended to up to 3 years. Central bank bills are issued through the PBOC's open market operation system and deposited with CCDC for trading in the CIBM.

3.   **Instruments issued by the Corporate Sector**

Corporate money market instruments in the China bond market are typically either commercial paper or repo agreements (see next section). Two types of commercial paper are typically issued in the CIBM: one with a tenor of 1 day to 1 year, with most tenors between 271 days and 365 days; and the second is the so-called super-short-term commercial paper, or SCP, with a tenor from 1 day to 270 days. In effect, SCP represents a shorter product within the commercial paper category.

a.   Commercial Paper (Short-Term Financing Bill)

Article 20 of the Administrative Measures for Debt Financing Instruments of Non-Financial Enterprises in the Inter-Bank Bond Market, promulgated by the PBOC in April 2008, stipulates that these measures also apply to short-term financing bills. Subsequently, NAFMII published its Guidelines on the Issuance of Commercial Paper of Non-Financial Enterprises in the Inter-Bank Bond Market. With these regulations, the PBOC and NAFMII effectively introduced the concept of a short-term financing bill to the CIBM.[62]

A short-term financing bill (official name) is a type of commercial paper and is defined as a note issued by domestic corporations that promise the payment of principal and interest within the stipulated period, which cannot exceed 1 year. Short-term financing bills are subject to registration with NAFMII and the supervision of the PBOC. They are presently deposited with SHCH and traded in the CIBM. When first issued, commercial paper was deposited with CCDC.

---

[61] In relation to the CCDC Bond Issuance System as well as other issuance systems, please refer to section E in this chapter.

[62] PBOC. 2008. Administrative Measures for Debt Financing Instruments of Non-Financial Enterprises in the Inter-Bank Bond Market (银行间债券市场非金融企业债务融资工具管理办法) (effective from 15 April 2008); PBOC Decree No. 1; NAFMII. 2008. Guidelines on the Issuance of Commercial Paper of Non-Financial Enterprises in the Inter-Bank Bond Market (银行间债券市场非金融企业短期融资券业务指引) (effective from 16 April 2008).

The term commercial paper refers to any debt financing instrument maturing within 1 year issued in the CIBM by nonfinancial enterprises. According to Article 2 of the NAFMII Rules for the Registration and Issuance of Debt Financing Instruments of Non-Financial Enterprises in the Inter-bank Market (非金融企业债务融资工具注册发行规则), last revised on 6 November 2015, "debt financing instrument" means any marketable securities issued in the CIBM by an incorporated nonfinancial enterprise. Please note that these instruments do not represent securities as defined under the Securities Law (see also section A.1).

Pursuant to Article 4 of the 2008 NAFMII Guidelines on the Issuance of Commercial Paper of Non-Financial Enterprises in the Inter-Bank Bond Market, the total outstanding amount of commercial paper issued must be less than 40% of the issuer's net assets. Article 5 of the guidelines states that proceeds from the issuance of commercial paper should be used for the issuer's production or operating activities that are in compliance with applicable national laws, regulations, and policies.

The specific use of proceeds must be disclosed clearly in its offering document (prospectus). Any change made to the use of proceeds before maturity is subject to prior disclosure. Such information disclosure to the CIBM needs to be made in accordance with the 2017 NAFMII Rules for Information Disclosure on Debt Financing Instruments of Non-Financial Enterprises in the Inter-Bank Bond Market (for more information on continuous disclosure in the CIBM, please see Chapter II.G).

According to Article 10 of the 2008 NAFMII guidelines, any commercial paper may be traded and transferred among institutional investors participating in the CIBM, starting from the business day immediately following the commercial paper's day of book-entry at an accredited securities depository.

b.   Super Short-Term Commercial Paper

On 21 December 2010, NAFMII published its Rules and Procedures for Super Short-Term Commercial Paper Business of Non-Financial Enterprises in the Inter-Bank Bond Market (Trial).[63]

The official designation "super short-term commercial paper" refers to any debt financing instrument maturing within 270 days issued in the CIBM. The issuer must be a nonfinancial enterprise that has legal person status and a high credit rating in the CIBM. SCP are traded on CFETS and its issuance documents are disclosed through the Chinamoney (CFETS) Network. When issuing SCP, an enterprise shall announce the issuance documents (prospectus) at least 1 working day before the issue date.

SHCH provides the services of registration, depository, and settlement for SCP. The use of proceeds from SCP is limited to working capital, similar to the case of commercial paper, and shall not be used for long-term investment.

4.   Negotiable Certificates of Deposit

An NCD (同业存单) is a book-entry time deposit certificate issued by deposit-taking financial institutions (banks) in the CIBM. Issuers of NCD are mainly small and medium-sized banks such as urban commercial banks whose investment entities are

---

[63] NAFMII. 2010. Rules and Procedures for Super Short-Term Commercial Paper Business of Non-Financial Enterprises in the Inter-Bank Bond Market (Trial) (银行间债券市场非金融企业超短期融资券业务规程(试行) No. 22.

national interbank lending market members (全国银行间同业拆借市场成员). The main investors in NCD issued in the CIBM are fund management companies and fund products, as well as large commercial banks.

Unlike in many developed financial markets, where the term NCD refers to a bank product outside the bond or money market, NCD issued in the PRC are considered a debt instrument tradable in the CIBM. In the PRC, NCD are not contained in a bank's general deposits and are not subject to any reserve requirements. Due to the typical tenor of an NCD, it is considered a money market instrument. At the same time, due to its integral role in financing and trading in the CIBM, NCD are often subsumed in bond trading and other debt financing instrument statistics.

In August 2013, the PBOC decided to allow the issuance of NCD in the CIBM to promote interest rate liberalization and offer relevant policies as a prelude to the market-oriented reform of deposit interest rates.[64] Hence, NCD function as substitutes for interbank deposits, improving the interest rate curves of the Shanghai Interbank Offered Rate (SHIBOR) quotes in the interbank lending market. Since 2014, the NCD market has undergone significant development: NCD are also used in repo transactions since NCD liquidity is high; as a result, the holding balance of NCD constituted about 47.2% of all assets under deposit at SHCH at the end of October 2019.[65]

NCD are a standardized financial product and they may be issued with a fixed interest rate or floating interest rate. Following PBOC regulations in 2017, the term of the fixed interest NCD may not be more than 1 year and is typically set at tenors of 1 month, 3 months, 6 months, 9 months, or 1 year. The interest rate is referenced to the SHIBOR for the same period. A floating rate NCD carries an interest rate commensurate with the SHIBOR. About 5% of the NCD issuance volume are floating rate NCD. A deposit-taking financial institution may, within its issuance limit amount for the current year, determine the issue amount and duration for each NCD, but a single-issuing amount shall not be less than CNY50 million.

5.   Repurchase Agreements

A repo is a contract for the sale of bonds or notes with a commitment by the initial seller (repo-seller, effectively a money borrower) to buy the same bonds or notes back from the initial buyer (repo-buyer, effectively a money lender) at a pre-agreed price on a pre-agreed designated future date after a pre-agreed fixed period of time.

Repo transactions in the China bond market feature one of two styles: pledged repo or outright repo. The vast majority of bond repos in the PRC are pledged repo transactions, which amount to roughly 97% of total transaction volume, while outright repos amount to only about 3%. For more details on repo in the China bond market, please refer to Chapter IV.G.

6.   Reverse Repurchase Agreements

The PBOC uses reverse repo in its open market operation as one of the tools to carry out its monetary policy objectives. Reverse repo represents a transaction in which the PBOC provides cash liquidity to its constituents or the market at large by purchasing specific debt financing instruments held by those constituents through a bidding process.

---

[64] PBOC regulations referring to the scope of general deposits include PBOC Announcement No. 209 (2011), PBOC Announcement No. 387 (2014), PBOC Announcement No. 105 (2015), PBOC Announcement No. 184 (2015), and PBOC Announcement No. 233 (2015).
[65] Shanghai Clearing House. 2019. *October Monthly Report.* www.shclearing.com/sjtj/tjyb/.

Reverse repo transactions commonly have a tenor of 7 days, but may also be concluded for longer or shorter periods. At the end of the reverse repo tenor, the PBOC will sell back the same securities in return for cash.

Please also see Chapter IV.G for a comprehensive description of the inter-bank bond repo market.

D.   Segmentation of the Market

Table 3.4 provides an overview of the par value of debt financing instruments issued in the CIBM, detailed into the different categories and types of instruments reviewed in section B of this chapter.

Table 3.4: Debt Financing Instrument Issuance in the CIBM
(CNY billion)

Instrument	2014	2015	2016	2017	2018	2019
Deposited with China Central Depository & Clearing Co., Ltd.						
Government bonds	1,569.6	1,861.2	2,945.8	3,866.2	3,541.1	4,009.1
Local government bonds	386.1	3,590.1	6,042.8	4,358.1	4,165.2	4,362.4
Policy bank financial bonds	2,221.1	2,413.9	3,347.0	3,201.5	3,434.0	3,660.2
Government-backed (agency) bonds	193.0	168.5	140.0	246.0	253.0	165.0
Commercial bank bonds and notes	80.4	187.4	365.7	381.7	515.5	433.0
Tier 2 and 1 (2019) capital instruments	344.7	251.9	257.4	482.4	400.7	1,164.6
Financial bonds (non-bank financial institutions)	–	–	90.5	73.4	185.3	187.5
Commercial paper of securities companies	386.1	226.7	88.8	31.2	–	–
Enterprise bonds	673.3	1,169.9	592.6	373.1	241.2	360.9
Asset-backed securities and similar	97.5	245.8	359.1	597.2	931.8	963.5
CCDC Subtotal	5,951.8	10,115.5	14,229.7	13,610.8	13,667.8	15,306.1

continued on next page

Table 3.4 *continued*

Instrument	2014	2015	2016	2017	2018	2019
Deposited with Shanghai Clearing House Co., Ltd.						
Commercial paper (except for SCP)	1,476.8	1,299.9	726.2	434.0	620.8	892.7
SCP	1,099.6	2,294.4	2,719.5	1,941.2	2,647.1	3,136.4
Medium-term notes	936.8	1,241.7	1,099.7	1,028.2	1,678.1	1,835.2
Private placement notes	1,024.0	877.9	602.9	494.0	544.4	616.5
Financial bonds (non-policy banks)	42.5	82.5	56.0	62.0	80.5	202.5
Green debt financing instruments	–	–	8.0	9.9	17.8	31.8
Government-backed agency bonds	60.0	60.0	85.0	40.0	-	207.0
Asset-backed notes and asset-backed securities	8.9	10.5	51.4	58.1	126.1	288.7
Other notes	1.2	5.5	3.9	2.1	0.0	1.4
SHCH Subtotal	**4,649.9**	**5,872.4**	**5,352.5**	**4,069.5**	**5,714.8**	**7,212.3**
Total debt financing instruments (other than NCD)	10,601.7	15,987.8	19,582.2	17,680.3	19,382.6	22,518.4
Negotiable certificates of deposit	897.6	5,297.6	12,993.1	20,187.2	21,083.2	17,970.6
Total debt financing instruments in CIBM	**11,499.2**	**21,285.4**	**32,575.3**	**37,867.5**	**40,465.8**	**40,489.0**

CCDC = China Central Depository & Clearing Co., Ltd.; CIBM = China Inter-Bank Bond Market; CNY = Chinese renminbi; NCD = negotiable certificates of deposit; SCP = super short-term commercial paper; SHCH = Shanghai Clearing House.
Note: ABS deposit balances have been diminishing toward nil and are no longer evident at SHCH.
Sources: CCDC. 2013. *Annual Review* (English); CCDC. 2017. *Bond Market Statistical Analysis Report 2014–2017*; CCDC. 2017. *Annual Report 2016–2017*; CCDC. 2017. *Bond Market Operation Analysis*; CCDC. 2018/12 统计月报: 2-01 债券发行量(按券种); SHCH. 2017. *Yearbook 2013–2017*; SHCH 2018/12 Monthly Report (web) 统计月报 表二 上海清算所固定收益产品发行量.

Detailed further information on the outstanding value of the different categories and types of bonds and notes, new issuances per period, and statistics on government and enterprise debt financing instruments in the China bond market can also be found on the websites of *AsianBondsOnline*, CCDC, and SHCH.

Appropriate links are also provided in Chapter VII and the appendixes.

E.   Methods of Issuing Bonds and Notes (Primary Market)

In cases when the issuance and trading of debt financing instruments are not covered by the Securities Law, the provisions of the Corporation Law, or other laws, the relevant administrative regulations issued by the regulatory authorities apply, depending on the industry, issuer, and type of securities or debt financing instruments.

In the CIBM, bonds can be issued by tender through the issuance system of the PBOC or by book-building. Currently, Treasury bonds and PFBs are issued by tender through the issuance system of the PBOC, which is operated by CCDC.

Credit products and other debt financing instruments, on the other hand, are issued in the CIBM mostly via book-building, using the central book-building platform operated by the CFAE on behalf of NAFMII. Securities companies issuing commercial paper typically use their own systems and client base to conduct book-building for their issuances.

Nonfinancial enterprises can also issue bonds by public tender, provided that they satisfy the relevant provisions of the Notice of the People's Bank of China (Financial Market Department) on the Relevant Matters Concerning the Issue of Bonds by Tender through the Issue System of the People's Bank of China (2010, No. 11), in which SHCH operates the issue system.

The different methods of issuance for individual types of debt financing instruments in the CIBM, and those employed by the various issuer types, are explained in further detail in this section.

1.   Issuance of Government Securities

Treasury bonds have been issued through electronic auction since 1996, where they are underwritten by government bond auction participants who will resell the Treasury bonds to the public market in different denominations. In the CIBM, government auction participants with special privileges are called market makers, not primary dealers as in many other markets; see also section M in this chapter for a description of these market participants and their functions.

After auction results are published, a distribution period of 1–2 days applies. Tender-winning participants have to pay for their successful subscription amount on the day following the auction. The period between the end of auction on auction day and the end of payment day is the distribution period.

Depending on the decision of the MOF, two types of auction may be applied in the primary market: the conventional auction method and the Dutch auction method.

a.   Issuance via Conventional Auction Method

The conventional auction method is also known as multiple price (multiple yield) auction method. Where the interest rate is the bidding object, the weighted average of the tender-winning interest rates becomes the coupon rate. For the tender-winning interest rates that are less than or equal to the coupon rate, the bond would be issued at face value; for the tender-winning interest rates that are greater than the coupon rate, the bond would be issued at the respective future value discounted with the coupon rate. This is the most common auction method and requires bids to be made on a yield basis.

Where the price is the bidding object, the weighted average of tender-winning prices would be the issuance price. For the tender-winning prices that are greater than or equal to the issuance price, the bond would be issued at the determined issuance price; for the tender-winning prices that are less than the determined issuance price, the bond would be issued at the individual tender-winning prices.

b. Issuance via Dutch Auction Method

A Dutch auction, or single price (single yield) auction (also referred to as uniform auction method in the CIBM) prescribes that all accepted tenders will be offered to auction participants at the same price. In the case of interest rate as the bidding object, the highest tender-winning interest rate would be the coupon rate; in the case of price as the bidding object, the lowest tender-winning price would be the issuance price.

2. Issuance of Financial Bonds

Financial bonds are typically issued through the underwriting method. Financial bonds may be underwritten by way of an agreement or by tendering (also referred to as bidding). If the issuance is based on an agreement, the issuer has to appoint a lead underwriter and a book runner. The lead underwriter needs to conduct and perform due diligence checks on the issuer and the statements by the issuer in the issuance documentation. A book runner should be appointed for agreed underwriting for the purpose of fair book-building. For an efficient issuance operation, the lead underwriter is often appointed as book runner.

Where a financial bond is issued in the form of underwriting by bidding, the issuer releases the following information to the underwriters:

    i.   the specific time and way of bid calling, the subject matter, how to determine the bid winner, emergency bidding, and the tendering plan—no later than 3 working days prior to the bidding; and

    ii.   a bid invitation at the beginning of a bid.

The actual issuance of a financial bond is processed through the Bond Issuance System of the PBOC, which is operated by CCDC or SHCH as part of their service provision in the CIBM.

The issuer itself is prohibited from purchasing its own financial bonds, nor may it do so in any disguised form, under provisions in the banking regulations.

3. Bonds and Notes Issued by the Corporate Sector

Debt financing instruments issued in the CIBM by enterprises or corporations may be issued via book-building or through a tendering process, which is also referred to as bidding.

Public offering is the most common issuance method for corporate or enterprise bonds. Of the overall issuance volume, private placements represent about 20%–25%.

While the registration for debt financing instruments with NAFMII is generally valid for a 2-year period (see also Chapter II.F for information on the regulatory process for debt financing instruments, or the registration process), the issuer can issue debt financing instruments via a single or multiple issuances through book-building or an invitation for bidding. An issuer who adopts the book-building method has to duly issue the debt financing instruments through the centralized book-building system operated by the CFAE on behalf of NAFMII (see section b below). An issuer who invites for bidding has to duly issue via the designated bond issuance system (e.g., that of the PBOC, which is operated by either CCDC or SHCH).

a.   Issuance via Tender (Public Offering)

The tender method is just one of the methods for pricing a bond issuance. There are no administrative barriers in terms of issue size or issuer credit rating for a tender issuance.

The tender (bidding) method is mainly used for the issuance of (i) Treasury bonds, (ii) central bank bills, and (iii) PFBs. If needed, smaller-sized debt financing instruments issued by nonfinancial enterprises may also use the method of issue by tender upon request from NAFMII as the registration authority in the CIBM.

For issuance by tender, taking into consideration the proposed use of the funds to be raised, issuers usually conduct an analysis of the demand and supply of funds available from the market and specific investor types, and then issue the bonds through a public offering with the determined tender or bidding method.

Issuance by tender in the CIBM means issuing bonds using the PBOC tender system, which is supported by CCDC and SHCH. The issuer must submit to the PBOC the necessary documents so as to use the PBOC tender system. The issuer and participants (underwriters) should conclude a written agreement on rights and obligations prior to the tender.

The issuer has to publicly disclose in accordance with a prior agreement with the investors at least 1 business day prior to the tender date through a website designated by NAFMII:

i.   indicate tender as the issuing method,
ii.   provide the tender documents, and
iii.   provide a list of participants in the tender.

Tender Methods

Tender methods are discussed below.

i.   Fixed Price Offer (Offer by Amount Tender)

The issuer will clearly indicate the total issuing amount, tenor, coupon rate, and price. Underwriters only bid for a committed underwriting amount through a fixed price offer.

ii.   Offer by Price Tender

The issuer will clearly indicate the total issuing amount and tenor. Underwriters only bid using a price and amount offer.

iii.   Offer by Rate Tender

The issuer will clearly indicate the total issuing amount, price, and tenor. Underwriters only bid for a coupon rate and for a specific underwriting amount.

iv.   Spread Tender

In the bidding document for floating rate notes, the issuer will clearly indicate the benchmark rate as guidance for the floating rate and the way it is determined. Underwriters only bid with an interest spread (the difference between coupon rate and benchmark rate) offer.

Currently, there are four types of benchmark rates in a floating rate bond issuance: (i) 1-year fixed official rate of interest, (ii) CIBM 7-day repo rate average, (iii) CIBM 7-day fixing repo rate, and (iv) SHIBOR.

Offers by price or rate tenders would generally employ the Dutch auction method, which may also be used for private placements.

Allocation Methods

Once a tender or bidding process has been carried out, a number of methods for the acceptance or allocation of successful bids may be applied. Such allocation methods for successful bids are discussed below.

i.   Proportional Bid Allocation

Each participant or underwriter's issue amount is allocated based on the ratio of its valid bid amount to the total valid issuing amount. If the total valid bid amount is less or equal to the total issuance amount, then all underwriters' valid bids are accepted; if the total valid bid amount is greater than the total issuance amount, then each underwriter's amount is allocated based on the ratio of its valid bid amount to the total valid issuance amount.

ii.   Single Price Bid Allocation

This method is also known as the allocation for the Dutch auction, or uniform price bidding method, and is used in an offer by price tender. All successful bids (where the price was accepted by the issuer or lead underwriter) are allocated at the determined price for the whole issuance.

iii.   Multiple Price Bid Allocation

This method is also known as the allocation for the conventional auction method and is used in an offer by yield or price tender. Here, all bids that came in at the determined yield or price, or were higher, are accepted by the issuer or lead underwriter and are allocated at the price at which they were offered. The issuer allocates the securities beginning with the lowest yield bid to the highest yield until the announced amount is fully subscribed. For price tenders, securities are allocated from the highest price to the lowest price until the issuer has allocated the total amount of the announced issue. The successful bids are awarded at their actual bid yield or price.

iv.   Hybrid Bid Allocation

As applied in the case of an offer by rate tender, the tender system will sort in ascending order all the underwriters' valid bid rates until all bids added up reach the total issuance amount. The highest rate is called the marginal rate point. The weighted mean of all the bid rates lower than the marginal rate point is the winning bid coupon rate. For those winning bid rates lower or equal to the coupon rate, the coupon rate will be used to calculate the respective underwriters' payment amount. For those winning bid rates higher than the coupon rate, each individual winning bid rate will be used to calculate the payment amount. Currently, the hybrid bidding method is typically only used in Treasury bond issuance. This is globally known as the auction method.

b.   Book-Building

Book-building is a global trend in bond issuance. Book-building means that the issuer and the lead underwriter jointly determine the range of bond yield, and the investors will place a purchase order at a preferable level in the yield range.[66] A so-called book runner is responsible for conducting the actual book-building and pricing operations, recording the investors' appetites on purchasing quantities at interested yields. The book runner generally serves as the lead underwriter. The book runner will collect all the orders and determine the actual rate (or price) and allocate the respective amounts.

At present, book-building is typically used for the issuance of debt financing instruments in smaller issue sizes and specific instrument types by nonfinancial firms, such as MTN and short-term financing bills (commercial paper).

Currently, the technical platform and support and service for the centralized book-building system for debt financing instruments in the CIBM are provided by the CFAE, under a mandate from NAFMII.

At the same time, CCDC also offers a book-building support service, including making available a dedicated, neutral book-building room within its premises to ensure that privileged information stays contained with the book runner.

c.   Private Placement

Private placements must be underwritten by a qualified underwriter(s) who meets certain criteria and requirements. The issuer appoints the lead underwriter who may form an underwriting syndicate if necessary.

An issuer may place debt financing instruments in the CIBM through a private placement (market practice refers to private placement bonds or notes) via qualified underwriter(s) either to institutional investors classified as such by NAFMII (SIIs) or institutional investors who are designated by the issuer and the lead underwriter for each issuance (DIIs). For more information on DIIs and SIIs, please refer to section N in this chapter.

By investing in privately placed debt financing instruments, SIIs are deemed to have executed the associated private placement agreement and accepted the rights and obligations of investors and the specific standards for information disclosure under the private placement (see Chapter II.G for a description of the disclosure requirements and practices in the case of a private placement).

The number of investors investing in each single private placement issue shall conform to applicable national law and regulations. The issuer and investors must agree to a regular monitoring of the credit rating, determine the specific credit rating follow-up (credit rating tracking) arrangement, and commit to such

---

[66] Parties involved in book-building include the issuer, lead underwriter, book-keeping manager or book runner, intermediary who provides services for issuance (if any), notary (if any), and other relevant entities.

specific arrangement in the private placement agreement. If disclosure in a language other than Chinese is to be allowed, this also has to be specified in the private placement agreement (see also section G in this chapter).

Private placement bonds have to be kept in custody in registered form under the actual name(s) of the respective bondholder(s).

d.   Note Issuance Programs

In the CIBM, the issuance of commercial paper, SCP, and other debt financing instruments by nonfinancial enterprises in the form of MTN is common and shall be registered with NAFMII. These issuances can be regarded as note issuance programs.

In the China bond market, MTN simply refer to debt financing instruments denominated in Chinese renminbi with a maturity of more than 1 year (typically 5–10 years) that are issued in tranches under a program and within the declared program amount. The concept of MTN in the CIBM was introduced by the PBOC in April 2008 to support the financing activities of domestic enterprises through bond issuances and to facilitate the domestic bond market's development.

In effect, MTN are note issuance programs that can be issued upon a successful registration with NAFMII and allow individual instruments to be issued under the approved amount in tranches between issuers who have financing needs and their appointed dealers or underwriters. Issuance requirements for MTN are less stringent than for corporate or enterprise bond issuance. At the same time, MTN may only be traded among, and be held by, institutional investors in the CIBM.

e.   Reverse Inquiries

Reverse inquiries–where investors approach the issuer of debt financing instruments or the appointed (lead) underwriter to offer to buy such debt financing instruments–are also evident in the China bond market. In such cases, the lead underwriter shall negotiate with the investors on the debt financing instrument conditions and price.

For details on the regulatory process for the issuance of debt financing instruments via a public offering, please refer to Chapter II.F.3.

4.   Bonds Issuance Systems in the Inter-Bank Bond Market

Issuance of bonds in the CIBM can occur in any number of dedicated issuance systems, including the PBOC Bond Issuance System, the MOF Government Bond Issuance System, and other bond issuance systems, such as those facilitated by CCDC and SHCH. The issuance method, the system used, and other details are publicly disclosed by the issuer before the issuance.

The PBOC Bond Issuance System is mainly used for issuances via tender of PFBs, ABS, and other financial bonds. The MOF Government Bond Issuance System is used for the issuance of Treasury bonds as well as local government bonds. Other bond issuance systems cover the issuance via book-building of enterprise bonds, ABS, and other bonds or debt financing instruments.

According to the 2015 NAFMII Rules, any corporate issuer that adopts the book-building method shall issue its debt financing instruments through the centralized book-building system (bond issuance system), which is operated by the CFAE on behalf of NAFMII. Any enterprise that invites for bidding shall duly issue its debt financing instruments via the designated bond issuance system (e.g., that of PBOC, which is operated by CCDC or SHCH). At the same time, commercial paper or other debt financing instruments issued by securities companies are typically issued by the issuer directly through their own platform.

F.   Governing Law and Jurisdiction (Bond and Note Issuance)

The governing law and jurisdiction for a bond issuance is of significance since potential issuers may consider issuing under the laws or jurisdiction of a country or market other than the place of issuance. The choice of governing law or the contractual preferences of stakeholders may affect the accessibility to a specific investor universe that may otherwise not be accessible if a bond were issued under the laws of the place of issuance.

At present, the governing law and jurisdiction for bond issuances within the territory of the PRC are limited to the laws of the PRC and its jurisdiction.

G.   Language of Documentation and Disclosure Items

It is envisaged that most ASEAN+3 markets participating in the ASEAN+3 Multi-Currency Bond Issuance Framework (AMBIF) will be able to accept the use of a common document in English. However, some markets may require the submission of approval-related information in their prescribed format and in the local language. In such cases, concessions from these regulatory authorities for a submission of required information in English, in addition to local language and formats, may be sought.

1.   General Requirements in the Inter-Bank Bond Market

In general, issuance documentation, applications and supporting documents, and disclosure information for the issuance of debt financing instruments in the CIBM must be in Chinese, particularly for public offerings. However, concessions are principally available for the issuance of Panda bonds for both issuance documentation published in the CIBM and continuous disclosure by the issuer.

Documentation to be submitted for registration and official filings with regulatory authorities need to be in Chinese. At the same time, documents to be submitted by a foreign investor to a custodian or bond settlement agent can be in English. If a bond settlement agent agreement between bank and investor is executed in English, it must be translated for filing with the PBOC.

Notwithstanding the above, issuers in the CIBM may make available to international investors an English version of the issuance announcement and key disclosure document prior to issuance if they so choose, including for a public offering. This practice has been observed for issuers that are part of an international company or group. Such announcements and initial disclosure information are for the convenience of investors only; the Chinese version remains the official document for the purpose of an offer.[67]

---

[67] The prospectus issued by Ford Automotive Finance (China) Limited in November 2017 is cited as one example of the provision of English documentation for selected investors; see www.1510649970156654153696.pdf.

2.   Language Concessions for Panda Bond Issuance

According to the Interim Measures for Administration of the Bond Issuance by Overseas Institutions in the National Inter-Bank Bond Market, echoed in the NAFMII Guidelines on Debt Financing Instruments of Overseas Non-Financial Enterprises (for Trial Implementation), all registration and offering documents shall either be in Chinese or in English accompanied by a Chinese version. In addition, all information disclosed during the life of the debt financing instrument shall be in Chinese, in principle. Where an overseas nonfinancial enterprise discloses information in English on other securities markets related to a material event that requires disclosure under the 2019 NAFMII Guidelines, the issuer shall, simultaneously or as soon as reasonably practicable thereafter, disclose such information in English in the CIBM and disclose a Chinese version or a Chinese summary within 7 business days upon the disclosure of the English version. In any case, the use of English for documentation or disclosure items will need to be prescribed in the offering circular for the Panda bond.

At the same time, the legal opinion issued by the foreign law firm (at the domicile of the nonresident issuer) is to be submitted in Chinese, or translated into Chinese if the original is issued in another language, since it forms part of the required documentation for the approval and/or registration process for Panda bonds in the CIBM.

3.   Panda Bonds Offered to Private Placement Investors

According to Article 29 of the 2019 NAFMII Guidelines, for debt financing instruments offered by a nonresident issuer (Panda bonds) through a private placement, the principal registration and offering documents (private placement agreement or private placement offering memorandum) shall be in Chinese or in English accompanied by a Chinese version.

Other documents may be either in Chinese or in English, as agreed between the issuer and the investors. Information disclosure during the life of such debt financing instrument may be made in Chinese or in English as agreed between the issuer and the investors.

In recent market practice, the use of English in the context of Panda bond issuance via a private placement has been limited to continuous disclosure, particularly the use of existing financial statements in English.

H.   Registration of Debt Financing Instruments in the Inter-Bank Bond Market

The term registration assumes a number of different meanings in the context of the CIBM. The primary meaning of registration is shared between the need for debt financing instruments issued by nonfinancial enterprises to be registered by NAFMII (expressed as 注册) and for said debt financing instruments to be subsequently registered with the respective CSD for transfer and settlement in their book-entry system (expressed as 登记); registration with a CSD is required to make a debt financing instrument tradable in the CIBM.

In the rules of the CSDs, bond registration is also used as a term to describe the deposit of bonds or debt financing instruments with a CSD in the account of a bondholder or investor. In fact, the official description of a CSD in the PRC refers to a bond registration, depository, and settlement institution. However, in this context, the bond registration part of the CSD function is understood to be for the admission of new debt financing instruments to the book-entry system following the application by an issuer. For the registration of ownership of debt financing instruments by investors in the book-entry systems of the CSDs, please refer to section L in this chapter.

In addition, the term registration may also refer to the participation of nonresident (foreign) investors in the CIBM who need to register their participation with the PBOC under the CIBM Direct market access scheme (see also Chapter II.N), or the participation of foreign-owned CRAs who may register with NAFMII to be eligible to carry out bond-rating activities in the CIBM.

These examples for the use of the term registration may not be exhaustive, also given the fact that the unofficial English translations of laws, regulations, and rules may naturally contain registration as the term chosen to express accreditation, licensing, or other admission concepts for market participants.

This section provides further details on the primary meaning of registration of debt financing instruments in the CIBM as mentioned above.

1.   Registration with National Association of Financial Market Institutional Investors

A nonfinancial enterprise or company wishing to issue debt financing instruments in the CIBM is required to register the proposed debt financing instruments with NAFMII. The registration process (注册) represents the issuance review and successful registration or rejection. NAFMII has been given a mandate by the PBOC as the market regulatory authority to carry out the registration process in its role as the SRO for the CIBM.

Central government bonds and local government bonds, financial bonds, and Panda bonds to be issued by nonresident financial institutions need not be registered with NAFMII, but instead are subject to separate approval or consent processes.

Chapter II.F contains a comprehensive description of the registration processes for debt financing instruments, including the eligibility criteria for issuers and instruments, necessary documentation and disclosure requirements, and the registration time frame.

2.   Registration with China Central Depository & Clearing Co., Ltd.

Debt financing instruments eligible for deposit in CCDC (mainly including central government bonds, local government bonds, PFBs, commercial bank bonds, central bank bills, enterprise bonds, government-backed agency bonds, and ABS) must be registered with CCDC upon issuance (登记) for these debt financing instruments to be traded, cleared, settled, and safekept in the CIBM.

3.   Registration with Shanghai Clearing House Co., Ltd.

Issuers of debt financing instruments that are eligible for deposit at SHCH—including commercial paper and SCP, MTN, PPN, Panda bonds, NCD, SDR-denominated bonds, PFBs, and other types of debt financing products—must register these instruments with SHCH upon issuance to ensure that they may be traded, cleared, settled, and safekept in the CIBM.

4.   Registration with China Foreign Exchange Trading System

Registration with CFETS is not required to ensure that market participants may trade debt financing instruments on the CFETS platform. At the same time, CFETS requires market participants to open a trading account and submit a net connection application accompanied by supporting documents, as set out in the Bond Market Admission Guide, which is available for download in English from the CFETS website.[68]

The connection application is intended to allow each investor to trade on CFETS while using the bond account(s) opened in their name at either CCDC or SHCH (or both) to clear and settle trades concluded on CFETS. Investors may also trade through bond settlement agents, who connect to the investor's trading account at CFETS based on a separate authorization from the investor. CFETS shall complete the account opening procedures within 3 working days after receiving the application documents.

Foreign investors who access the CIBM through the CIBM Direct, QFII, or RQFII schemes will authorize a bond settlement agent to connect their bond account(s) to the trading account at CFETS and trade on their behalf.

I.   Listing of Debt Financing Instruments

The listing of bonds and notes does not apply to the CIBM. To ensure the equivalent functions of a bond listing (i.e., the visibility of debt instruments), the initial and continuous disclosure obligations of the issuer, and the ready availability of bond pricing or valuations, most debt financing instruments issued in the CIBM are required to be registered with NAFMII, while their disclosure information is available from DCM-FANS and other websites designated by NAFMII, as well as the CCDC and SHCH websites, with transaction data and traded price information available on the trading platform operated by CFETS.

Please see the previous section on the registration of debt financing instruments with NAFMII. More information on disclosure and the available information on debt financing instruments for interested parties can be found in Chapter II.G and Chapter IV.E.

For a comprehensive description of the listing requirements and listing application and approval process for debt securities in the exchange bond market, please see the *ASEAN+3 Bond Market Guide for the Exchange Bond Market in the People's Republic of China*.[69]

J.   Methods of Trading Bonds and Notes (Secondary Market)

Trading in the CIBM is conducted either on the electronic platform of CFETS or, to a lesser degree, through the proprietary systems of money brokerage companies (money brokers). CFETS fulfills the function of offering a common, standardized trading platform for all debt financing instruments offered in the CIBM, with full integration into the clearing and settlement process. Money brokers fulfill the desired function of intermediation between counterparties who do not know each other.

Indirect participants, such as nonfinancial enterprises (e.g., corporates), access the trading activities on CFETS through the CFAE, with quotes relayed from CFETS and execution occurring on CFETS; in this context, the CFAE acts as an order-routing mechanism. Similarly, nonresident investors accessing the CIBM via Bond Connect place their orders through the international fixed income trading platform they are connected to (e.g., Bloomberg or TradeWeb), but trades are executed on CFETS according to CFETS trading practices.

---

[68] See http://new.chinamoney.com.cn/english/svcfop/.
[69] See https://asianbondsonline.adb.org/abmg.php.

On the CFETS platform, trades may be concluded through bilateral negotiation or the so-called one-click method. The practice of bilateral negotiation is applied to all CIBM products, while one-click trading (点击成交) is only applied to cash (outright) bond trading and to interest rate derivatives. Counterparties can use CFETS features to request and obtain quotes, or they can quote prices for debt financing instruments. The systems and platforms offered by money brokers will capture only trades between participants and the money broker.

The legal basis for trading, for example, corporate bonds in the CIBM is contained in the Administrative Measures for the Issuance and Trading of Corporate Bonds (公司债券发行与交易管理办法), issued by the PBOC in 2015. NAFMII, as the SRO for the CIBM, issued the Self-Regulatory Rules for Bond Trading in the Inter-Bank Bond Market to define and commit market participants to market practices and conventions.

For further information on the trading methods, trading platforms, and trading conventions in the CIBM, please refer to the relevant sections in Chapter IV.

K.   Bond and Note Pricing and Valuation

In the CIBM, the price or yield of debt financing instruments is determined through executed transactions on the CFETS platform or quotations from market participants. Prices are displayed on the access and information systems of CFETS and simultaneously or subsequently distributed to participants, information vendors, and other parties.

1.   China Foreign Exchange Trading System

As the common trading platform for the CIBM, CFETS—also known as Chinamoney—provides market maker's quotes and traded prices or yields for debt financing instruments, as well as trading volume, on its website (Figure 3.1). Quotes are listed by market maker and bond code, while debt financing instrument prices and yields are listed by bond code.

For more information on CFETS and its trading platform, please see Chapter IV.B.

Figure 3.1: Inter-Bank Bond Market Bond Traded Prices at CFETS

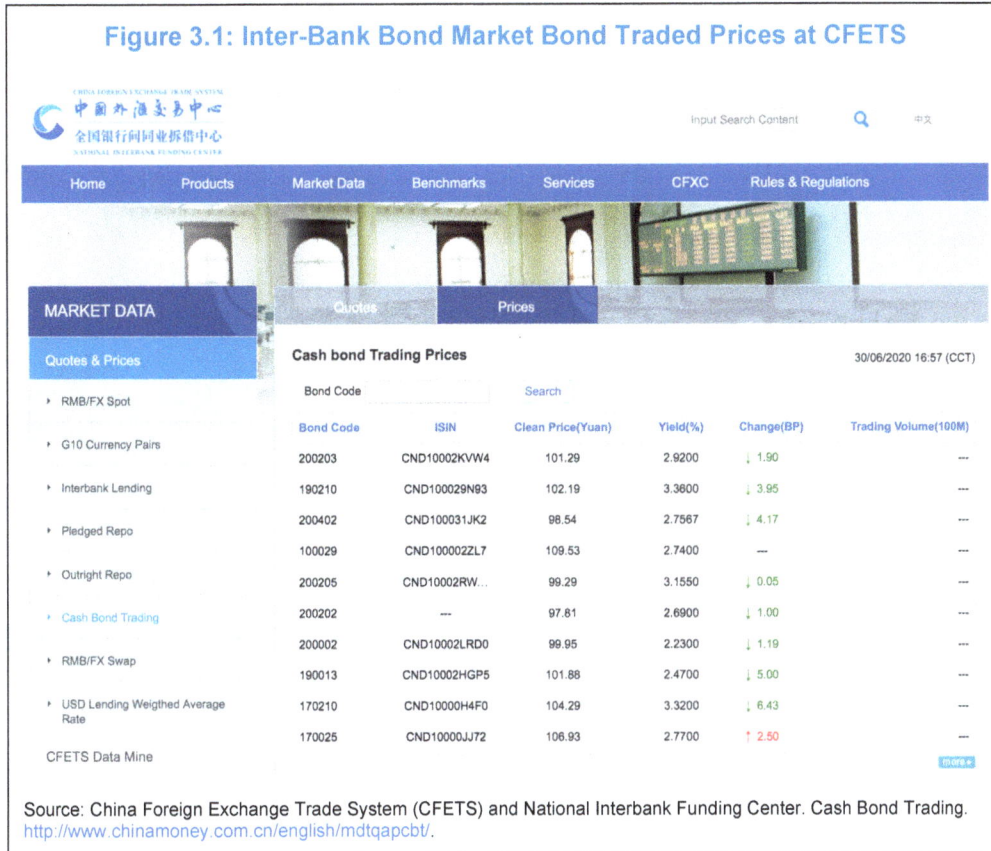

Bond Code	ISIN	Clean Price(Yuan)	Yield(%)	Change(BP)	Trading Volume(100M)
200203	CND10002KVW4	101.29	2.9200	↓ 1.90	---
190210	CND100029N93	102.19	3.3600	↓ 3.95	---
200402	CND100031JK2	98.54	2.7567	↓ 4.17	---
100029	CND100002ZL7	109.53	2.7400	---	---
200205	CND10002RW...	99.29	3.1550	↓ 0.05	---
200202	---	97.81	2.6900	↓ 1.00	---
200002	CND10002LRD0	99.95	2.2300	↓ 1.19	---
190013	CND10002HGP5	101.88	2.4700	↓ 5.00	---
170210	CND10000H4F0	104.29	3.3200	↓ 6.43	---
170025	CND10000JJ72	106.93	2.7700	↑ 2.50	---

Cash bond Trading Prices   30/06/2020 16:57 (CCT)

Source: China Foreign Exchange Trade System (CFETS) and National Interbank Funding Center. Cash Bond Trading. http://www.chinamoney.com.cn/english/mdtqapcbt/.

2.   China Central Depository & Clearing Co., Ltd.

As part of its function to effectively support the CIBM, CCDC also features the ChinaBond Pricing Center. CCDC started creating the market's first yield curve in 1999 and established a series of bond pricing valuations in 2006. In 2010, ChinaBond Pricing Center, as a unit of CCDC, started commercial operation. By 2013, ChinaBond had fully covered bond valuations for all CNY-denominated debt financing instruments traded in the CIBM and has since expanded into other valuation and index products; see Chapter IV.F for further details.

Today, ChinaBond provides daily valuations for more than 14,000 bonds and notes denominated in Chinese renminbi and traded in the CIBM, regardless of whether an individual instrument was traded that day. Bond valuations are carried out daily at 5:30 p.m. based on a number of defined bond valuation indicators.

In 2007, fund companies began to use ChinaBond yield curves and valuations to appraise debt financing instruments traded in the CIBM, while listed banks started to use ChinaBond valuations as a measurement of bond fair value from 2008; subsequently, the then CBRC recommended ChinaBond valuations as a credible reference for the measuring of bond fair value in its Operation Guide for Commercial Banks on Bond Fair Value Valuation. In 2009, ChinaBond valuations became the reference indicator for the monitoring of abnormal trading activities in bonds traded in the CIBM.

In 2013, the application of ChinaBond valuations was extended to use in collateral management by trading counterparties. Since 2015, the Association of Asset Management Companies of China has mandated that all debt securities traded on an exchange require a third-party valuation; this extended the application of the ChinaBond valuations into the exchange market.

In addition, the ChinaBond Pricing Center also conducts an analysis of market prices and financial statements of issuers, by observing the credit spreads given by investors to each bond, and calculates a so-called market implied credit rating.

ChinaBond also analyzes the quotations (bids) provided in the CIBM, showing the best quotations for individual debt financing instruments on its website as a service for the easy orientation of market participants (Figure 3.2).

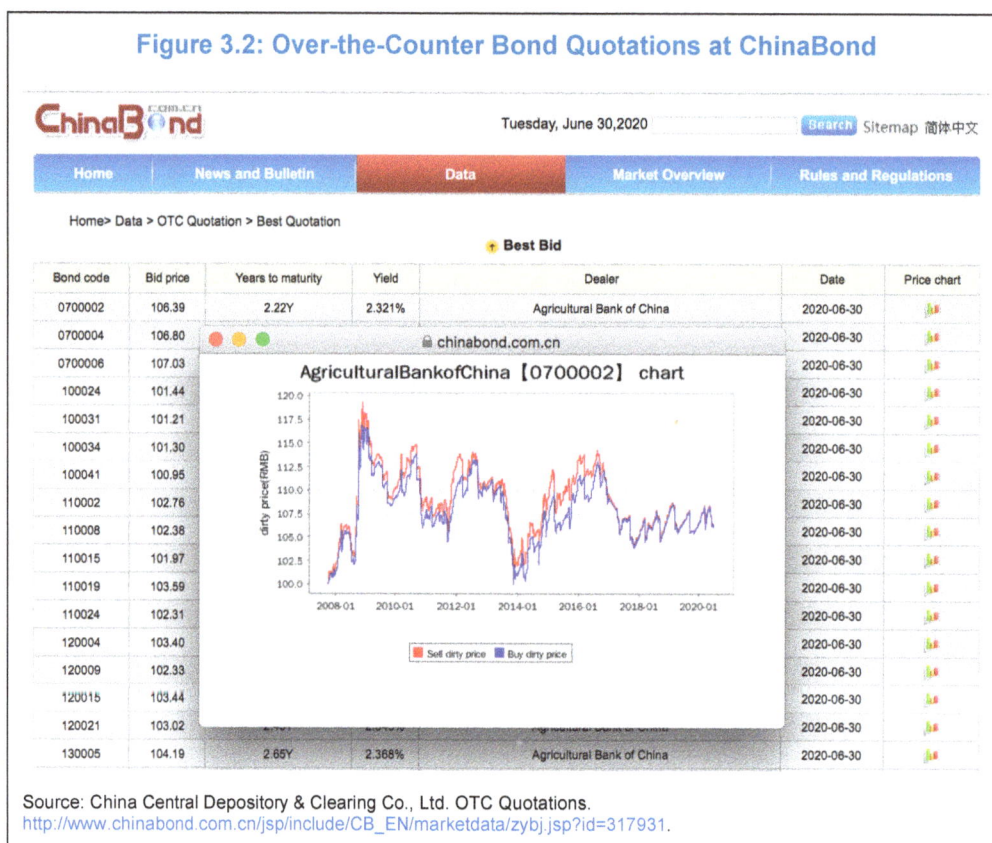

Figure 3.2: Over-the-Counter Bond Quotations at ChinaBond

Source: China Central Depository & Clearing Co., Ltd. OTC Quotations.
http://www.chinabond.com.cn/jsp/include/CB_EN/marketdata/zybj.jsp?id=317931.

3.   Shanghai Clearing House Co., Ltd.

SHCH pays close attention to the fair valuation of debt financing instruments and has established a market-recognized valuation system for bonds and other debt financing instruments. Today, SHCH provides daily valuations for more than 30,000 debt financing instruments of 19 different types in the CIBM, including credit bonds and government bonds.[70] The indicators for each instrument include dirty price, clean price, yield to maturity, accrued interest, duration, and convexity, among others. The tenor of these debt financing instruments does not have to be more than 1 year and the large number of instruments valued is the result of the inclusion of short-term instruments such as commercial paper varieties and NCD.

Debt financing instruments valuations are released through the official SHCH website daily at about 6 p.m. (Figure 3.3). At the time of writing, the SHCH website with valuation information was only available in Chinese.

---

[70] SHCH provides daily pricing for debt financing instruments such as local government bonds, enterprise bonds, financial bonds, ABN, SCP and commercial paper, PPN, MTN, and NCD.

Figure 3.3: Shanghai Clearing House Bond Valuation Web Page

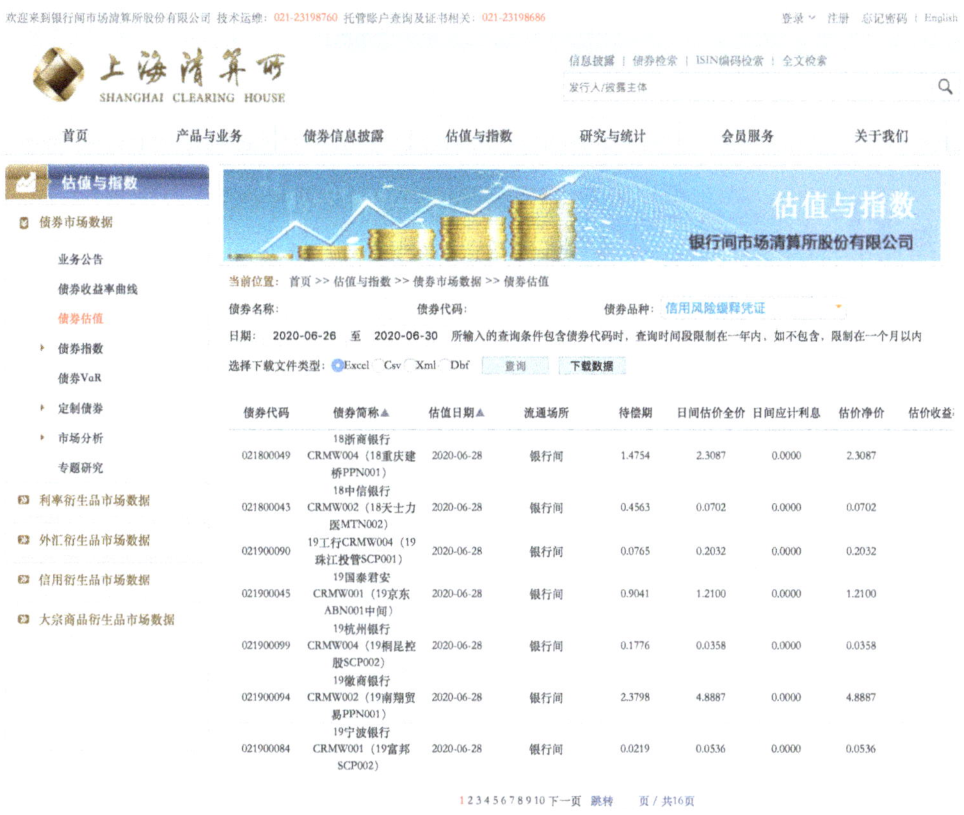

债券代码	债券简称▲	估值日期▲	流通场所	待偿期	日间估价全价	日间应计利息	估价净价	估价收益
021800049	18浙商银行CRMW004（18重庆建桥PPN001）	2020-06-28	银行间	1.4754	2.3087	0.0000	2.3087	
021800043	18中信银行CRMW002（18天士力医MTN002）	2020-06-28	银行间	0.4563	0.0702	0.0000	0.0702	
021900090	19工行CRMW004（19珠江投管SCP001）	2020-06-28	银行间	0.0765	0.2032	0.0000	0.2032	
021900045	19国泰君安CRMW001（19京东ABN001中间）	2020-06-28	银行间	0.9041	1.2100	0.0000	1.2100	
021900099	19杭州银行CRMW004（19桐昆控股SCP002）	2020-06-28	银行间	0.1776	0.0358	0.0000	0.0358	
021900094	19徽商银行CRMW002（19南翔贸易PPN001）	2020-06-28	银行间	2.3798	4.8887	0.0000	4.8887	
021900084	19宁波银行CRMW001（19富邦SCP002）	2020-06-28	银行间	0.0219	0.0536	0.0000	0.0536	

Source: Shanghai Clearing House. Bond Valuation. http://www.shclearing.com/cpgz/zqjqysp/zqgz/.

L. Transfers of Interests in Bonds and Notes

The transfer of interests in, or ownership of, debt financing instruments in the CIBM depends on the type of instrument and, by extension, the depository in which such instruments are registered, deposited, and settled. Debt financing instruments will need to be registered with a CSD at issuance to be traded or transferred in the CIBM.

CCDC and SHCH support or provide services for the issuance, registration, securities depository or safekeeping, and settlement of debt financing instruments traded in the CIBM. They also facilitate the interest payment and redemption, as well as other ancillary services.

Institutional investors in the CIBM, as well as securities firms and commercial banks acting for their own purposes or their clients, open one or more bond account(s) (e.g., pledge or repo accounts) with CCDC or SHCH, either directly or through a bond settlement agent (see section M in this chapter).

For an investor or other account holder to claim ownership of debt financing instruments in the CIBM, these debt financing instruments will need to be recorded in their bond account(s). On the other hand, Bond Connect allows nonresident investors to enter the CIBM under a nominee account arrangement through the omnibus account maintained by the CMU at CCDC or SHCH.

This section details the transfer of interests in (i.e., the ownership of) debt financing instruments from a number of perspectives.

1.   Government Securities

CCDC is the depository authorized by MOF for managing the registration of Treasury bonds and act as the central register for these debt instruments. In addition, CCDC also registers central bank bills issued by the PBOC as part of its open market operation.

CCDC maintains a book-entry system to record investors' holdings of debt financing instruments registered and deposited with it, and manages investors' rights and interests. CCDC records transfers of debt financing instruments among bond accounts in its book-entry system on settlement day, upon having received trading data from CFETS and matching those to settlement instructions from its account holders. At settlement, debt financing instruments are transferred from the seller's bond account to the buyer's bond account, with the corresponding cash being settled through the National Interbank Funding Center (NIFC).

2.   Other Debt Financing Instruments

Depending on the type of debt financing instrument, the transfer of ownership will be recorded in bond accounts of investors in the book-entry systems of either CCDC or SHCH. In addition, CCDC and SHCH will record pledges, or release such pledges, upon instructions from bond account holders. Upon completed settlement, the transfer of debt financing instruments between bond account holders becomes irrevocable.

3.   Cross-Market Transfer

The concept of cross-market transfer is unique to the China bond market, owing to its multiple bond market segments. Debt financing instruments (bonds) registered with CCDC in the CIBM—such as Treasury bonds, local government bonds, SOE bonds, and local enterprise bonds—may also be listed, deposited, traded, and settled in the exchange bond market, where the term debt securities is used for these instruments.

Bond account holders in the CIBM are able to have part or all of their holdings in eligible debt instruments transferred between bond accounts they maintain in the CIBM and accounts with CSDC in the exchange bond market. Positions in central and local government debt instruments, as well as many enterprise bonds, are fungible between the CIBM and exchange market, with the exception of PFBs (Table 3.5).

Upon instruction, CCDC will transfer debt financing instruments from the bond accounts of their participants in their book-entry system to the bond account maintained by CSDC in their book-entry system. Functioning like a nostro account, CSDC will then record the transfer in its own book-entry system by recording the transferred holding in the investor's bond account in the CSDC's book-entry system, following which the holding is tradable and can be settled in the exchange bond market.

Table 3.5: Fungibility of Debt Financing Instrument among Major Market Segments

Inter-Bank Bond Market		Exchange Bond Market
Nonfungible Instruments	**Fungible Instruments**	**Nonfungible Instruments**
Policy bank financial bonds, medium-term notes, commercial paper, super-short-term commercial paper, private placement notes, SME collective notes, negotiable certificates of deposit	Treasury bonds, local government bonds, government-backed (agency) bonds, state-owned enterprise bonds, local enterprise bonds, local enterprise collective bonds, project revenue bonds	Corporate bonds, convertible bonds, policy bank financial bonds

SME = small and medium-sized enterprises.
Sources: ChinaBond. 2019. *Monthly Bulletin of Statistics: 3-04 Cross Market Bond Balance* (登录中国债券信息网:统计月报:3-04 跨市场债券托管量); Standard Chartered Bank; and ASEAN+3 Bond Market Forum Sub-Forum 1 team.

The actual process of a cross-market transfer from the CIBM to the exchange bond market requires an application to CCDC by the account holder wishing to transfer its debt financing instruments and includes the following steps:

Step 1: The applicant completes an application form for cross-market transfer.
Step 2: The applicant has to fax the application form to CCDC and, at the same time, send a cross-market transfer instruction to CCDC in the depository system.
Step 3: As a result of the cross-market transfer instructions, a book-keeping notice is generated in the CCDC system.
Step 4: CSDC will effect the book-entry transfer in accordance with the cross-market transfer book-keeping notice.

Since the transfer of debt instrument holdings occurs between accounts of the same investor, there is no change in legal ownership of the instruments as a result of the transfer.

4.   Prohibited Transfers

In principle, the transfer of ownership of debt financing instruments in the CIBM requires an underlying trade concluded on the CFETS platform or recorded in CFETS after agreement between counterparties, and a settlement instruction to the CSD from a bond settlement agent, a direct participant, or an indirect participant. In addition, the CSDs carry out transfers of debt financing instruments to service clearing or settlement obligations for direct trading participants in the CIBM, as well as for bond settlement agents.

At the same time, a CSD may not carry out a transfer as instructed by the bond settlement agent or direct participant, if such a transfer order may cause a violation of laws, regulations, or rules in the CIBM.

However, a transfer may also occur as a result of other underlying causes such as a court order for the freezing (or unfreezing) of assets, an inheritance, or other directions by the relevant authorities. In such cases, CCDC or SHCH will carry out the transfer in line with the legal documents presented.

5. Custodian Point of View

In the CIBM, custodians are typically referred to as bond settlement agents, provided they have obtained a so-called Type A license, which allows them to both trade and settle debt financing instruments for themselves and on behalf of other market participants without direct access to the CIBM, or Type C participants, which include foreign investors.

Bond settlement agents maintain separate bond accounts with CCDC and SHCH for their proprietary business (also called bond primary account) and client business (bond secondary accounts), one for each investor. Prior to commencing the bond settlement agency service, bond settlement agents execute a participant agreement with the CSD and, in turn, will conclude a client agreement on the provision of such bond settlement agency services with Type C investors.

Bond settlement agents will only place orders in the CIBM or instruct settlements to the respective CSD when so authorized by the investor. At the same time, the CSD will accept settlement instructions as given by the bond account holder and effect transfers of holdings in their book-entry systems if trading records are evident and settlement instructions match.

M.   Market Participants

In the CIBM, market participants are made up of the many members of NAFMII, which include commercial banks and non-bank financial institutions, securities firms and investment banks, asset managers, and insurance companies as investors and/or service providers. Please also see Chapter II.H for relevant details on membership in NAFMII.

Issuers of debt financing instruments and relevant intermediaries are required to be members of NAFMII. Investors that would like to invest in PPN shall be NAFMII members, while membership is not mandatory if investors invest in other bond types in the CIBM.

Foreign institutional investors are able to participate in the CIBM—under the QFII, RQFII, or CIBM Direct market access schemes (see Chapter II.N for details)—by appointing one or more bond settlement agents, who also act as trading participants on behalf of the foreign investors, or by accessing Bond Connect through nominee accounts of the CMU at CCDC or SHCH.

Issuers consist of the central and local governments and their agencies, as well as listed and unlisted companies and enterprises. Please see also section B in this chapter for a complete description of the typical debt financing instruments in the CIBM and their issuers.

In addition, a number of market institutions and infrastructure providers also offer service provisions in support of debt financing instrument issuance, trading, clearing, and settlement, as well as credit rating and valuation services.

1. Issuers in the Inter-Bank Bond Market

The CIBM features a wide range of issuers, from the central government of the PRC (in the form of Treasury bonds) and local governments and their agencies, to policy banks and other state-controlled entities. Key among the issuers related to the government are SOEs. For the most part, their issuances (enterprise bonds) are treated the same as corporate bonds, including when considering the credit rating. In addition, the PBOC issues central bank bills in the CIBM as part of its open market operation.

From the private sector, many large or larger companies issue their bonds in the CIBM, in particular banks and non-bank financial institutions. A particular section of issuers is represented by nonlisted companies, including SMEs that also issue a particular type of debt financing instruments. Please also see section B in this chapter for a description of the debt instruments issued in the CIBM and their issuers.

At the time of registration of debt financing instruments by nonfinancial enterprises to be issued in the CIBM, NAFMII, as the registration authority, applies a categorization to issuers according to specific criteria in case of public offerings. The categorization of an issuer determines the actual registration process and disclosure obligations; see also Chapter II.F.3 for a comprehensive description of the issuance regulatory process for public offerings and the distinctions made for each issuer category.

In the RPR (2020), NAFMII distinguished between four issuer categories, grouped into mature and basic-level enterprises, using size, market recognition, and issuance history and experience as key criteria. Please also see the explanation of the grouping and individual categories in Chapter II.F.3 for guidance.

For example, pursuant to Article 7 of the RPR (2020), an enterprise that meets all of the following criteria is classified as a mature enterprise, or Category I or II issuer:

i.   a high level of market recognition or prominent industry status, sound corporate governance, and production and operations that comply with national macroeconomic and industrial policies;

ii.   a stable financial situation with the size, capital structure, and profitability meeting the specific requirements of its industry classification;[71]

iii.   mature public information disclosure for no less than three separate issuances of debt financing instruments (or other debt instruments) in the last 36 months, and debt financing instrument issuance to the public of not less than CNY10 billion in that period;

iv.   no default on or delayed payment of principal and interest within the last 36 months, for both the issuer and parent company, if applicable;

v.   no violation of laws and regulations, breaches of NAFMII self-regulations, investigations by competent authorities, or administrative or criminal penalties; and

vi.   other conditions set by NAFMII in accordance with investor protection requirements.

The classification as a mature enterprise also includes select eligibility criteria by industry (Table 3.6).

---

[71] The appendix of the RPR (2020) contains a table detailing the minimum asset size, maximum assets-to-liabilities ratio, and minimum return-on-assets percentage prescribed for a mature enterprise (issuer), according to four industry groupings.

Table 3.6: Business and Financial Indicators for Category I Issuers

Industry	Total Assets (CNY billion)	Debt Ratio (%)	Return on Assets Ratio (%)
Telecommunications, utilities, transportation, energy	>100	<85	>3
Information technology, large-scale manufacturing, textiles and apparel and consumer products, metals, automobiles and auto parts, medicine, raw materials	>100	<80	>3
Hotels, restaurants and leisure, tourism, media and culture, agriculture, forestry, animal husbandry, fishing, wholesale and retail trade	>80	<75	>3
Civil construction, infrastructure construction, comprehensive and other categories	>120	<85	>3

CNY = Chinese renminbi.
Source: National Association of Financial Institutional Investors.

A mature enterprise not satisfying the additional quantitative criteria (including asset size and recent issuance volume) for Category I shall be classified as a Category II issuer. Issuers not meeting the criteria prescribed for mature enterprises are classified as basic-level enterprises (Categories III and IV), which are further distinguished by past issuance volume and experience. Furthermore, an issuer will lose its category status if it no longer fulfills the respective conditions for such status.

As of April 2020, NAFMII alone reported more than 4,400 nonfinancial enterprise issuers in the CIBM, with an outstanding balance of debt financing instruments of about CNY12.4 trillion.

2.   Investors in the Inter-Bank Bond Market

Investors in the CIBM are nearly exclusively institutional investors such as commercial banks and non-bank financial institutions, insurance companies, securities companies, funds management companies, enterprises, and public institutions. At the end of December 2019, CCDC maintained 24,397 bond accounts for institutional investors in the CIBM. Table 3.7 provides a breakdown of investor types and their bond accounts and holdings with CCDC.

In addition, CCDC alone maintains nearly 23 million additional "sub-custody" bond accounts for investors from the commercial banks' counter market, which are kept as subaccounts under the commercial banks that are on-selling debt financing instruments to general investors, including retail investors.[72] In CCDC terminology, the accounts in Table 3.7 are referred to as "first-tiered custody" bond accounts.

---

[72] At the end of December 2019, the exact number of "sub-custody" accounts reported by CCDC was 22,927,508.

Table 3.7: Overview of Inter-Bank Bond Market Bond Accounts at CCDC

Type of Account Holders	Number of Bond Accounts	Breakdown by Account Category		
		A	B	C
1. Policy financial banks	3	1	2	–
2. Commercial banks	1,538	60	1,458	20
2.1 National commercial banks and their branches	80	17	55	8
2.2 City commercial banks	145	29	116	–
2.3 Rural commercial banks	1,139	8	1,131	–
2.4 Rural cooperative banks	15	–	14	1
2.5 Village banks	80	–	70	10
2.6 Foreign banks	67	6	60	1
2.7 Other banks	12	–	12	–
3. Credit unions	530	–	463	67
4. Insurance agencies	183	–	166	17
5. Securities companies	135	54	81	–
6. Fund companies and foundations (pension and provident funds)	59	–	56	3
7. Other financial institutions	349	5	335	9
8. Nonfinancial institutions	265	–	1	264
9. Unincorporated products	20,196	–	20,115	81
Of which, commercial banking wealth management products	1,611	–	1,611	–
10. Foreign institutions	1,120	–	2	1,118
11. Others in CIBM	19	3	15	1
Total CIBM accounts at CCDC	**24,397**	**123**	**22,694**	**1,580**

CCDC = China Central Depository & Clearing Co., Ltd; CIBM = China Inter-Bank Bond Market.
Notes: Data as of December 2019. The account categories refer to the ability to settle. "A" can settle for one's own and other institutions. "B" can settle only for one's own institution. "C" needs to use a settlement agency to participate in the CIBM.
Sources: Adapted by ASEAN+3 Bond Market Forum Sub-Forum 1 team from ChinaBond. 2019. *December Monthly Bulletin of Statistics. 3-02 Bond Balance* (Investor Type: 债券托管量(按投资者)) and 3-08 (Total Number of Investors: 投资者数量).
https://www.chinabond.com.cn/cb/eng/yjfx/zzfx/yb/20200103/153505906.shtml and
https://www.chinabond.com.cn/cb/cn/yjfx/zzfx/yb/20200103/153505771.shtml.

The market distinguishes between direct investors, who are able to participate at auction and in tenders directly but without being able to distribute the acquired debt financing instrument to the secondary market, and indirect investors, who may only purchase debt financing instruments in the secondary market. Investors may maintain bond accounts with both CCDC and SHCH.

Table 3.8: Overview of Inter-Bank Bond Market Bond Accounts at SHCH

Type of Account Holders	Number of Bond Accounts	Breakdown by Account Category		
		A	B	C
1. Policy financial banks (政策性银行)	3	–	3	–
2. Deposit-taking financial institutions (存款类金融机构)	2,237	55	2,172	10
3. Non-bank financial institutions (非银行类金融机构)	266	–	266	–
4. Securities companies (证券类金融机构)	159	–	159	–
5. Insurance agencies (保险类金融机构)	140	–	132	8
6. Nonfinancial institutions (非金融机构法人)	288	–	278	10
7. Unincorporated products (非法人产品)	19,326	–	19,325	1
8. Foreign institutions (境外机构)	1,024	–	4	1,020
9. Others (其他)	68	–	64	4
Total bond accounts	**23,511**	**55**	**22,400**	**1,056**

Notes: Data as of the end of November 2019. The account categories refer to the ability to settle. "A" can settle for one's own and other institutions. "B" can settle only for one's own institution. "C" needs to use a settlement agency to participate in the China Inter-Bank Bond Market.
Source: Shanghai Clearing House.

At the end of November 2019, SHCH reported 23,511 bond accounts for institutional investors in its book-entry system; a breakdown of the total number of bond accounts is provided in Table 3.8, with an example of the distribution by account type provided.

a.   Commercial Banks

Commercial banks—including state-owned commercial banks, joint-stock commercial banks, foreign banks, city commercial banks, rural commercial banks, and other commercial banks—are major institutional investors in the CIBM.

At present, state-owned banks, city commercial banks, and joint-stock commercial banks are the most active trading participants in the CIBM, and act as direct investors at auction and in tenders, as primary dealers for the PBOC's open market operation, as well as market makers for the CIBM. Their bid–ask quotes play an important role for guiding the market, including for the price-finding mechanism. Commercial and other banks are licensed by CBIRC and their activities in the CIBM are regulated by the PBOC.

b.   Non-Bank Financial Institutions

Non-bank financial institutions are important institutional investors with investing power in the CIBM, including financial leasing companies belonging to large enterprise groups, investment trust companies, and other financial leasing companies.

c.   Securities Companies

Securities companies are important institutional investors in the CIBM. Subject to their financial strength, their principal bond investment size may not be big. But securities companies play multiple roles as proprietary investors, financial intermediary institutions, and market makers. Securities companies are regulated by CSRC.

d.   Insurance Companies

Due to the significant amount of recurring premium income, insurance companies are important institutional investors in debt instruments, including in the CIBM. Insurance companies mostly act as direct investors. Some of the larger insurance companies, such as China Life Insurance and China Pacific Insurance Group, have also been appointed by the PBOC to act as CIBM market makers.

e.   Investment Funds

Participation by investment funds in the CIBM has grown strongly in recent years. Among them, bond funds and money market funds invest the most in the bond market. Money market funds in particular have become significant institutional investors in short-term (discount) Treasury bonds and central bank bills.

f.   Nonfinancial Institutions

Nonfinancial institutions refer to all types of enterprises and public institutions. These entities may have idle funds that are available for investment in debt instruments for value preservation, income generation, and appreciation. These institutions enter the CIBM by placing their orders via the CFAE, which routes these orders to the trading platform of CFETS for execution. Nonfinancial institutions are presently not able to use the services of a bond settlement agent. Nonfinancial institutions mostly invest in central bank bills, short-term (discount) Treasury bonds, and financial bonds.

g.   Pension and Provident Funds

The National Social Security Fund (NSSF) and the occupational pension scheme for government employees, established in 2015, have been active participants in the CIBM in recent years. The NSSF is classified as a sovereign wealth fund and serves as the national social security reserve fund to supplement and adjust social security spending, such as social insurance, in view of an aging population. The funding sources of the NSSF include fiscal allocation from the central government, the transfer of state-owned capital and fund investment proceeds, as well as capital raised by other methods approved by the State Council.[73]

---

[73] Text adapted by ABMF SF1 from the National Social Security Fund website: http://www.ssf.gov.cn/Eng_Introduction/201206/t20120620_5603.html.

Due to their prudential nature, the NSSF and other pension funds are required to focus on capital preservation and income generation, which makes them prime investors in government and government-linked debt financing instruments. The NSSF has been able to invest directly in the CIBM since April 2015, and may invest up to 20% in high-quality corporate debt financing instruments.

h.   Qualified Overseas Institutional Investors

Overseas central banks; foreign currency authorities; sovereign wealth funds; RMB clearing banks in Hong Kong, China and Macau, China; and any foreign institutional investor who is qualified as a QOII may access the CIBM to trade cash bonds and carry out other transactions approved by the PBOC without a cap on investment volumes and fund transfers. Other transactions may include foreign exchange hedging products, bond lending, bond forwards, interest rate swaps, and forward rate agreements.

Pursuant to PBOC Notice No. 3 (2016), foreign institutional investors who are able to participate in the CIBM are summarized as QOII. This grouping includes QFII and RQFII accessing the CIBM.

Foreign central banks and currency authorities, and RMB clearing banks in Hong Kong, China and Macau, China, have been able to invest in the CIBM since August 2010 when the PBOC introduced market access to foreign entities under the RQFII scheme to allow for inflows of offshore Chinese renminbi back into the domestic market.

QFII include asset management companies, insurance companies, securities firms, commercial banks, pension funds, charitable foundations, endowment funds, and sovereign wealth funds. For a detailed explanation of the QOII concept and information on the QFII and RQFII schemes and their underlying regulations, please refer to Chapter II.N.

Investment in the CIBM by QOII has increased steadily over the past several years (Figure 3.4), in line with the continuous measures by policy bodies and regulatory authorities to further liberalize access to the China bond market and capital market at large.

At the end of November 2019, CCDC maintained 1,095 bond accounts for overseas institutions, with the balance of bonds under custody reaching approximately CNY1.87 trillion, accounting for 85% of the total amount of bonds held by foreign institutions in the PRC. At the end of November 2019, SHCH maintained 1,024 bond accounts for overseas institutions, with a balance of approximately CNY0.33 trillion, representing 15% of the total amount of bonds held by foreign investors.

However, at the end of November 2019, foreign ownership of debt financing instruments and debt securities still only accounted for approximately 3.6% of the CIBM total, representing CNY2.2 trillion, or the equivalent of approximately USD313 billion at the time.

Please also see Chapter II.N for applicable regulations and limitations for nonresidents.

Figure 3.4: Foreign Holdings of CNY-Denominated Bonds

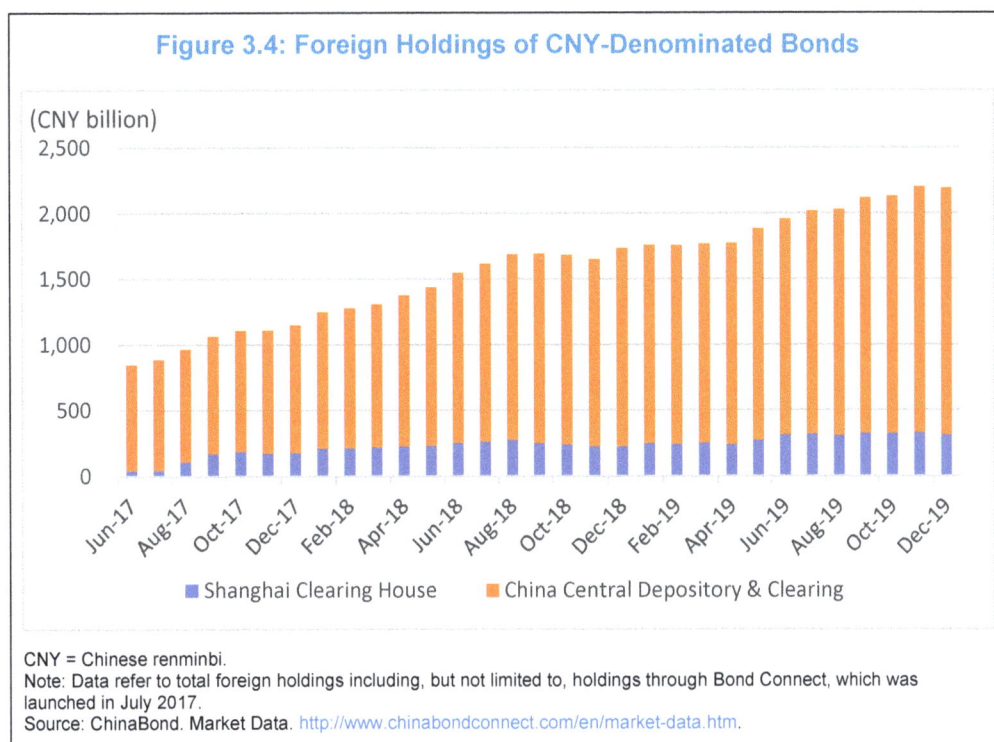

CNY = Chinese renminbi.
Note: Data refer to total foreign holdings including, but not limited to, holdings through Bond Connect, which was launched in July 2017.
Source: ChinaBond. Market Data. http://www.chinabondconnect.com/en/market-data.htm.

3.   Parties Involved in Debt Securities Issuance

The intermediary roles in the CIBM include primary dealers, dealers and underwriters, commercial banks, accounting firms, law firms, CRAs, and other entities.

a.   Primary Dealers

In contrast to other established markets, the term primary dealer in the CIBM is given to financial institutions that are able to deal directly with the PBOC (e.g., as constituents of the open market operation of the PBOC). This stems from the origins of the CIBM, which started operation in 1997 as an interbank market for the purpose of the PBOC conducting its open market operation with newly created monetary tools and the fulfillment of the refinancing needs of its constituents.

The traditional role of primary dealers (as principal actors in the primary market), particularly for sovereign bond issuances, is partly subsumed in the CIBM by the market makers (see section e below). Primary dealers may choose to also participate in government bond issuances through auction or tender in addition to being members of the interbank market. Primary dealers may also be market makers, and vice versa.

Primary dealers are selected by the PBOC.

b.   Securities Companies

Securities firms (in regulations described as securities companies) act as dealers and financial intermediaries, such as a bond settlement agent, for domestic and foreign investors wanting to access the CIBM. Dealers sell debt financing instruments issued in the CIBM as a selling agent or in an underwriter capacity. Securities companies are licensed by CSRC and the issuance of debt instruments by securities companies is also regulated by CSRC but subject to registration with NAFMII.

c.   Commercial Banks

Commercial banks may act as an underwriter or selling agent for debt financing instruments to be issued in the CIBM, as well as a bond settlement agent or a custodian. Commercial banks are licensed by CBIRC and need not be separately licensed or approved by the PBOC for participation in the CIBM or to act as underwriter for financial bonds.

However, if a commercial bank would like to act as market maker (see section e below), it will need to be appointed to that role by the PBOC. If a commercial bank would like to underwrite debt financing instruments issued by nonfinancial enterprises (corporates), it will need to obtain an Underwriting License for Debt Financing Instruments of Non-Financial Enterprises from NAFMII.

d.   Underwriters

Underwriters are financial institutions—securities firms or commercial banks—that commit to selling debt financing instruments for an issuer to investors in the CIBM. Underwriting is conducted on a firm commitment or an agency basis.

NAFMII introduced the debt financing instrument underwriting business members (债务融资工具承销业务相关会员) category in 2011. This member category is divided into the following three categories:

i.   members who have been engaged in debt financing instrument underwriting as lead underwriting members (主承销类会员),

ii.   members who have been engaged in debt financing instrument underwriting as underwriting members (承销类会员), and

iii.   members who are interested in and intend to be debt financing instrument underwriting members (意向承销类会员) in the CIBM and are voluntarily participating in the market evaluation by NAFMII.

Underwriters active in the CIBM need to obtain a license from NAFMII for the underwriting of debt financing instruments issued by nonfinancial enterprises (corporates); separate licenses exist for lead underwriters and underwriters. The lead underwriting licenses are divided into two categories, A and B.

In case an issuer appoints more than one underwriter, regulations require the designation of a lead underwriter. In the case of a public offering, the (lead) underwriter is required to submit issuance and disclosure documentation to NAFMII for the registration of the debt financing instruments. The (lead) underwriter also has an obligation to assist the issuer to conduct a debt financial instrument holders meeting if so required (see section S in this chapter for more details). If the issuer is a nonresident entity issuing Panda bonds, the (lead) underwriter acts as post-registration manager, aiding in debt financial instrument holder meetings as well as supporting the provision of continuous disclosure information as may be prescribed in the issuance documentation (please see Chapter II.G for more information).

An underwriter needs to meet the following criteria to conduct underwriting activities:

i.   registered capital of no less than CNY200 million,
ii.   relatively strong capabilities in distributing bonds,
iii.   qualified professionals engaged in bond market business and bond distribution channels,
iv.   committed no serious illicit act within the most recent 2 years, and
v.   other conditions as required by the PBOC.

A type A lead underwriter can carry out the underwriting of debt financing instruments issued by nonfinancial enterprises throughout the country; a type B lead underwriter can carry out lead underwriting business within a limited scope, must be a bank, and needs to work with a type A lead underwriter to jointly develop the lead underwriting business for 1 year.

In addition, NAFMII has established a market-based evaluation system to see if the applicants (such as banks) are eligible to be underwriters or lead underwriters of debt financing instruments in accordance with their scores.

Underwriters or debt financing instrument underwriting business members are evaluated and accredited by NAFMII through the member market evaluation index system, according to the following three types of indicators: (i) institutional qualification and business evaluation, (ii) market evaluation, and (iii) evaluation by the NAFMII Secretariat.

At the end of November 2019, there were 41 type A lead underwriters, consisting of major domestic banks and securities dealers, and 26 type B lead underwriters, most of them medium-sized city commercial banks and rural commercial banks.

As for underwriters, there were 65 at the end of November 2019. In addition to smaller urban or rural commercial banks, there are also types of institutions such as Insurance Asset Management Companies (which belong to the Insurance Asset Management Association of China), trusts, and financial companies.[74]

As of November 2019, six foreign banks had obtained the qualification for underwriting business in the CIBM. Among them, Deutsche Bank and BNP Paribas obtained a type A qualification, while HSBC and Standard Chartered Bank obtained a type B qualification, and J.P. Morgan and Citibank obtained underwriter licenses.

The PBOC restricted the business scope of foreign banks that have obtained a type B qualification to the underwriting of debt financing instruments issued by foreign nonfinancial enterprises.

At the time of the compilation of this bond market guide, NAFMII had issued the following self-regulatory rules and guidelines specific to underwriters or underwriting business:

---

[74] The Insurance Asset Management Association of China, established in September 2014, is the national SRO for the Chinese insurance asset management industry under the supervision of CBIRC. At the end of 2018, the association had 554 members from all sectors of the financial market, including 535 institutions and 11 renowned Chinese and foreign economists. For more details, see http://www.afca-asia.org/Portal.do?method=columnView&channelID=43.

- Guidelines on Post-Registration (Follow-Up) Management by Lead Underwriter of Debt Financing Instruments of Non-Financial Enterprises in the Inter-Bank Bond Market (银行间债券市场非金融企业债务融资工具主承销商后续管理工作指引) (6 April 2010) (an English translation is available from NAFMII)[75]
- Rules on Market Evaluation of NAFMII Members Participating in the Underwriting of Debt Financing Instruments of Non-Financial Enterprises (中国银行间市场交易商协会非金融企业债务融资工具承销业务相关会员市场评价规则) (8 April 2011)
- Code of Conduct for Underwriting Staff of Debt Financing Instruments of Non-Financial Enterprises in the Inter-Bank Bond Market (银行间债券市场非金融企业债务融资工具承销人员行为守则) (7 April 2012)
- Model Underwriting Agreement for Debt Financing Instruments of Non-Financial Enterprises in the Inter-Bank Bond Market (银行间债券市场非金融企业债务融资工具承销协议文本) (2 September 2013)
- Model Underwriter Syndicate Agreement for Debt Financing Instruments of Non-Financial Enterprises in the Inter-Bank Bond Market (银行间债券市场非金融企业债务融资工具承销团协议文本) (2 September 2013)
- Rules on Market Evaluation of NAFMII Members Participating in the Underwriting of Debt Financing Instruments of Non-Financial Enterprises (中国银行间市场交易商协会非金融企业债务融资工具承销业务相关会员市场评价规则) (8 April 2011)
- NAFMII Market Evaluation Criteria for Intended Underwriting Members (Banks Category) (中国银行间市场交易商协会意向承销类会员（银行类）市场评价标准) (8 July 2016)
- NAFMII Material Description for Intended Underwriting Members (Banks Category) to Participate in the Underwriting Business Market Evaluation (中国银行间市场交易商协会意向承销类会员（银行类）参与承销业务市场评价相关材料说明) (8 July 2016)
- NAFMII Materials List for Intended Underwriting Members (Banks Category) to Participate in the Underwriting Business Market Evaluation (中国银行间市场交易商协会意向承销类会员（银行类）参与承销业务市场评价相关材料清单) (8 July 2016)
- NAFMII Market Evaluation Criteria for Intended Underwriting Members (Trust Company Category) (中国银行间市场交易商协会意向承销类会员（信托公司类）市场评价标准) (7 September 2017)
- NAFMII Material Requirements for Intended Underwriting Members (Trust Company Category) to Participate in the Underwriting Business Market Evaluation (中国银行间市场交易商协会意向承销类会员（信托公司类）参与承销业务市场评价相关材料要求说明) (7 September 2017)
- NAFMII Materials List for Intended Underwriting Members (Trust Company Category) to Participate in Underwriting Business Market Evaluation (中国银行间市场交易商协会意向承销类会员（信托公司类）参与承销业务市场评价相关材料清单) (7 September 2017)

The license related to financial bonds is regulated by the PBOC. The underwriting of financial bonds does not require a specific license from the PBOC.

With the introduction of the revised Rules and Procedures for Meeting of Debt Financing Instrument Holders of Non-Financial Enterprises in the Inter-Bank Bond Market by NAFMII (published in December 2019 and effective in July 2020), underwriters are also formally recognized as a convener of debt

---

[75] See http://www.nafmii.org.cn//english/lawsandregulations/selfregulatory_e/201801/t20180110_67081.html.

financing instrument holder meetings, if so appointed by the issuer (see section R in this chapter for more details).

e.   Market Makers

The market maker (债券市场做市商) system is essential to efficiently run and develop the CIBM. According to Article 2 of the Provisions for Administering National Inter-Bank Bond Market Makers, issued by the PBOC on 9 January 2007, market maker refers to financial institutions that conduct market making activities in the CIBM upon the approval of the PBOC and enjoy the provisioned rights while assuming the corresponding obligations.[76] As of the middle of December 2019, the CIBM featured 30 market makers and 55 probationary market makers (the Chinese term "债券市场尝试做市机构 defines them as organizations with a probationary status to be a market maker in the future). The latter group comprised 48 comprehensive market makers and 7 specialized market makers.[77] Market makers are licensed and appointed by the PBOC and their performance is evaluated by NAFMII.

Pursuant to the Provisions on the Administration of Market Makers in the National Inter-Bank Bond Market (published 9 January 2007), those financial institutions wishing to apply for the role of a market maker need to be established in accordance with the laws of the PRC and shall meet the following requirements:[78]

    i.   registered capital or net capital of not less than CNY1.2 billion;
    ii.   active and within the top 80 cash transactions in the previous year when the application was submitted;
    iii.   before submitting the application, have already tried the market-making business in the CIBM and have the necessary experience and capabilities;
    iv.   sound internal management system and operating procedures, and a sound internal risk control mechanism, incentives, and assessment mechanism;
    v.   strong bond market research and analysis capabilities;
    vi.   relevant business departments with more than five qualified bond practitioners with reasonable post settings and clear responsibilities;
    vii.   no illegal or major violations in the 2 years before the application is submitted; and
    viii.   other conditions stipulated by the PBOC.

A market maker may be entitled to (i) the convenience of purchasing bonds in the primary market; and (ii) gaining priority to become a member of the underwriting syndicates for government bonds or bonds of governmental development financial institutions, or a primary dealer for participation in open market operation.

A market maker, in accordance with the relevant requirements, continuously makes bilateral quotations for the purchase and sale of those debt financing instruments in the CIBM for which market making is required, and then transacts with other market participants on the basis of its quotations. Nonfinancial institutions placing orders via the CFAE are only able to enter into trades with market makers, which send their quotes to CFAE for display.

---

[76] See http://www.asianlii.org/cn/legis/cen/laws/pfanibmm628/.
[77] For a list of market makers, please refer to http://www.chinamoney.com.cn/english/mdtmmbrmm/.
[78] See http://www.fdi.gov.cn/1800000121_23_60931_0_7.html.

In recent years, market makers have quoted more varieties across more maturities of bonds, which has enhanced the quality and continuity of quotations in the market. The added variety has also improved CIBM liquidity as well as strengthened the formation of a market yield curve and better price discovery.

At the time of compilation of this bond market guide, NAFMII had issued the following self-regulatory rules related to market making:

- Guidelines on Market Making Operations in the Inter-Bank Bond Market (银行间债券市场做市业务指引) (4 August 2016), and
- Assessment Indicators for Market Making Operations in the Inter-Bank Bond Market (银行间债券市场做市业务评价指标体系) (4 August 2016).

f.   Trustee Agent or Bond Trustee

The concept of a bond trustee (受托管理人) was introduced for debt financing instruments registered with NAFMII, together with corresponding rules, in December 2019 with effectivity from July 2020. Previously, some of the functions typically associated with a trustee agent, such as the administration of bondholder meetings, were performed in the CIBM by the lead underwriter.

Bond trustees could be the lead underwriter of a debt financing instrument, a financial asset management company, a trust company acting as an underwriter, or a law or other professional firm with experience in the debt financing instrument business.

The function of a trustee agent continues for debt financing instruments in the CIBM not registered with NAFMII such as financial bonds or other instruments approved by the PBOC. However, the PBOC may also introduce a formal trustee concept in the future.

Please see sections Q and S in this chapter for more information on CIBM practices commensurate with the typical obligations of a bond trustee.

g.   Guarantor

In the event that an issuer of debt financing instruments needs to improve their attractiveness or chances to be able to issue at all, a guarantor with an appropriate credit rating may be appointed. Guarantors may be commercial banks, securities companies, or other enterprises. A guarantor does not need approval from the PBOC.

h.   Bond Settlement Agent

Bond settlement agent is the term used in the CIBM for a qualified institution to provide the combined service of facilitating trading and settlement for foreign investors and those domestic investors that are not able to directly participate in the CIBM. Bond settlement agents can be securities firms or commercial banks. Depending on their license, bond settlement agents may also carry out securities trading on behalf of their clients, in addition to settlement and safekeeping services. Foreign investors wanting to invest in the CIBM through CIBM Direct will need to appoint a bond settlement agent as their primary service provider in the CIBM.

Pursuant to the Administrative Rules for the Issuance of Financial Bonds in the National Inter-Bank Bond Market and the Notice of the People's Bank of China on the Relevant Issues Concerning Launching the Bond Settlement Agent

Business, the term "bond settlement agent" refers to a financial corporation authorized by other market participants to conduct bond settlement and other business transactions for them. Bond settlement agents need to obtain PBOC approval prior to commencing their activities.

The bond settlement agent business includes

i.   opening of a trading account at and network connection with CFETS in the name of the client;

ii. opening or canceling of a bond custody account for a client in the client's name at CCDC or SHCH, and related activities;

iii. carrying out settlement activities for a client according to the instructions of the client;

iv. receiving (for a client) payment of bond interest and repayment of bond principal; and

v.   conducting bond transactions with clients, including cash bond transactions and reverse repo transactions with nonfinancial institutions.

At the time of compilation of this bond market guide, the PBOC had approved 49 bond settlement agents, of which 19 institutions had the capabilities to service foreign investors. A list of bond settlement agents accessing CFETS is available from the CFETS website, if presently only in Chinese.[79]

i.   Central Securities Depositories

The CIBM is serviced by CCDC and SHCH as CSDs with a focus on different debt financing instrument types and maturities. Both CSDs are state-owned financial market infrastructures responsible for the registration, clearing, settlement, safekeeping, margin management, and collateral management for direct and indirect transactions in debt financing instruments under their remit. In addition, SHCH may act as central counterparty (CCP) in the transactions executed by its account holders on CFETS, across all instrument types deposited with SHCH, if both trading counterparties are clearing members and agree to use the CCP service; this can be decided at the time of trade or when instructing SHCH. The use of the CCP for fixed income transaction settlement is not mandatory.

CCDC was established in 1996 under the approval of the State Council and was subsequently appointed by the MOF as the general depository for Treasury bonds and operator of the Bond Issuance System managed by the PBOC.

SHCH focuses on newer debt financing instruments and other products, and also clears and settles foreign exchange and derivatives transactions, as well as structured products. SHCH was established on 28 November 2009 under a directive of the PBOC.

Both CCDC and SHCH maintain accounts for the CMU of the Hong Kong Monetary Authority as part of the Bond Connect market access scheme. The CMU is the nominee holder of the debt financing instruments registered with either CCDC or SHCH.

---

[79] See http://www.chinamoney.com.cn/chinese/mtmemrmb/.

j.   Law Firms

A law firm or legal counsel is required to provide a legal opinion on the issuer, the issuance documentation, and disclosure items for debt financing instruments intended to be registered with NAFMII or otherwise issued in the CIBM.
Law firms involved in the issuance of debt financing instruments in the CIBM do not require approval from the PBOC. However, law firms acting for issuers in the CIBM need to be registered with NAFMII.

In addition, law firms at the domicile of a nonresident issuer of Panda bonds are involved in the issuance of such bonds in the CIBM, as regulations require them to provide a legal opinion on the issuer at the time of the registration of the proposed debt financing instrument with NAFMII or the request for approval from the PBOC, as the case may be. Please also see Chapter II.F for the complete description of the regulatory processes for issuances by nonresidents.

k.   Accounting Firms

Accounting firms involved in the financial audit of issuers of debt financing instruments in the CIBM, compilation or audit of the relevant financial statements, or compilation of issuance documentation and supporting documents are subject to supervision by the MOF as the regulator for accounting subjects in the PRC. Accounting firms must be a member of NAFMII to provide services to issuers.

N.   Definition of Professional Investors

Traditionally, the underlying laws and regulations governing the CIBM contained no formal concept or definition of a professional investor category. Instead, the use of the term "professional" had often been taken to mean experienced At the same time, investors in the CIBM have nearly exclusively been financial firms or professional investment institutions, by their own assessment and using typical definitions applied in the international bond markets. In addition, a registration with NAFMII prior to participation in the CIBM ensured a vetting of qualifications.

The introduction of the Rules for Private Placement of Debt Financing Instruments of Non-Financial Enterprises in the Inter-Bank Bond Market by NAFMII in 2011, defining the concept of DIIs, formalized the existence of a category of institutional investors that—for all intents and purposes—could be considered professional by international standards. In late 2015, NAFMII added the category of SII and even published a positive list of such investors specializing in investments in debt financing instruments.

1.   Designated Institutional Investors

On 29 April 2011, NAFMII issued the Rules for Private Placement of Debt Financing Instruments of Non-Financial Enterprises in the Inter-Bank Bond Market (银行间债券市场非金融企业债务融资工具非公开定向发行规则), No. 6 (2011 Rules). Through these rules, NAFMII introduced both the private placement method (非公开定向发行, see Chapter III.E for a definition of this issuance method) and the concept of DIIs (特定机构投资人) or private placement investors (定向投资人).

The 2011 Rules stipulated that the term "private placement" (非公开定向发行) refers to the issuance of debt financing instruments by nonfinancial enterprises to a category of DIIs (特定机构投资人) in the CIBM, in effect a private placement to institutional investors who are subject to eligibility criteria and compliance with certain practices to maintain their status. Stipulating a private placement also meant that such placements can only be transferred within the scope of DIIs, creating a closed, near-professional market.

Consequently, debt financing instruments issued via the private placement method (非公开定向发行方式发行的债务融资工具) are referred to as privately placed debt financing instruments (非公开定向债务融资工具), or simply private placement instruments (定向工具).

The term private placement investors (定向投资人) used in the rules stems from the prescribed practice that an issuer or its appointed underwriter had to specifically identify (i.e., designate), upon every issuance, a list of institutional investors to which the debt financing instruments could be offered and issued.

Private placement investors who want to invest in private placement instruments should issue a written confirmation letter to NAFMII and confirm they are aware of the investment risk(s) of the private placement instruments, have the ability and willingness to assume the investment risk of the privately placed instruments, voluntarily accept the management by NAFMII of the CIBM participants, and fulfill any membership obligations.

2. Specialized Institutional Investors

The Rules for the Registration and Issuance of Debt Financing Instruments of Non-Financial Enterprises (非金融企业债务融资工具注册发行规则), issued by NAFMII on 6 November 2015 (2015 Rules), revised the 2011 Rules and introduced the concept of the SII (专项机构投资人).

Under the 2015 Rules, enterprises were able to issue private placement instruments to DIIs as well as SIIs. Article 20 of the 2015 Rules stipulated that SIIs refer to institutional investors who, in addition to having significant experience in CIBM investment and risk identification, are familiar with the risk characteristics and investment process of private placement instruments, have the willingness and ability to take risks, voluntarily accept the market participant management of NAFMII as the SRO for the CIBM, and fulfill any member obligations.

SIIs are selected by NAFMII in accordance with market principles and in line with the procedures determined by its Governing Council. For SIIs to invest in private placement instruments, they may have to sign a "private placement agreement" (定向发行协议), accept the rights and obligations stipulated in the agreement, and recognize the specific level of information disclosure described in the agreement.

To clarify the new rules and standardize the selection process for private placement investors, NAFMII issued the Provisions for the Selection of Specialized Institutional Investors of Private Placement Notes (定向债务融资工具专项机构投资人遴选细则) on 26 November 2015 and published a formal definition of an SII. Pursuant to Article 3 of the provisions, an institution that meets one of the following conditions may become an SII:

    i.   PBOC open market business-level dealer (中国人民银行公开市场业务一级交易商),

    ii.   market maker in the Inter-Bank Bond Market (银行间债券市场做市商),

    iii.   Inter-Bank Bond Market bond settlement agent (银行间债券市场债券结算代理人),

    iv.   debt financing instruments underwriting agency (债务融资工具承销机构),

    v.   credit risk mitigation tool core trader or credit risk slow-release voucher creation institution (信用风险缓释工具核心交易商或信用风险缓释凭证创设机构), or

vi.   institutional investor whose average deposited debt financing instruments reach a certain size (债务融资工具平均托管量达到一定规模的机构投资人).

In Article 4 of the provisions, NAFMII listed 120 SIIs that fulfilled the criteria established in Article 3. The list is reviewed on an annual basis. At the time of the compilation of this bond market guide, the list contained 180 investors.

3.   Wholesale Investors versus Retail Investors

Regulations relevant for the CIBM do not carry an official definition of what constitutes, for example, a wholesale investor or a retail, general, or public investor. References to the term wholesale in the primary market can usually be found in relation to Treasury bonds and other public sector bonds, which are underwritten by syndicated participants, and to other types of bonds offered through a book-building or subscription process. References to retail in the primary market tend to describe the issuing of bonds to the public through a resale from syndicated participants.

O.   Credit Rating Requirements

This section details the actual domestic credit rating requirements for debt financing instruments issued in the CIBM and the application of those credit rating requirements in the issuance process. For information on CRAs and their underlying regulations, please refer to Chapter II.O.

1.   Credit Rating Overview

The PBOC serves as the main supervisory authority of the credit rating industry. As such, it is mainly responsible for drafting relevant rules and regulations governing the credit rating system and for drawing up development strategies and policies, among other responsibilities (Table 3.9). CSRC supervises credit ratings in the exchange bond market, while NDRC oversees credit ratings for enterprise bonds. Issuers pay the credit rating cost and request CRAs to evaluate bonds.

Table 3.9: Credit Rating Regulations and Provisions for the Inter-Bank Bond Market

Regulations and Measures on the Credit Ratings for the Issuance of Bonds and Notes   • Administrative Rules for the Issuance of Financial Bonds in the National Inter-Bank Bond Market   • Administrative Measures for Debt Financing Instruments of Non-Financial Enterprises in the Inter-Bank Bond Market   • Provisional Administrative Rules on International Development Institutions' Issuance of RMB Bonds
People's Bank of China Announcement No. 22, 2004   • Notice of the People's Bank of China on Strengthening the Management of Credit Rating Practices in the Inter-Bank Bond Market   • Guiding Opinions of the People's Bank of China for the Management of Credit Ratings   • Specification for Credit Rating in the Credit Market and Inter-Bank Bond Market

Source: ASEAN+3 Bond Market Forum Sub-Forum 1 team compiled from public domain sources.

In November 2006, the PBOC released the Specification for Credit Rating in the Credit Market and Inter-Bank Bond Market, which contained a unified definition for the classification, symbol, and meaning of short-, medium-, and long-term credit ratings in the CIBM.

Table 3.10: Credit Rating Ranks for Short-Term Bonds in the Inter-Bank Bond Market

Credit Rank	Meaning
A-1	Strongest capacity to repay the loan and accrued interest, with the highest security
A-2	Relatively strong capacity to repay the loan and accrued interest, with relatively high security
A-3	Moderate capacity to repay the loan and accrued interest, with security that is vulnerable to an unfavorable economic environment
B	Relatively weak capacity to repay the loan and accrued interest, and somewhat vulnerable to default risk
C	Very weak capacity to repay the loan and accrued interest, with relatively high default risk
D	Unable to repay the loan and accrued interest

Note: Slight adjustment to each rank is not allowed.
Source: People's Bank of China.

Table 3.11: Credit Rating Ranks for Medium-Term and Long-Term Bonds in the Inter-Bank Bond Market

Credit Rank	Meaning
AAA	Extremely strong capacity to pay the debt, free from the influence of an unfavorable economic environment, and extremely low default risk
AA	Very strong capacity to pay the debt, insignificantly affected by an unfavorable economic environment, and very low default risk
A	Relatively strong capacity to pay the debt, relatively easy to be affected by an unfavorable economic environment, and relatively low default risk
BBB	Moderate capacity to pay the debt, somewhat significantly affected by an unfavorable economic environment, and moderate default risk
BB	Relatively weak capacity to pay the debt, significantly affected by an unfavorable economic environment, and relatively high default risk
B	The capacity to pay the debt somewhat mainly dependent on a sound economic environment, and very high default risk
CCC	The capacity to pay the debt extremely dependent on a sound economic environment, and extremely high default risk
CC	Relatively weak protection in case of bankruptcy or reorganization, with capacity to pay the debt that can hardly be guaranteed
C	Unable to pay the debt

Note: Except for AAA, CCC, and ranks below CCC, a "+" or "−" can be used for a slight adjustment to indicate a slightly higher or lower grade than that of the corresponding rank.
Source: People's Bank of China.

Table 3.10 shows the credit rating ranks for short-term bonds and Table 3.11 for medium-term and long-term bonds in the CIBM. The credit rating ranks for short-term bonds in the CIBM can be divided into six levels in four classes: A-1, A-2, A-3, B, C, and D. No slight adjustment may be made to each rank. The ranks of credit rating for medium-term and long-term bonds are divided into nine levels in three classes: AAA, AA, A, BBB, BB, B, CCC, CC, and C. Slight adjustments are possible and expressed by the use of "–" and "+" indicators.

2.   General Credit Rating Practices in the Inter-Bank Bond Market

In the CIBM, the credit rating business is examined and supervised by the PBOC. Pursuant to PBOC regulations and depending on the type of offering, all institutions planning to issue bonds in the CIBM and the bond itself have to be rated by a bond CRA that is registered with NAFMII.

The credit rating requirement is mandatory for public offerings of debt financing instruments, including Panda bonds, and one rating is accepted for the registration of debt financing instruments with NAFMII. An exception exists for commercial paper and SCP, for which only an issuer rating is required due to the very short tenor of these instruments. A credit rating for debt financing instruments issued via private placements, also including Panda bonds, is not mandated for registration with NAFMII, and may be subject to agreement between issuer and investors. An issuer may choose to have different bond issues or issuance programs rated by different CRAs, which in consequence may lead to multiple issuer ratings.

In addition to the initial credit rating for the bonds, the qualified CRA is required to perform the so-called track rating (i.e., a periodical review of the credit rating at issuance during the lifecycle of the bonds). The issuer should include the track rating arrangements in the issuance and disclosure documentation upon issuance and in the registration application with NAFMII, and publish the same via a website accredited by NAFMII such as DCM-FANS. Domestic government bonds and PFBs are exempted from the credit rating requirements.

The CRA should also rate the issuer planning to issue a guaranteed bond, a bond with a mortgage, or a bond with appreciated value if a guarantee or security service is provided.

The issuance of a financial bond is subject to credit rating by a competent CRA. After the issuance of a financial bond, the CRA shall conduct a follow-up credit rating for the bond on an annual basis. In the event of the occurrence of any important event that may affect the credit rating of the financial bond, the CRA shall adjust the credit rating of the financial bond in a timely manner and disclose the relevant information to the investors.

3.   Credit Rating Practices for Panda Bonds

Pursuant to the relevant regulations of the PBOC and the MOF, and the rules of NAFMII, a minimum of one credit rating assigned by a qualified CRA in the CIBM is accepted for the registration of Panda bonds. Most Panda bond issuers have an investment-grade rating by an international CRA as an observed practice, which is equivalent to a AAA rating in the PRC.

On 25 September 2018, the PBOC and the MOF officially implemented the Interim Measures for the Administration of the Issuance of Bonds by Overseas Institutions in the National Inter-Bank Bond Market (PBOC and MOF Announcement No. 16, 2018). Article 7 of these measures stipulates that credit rating reports and follow-up rating arrangements (if any) are optional. At the same time, if an overseas institutional issuer wishes to publicly disclose a credit rating (report), the credit rating shall be issued by a CRA accredited in the CIBM and registered with NAFMII.

With the above measures coming into effect, the Interim Measures for the Administration of the Issuance of RMB Bonds by International Development Institutions (2010 Revision) were formally abolished.

4.   Credit Rating Practices for Private Placements

In the case of an issuance of debt financing instruments via a private placement, including Panda bonds, a credit rating is not mandatory. In fact, the issuance documentation and disclosure practices agreed between issuer and investors can include specific provisions for the credit rating and tracking practices for each individual issuance, as stipulated in particular for Panda bonds, in Article 23 of the NAFMII Guidelines for Panda bond issuance.

5.   Credit Rating Practices for Commercial Paper

Pursuant to Article 9 of the NAFMII Guidelines on the Issuance of Commercial Paper of Non-Financial Enterprises in the Inter-Bank Bond Market, promulgated in 2008, if the main credit level of an enterprise becomes lower than the credit level at the time of issuance registration, the issuance registration of commercial paper will automatically expire, and NAFMII will publicly announce this development.

P.   Financial Guarantee Institution

The issuance of bonds within the PRC does not require the issuer to provide guarantees for bond issuance, but the issuer of debt financing instruments can independently adopt third-party guarantees, asset mortgages, pledge guarantees, and other credit enhancement mechanisms to improve solvency or the attractiveness of the debt securities to be issued.

One such institution providing financial guarantee services or corporate credit enhancement services for debt financing instruments in the CIBM is the China Bond Insurance Co. Ltd., based in Beijing.[80]

Q.   Market Features for Investor Protection

The CIBM features a number of mechanisms that are aimed at protecting general or public investors. In the Opinions of the General Office of the State Council on Further Strengthening the Protection of the Legal Rights and Interests of Small and Medium-Sized Investors in the Capital Market, 2013, the safeguarding of the legitimate rights and interests of small and medium-sized investors was declared the top priority of the regulatory authorities in the securities and futures markets.

Investor protection is also highlighted in the regulations governing Panda bond issuance in that the nonresident issuer has to appoint an independent entity to ensure that certain investor protection mechanisms are in place (see section 3 for details).

Features in the CIBM, and those inherent to the capital market in the PRC, with a specific focus on investor protection are explained in the following sections.

---

[80] This has been reported by Bloomberg. The website of China Bond Insurance Co., Ltd. is presently only available in Chinese at http://www.cbicl.com.cn.

1.   Regulatory Framework

As guidance to regulatory authorities on how to further develop the capital market, the State Council published its Opinions on Further Promoting the Healthy Development of the Capital Market in 2014. Article 29 emphasized the improvement of the investor suitability system to strictly manage the appropriateness of investors; strengthen the voting mechanism of small and medium-sized investors in public companies, optimize the investor return mechanism, and improve the diversified dispute resolution and investor damage compensation mechanism. The State Council has also advocated for institutional investors, such as securities investment funds, to participate in the performance reviews of listed companies to exercise their rights on behalf of public investors (公众投资者).

The PBOC established a set of mechanisms to ensure the proper sharing of risks among issuers, market participants, intermediaries, and investors. These mechanisms specify obligations and responsibilities of underwriters, accounting firms, law firms, CRAs, and other intermediaries.

NDRC emphasizes protecting the investors' interests and encourages and guides issuers and underwriters to explore effective methods to improve credit worthiness and raise funds. NDRC also focuses on a reduction of risk and has introduced the concept of bondholders' meetings for enterprise bonds, a debt proxy system, and the mortgage assets supervisor system. It requests issuers to formulate a practical and feasible debt repayment plan and safeguard measures, and encourages issuers to obtain a guarantee for the debt repayment.

NAFMII promotes investor protection mechanisms in the nonfinancial enterprise debt capital market. It formulated self-regulatory rules, such as the Rules and Procedures for Meeting of Debt Financing Instrument Holders of Non-Financial Enterprises in the Inter-Bank Bond Market (银行间债券市场非金融企业债务融资工具持有人会议规程), revised with effect from 1 July 2020. The NAFMII document sets clear conditions for the need to organize a debt financing instrument holder meeting.

Under these rules, the issuer shall agree in the prospectus or other offering document on the convener (召集人) of the debt financing instrument holder meeting. The convener is responsible for organizing a debt financing instrument holder meeting to solicit and collect the views of holders of debt financing instruments on material events, and to perform the duties of information disclosure and support the raising of required documentation and their retention.

Under provisions in the PBOC's Guidelines on the Issuance of Non-Financial Enterprises Medium-Term Notes in the Inter-Bank Bond Market, the issuer shall state the applicable investor protection mechanism(s) in the offering document when issuing MTN, including effective measures to be taken to cope with any downgrading of the credit rating, a deterioration of the financial status of the issuer, or other situations that may affect investors' interests, as well as details on claim arrangements in case of events of default.

2.   Investor Complaints

Investor complaints in the CIBM are handled by NAFMII. As the SRO in the CIBM, NAFMII mediates disputes between its members. For this, NAFMII promotes communication among the parties to reach agreements. With regard to alleged misconduct that may violate self-regulatory rules, NAFMII takes self-disciplinary actions on the members after an in-depth investigation. For activities that might violate relevant laws and regulations, NAFMII may transfer the cases to the competent authorities in accordance with the law enforcement arrangements in the CIBM.

3.   Bond Trustee Concept

Until the end of 2019, the CIBM had not featured a formalized concept for a bond trustee or debt financing instrument holder's representative similar to the one available in the exchange bond market, or in other regional markets. In December 2019, NAFMII introduced guidelines for a bond trustee concept and related transitional notices as well as their application in rules for debt financing instrument holder meetings for debt financing instruments (to be) registered with NAFMII. These guidelines and rules take effect from 1 July 2020. Please see section S in this chapter for more details on the bond trustee concept.

At the same time, past regulations already required the inclusion of provisions for bondholder representation, meetings, and resulting procedures in the issuance documentation for debt financing instruments to ensure that basic investor protection features were in place.

As an example, Article 25 of the PBOC Interim Measures (for Panda bond issuance) stipulated that overseas issuers shall establish investor protection mechanisms and engage an entity within the PRC that is independent from the issuer to safeguard the interest of debt financing instrument holders during the life of the debt financing instrument. Such independent entities shall act diligently, independently, and fairly, and oversee the issuer to implement the investor protection mechanisms including, among other things, disclosing material events and convening debt financing instrument holder meetings. This function was also referred to in market practice as a "post-registration manager" and is typically performed by the (lead) underwriter of a bond issuance. In principle, the referenced entity performs a function similar to a dedicated bond trustee or bondholders' representative in other markets.

4.   Introduction and Application of Investor Protection Covenants

As part of its commitment to ensuring investor protection in the CIBM, NAFMII has been promoting the introduction and use by market participants of investor protection covenants. NAFMII first published examples of investor protection clauses in September 2016 and formally published its Model Investor Protection Clauses (投资人保护条款示范) in April 2019.

Please also see Chapter IX.A.1 for more information on the model clauses.

5.   Deposit Insurance

The PRC introduced a bank deposit insurance scheme on 31 March 2015. The insurance scheme took effect on 1 May 2015. The Deposit Insurance Act, passed by the 67th Executive Meeting of the State Council, gave rise to the launch of the insurance program, which covers deposits of up to CNY500,000.

6.   Investor Protection Fund or Similar Mechanism

Due to the nature of the CIBM as an OTC market, a single investor protection fund or similar mechanism is not available. At the same time, the CIBM features inherent investor protections through market mechanisms such as investor screening and the eligibility criteria and registration of market participants including issuers, investors, and intermediaries.

7.   Foreign Investors

Foreign institutional investors designated as QOII—including QFII and RQFII (see also Chapter II.N for more details)—are afforded the same rights as domestic investors and occupy the same creditor positions as domestic investors, including in the event of nonpayment of interest or principal on a bond or note, a default by the issuer or the issuer's bankruptcy or insolvency.

Most institutions and market infrastructure providers in the CIBM—or securities market at large—provide information in English in official materials and on their websites.

R.   Debt Financing Instrument Holder Meeting

Rules for debt financing instrument holder meetings related to debt financing instruments issued in the CIBM are defined through NAFMII rules and guidelines since they are not contained in fundamental or key legislation such as the Company Law.

To effectively support the concept of a debt financing instrument holders meeting, NAFMII established an investor protection framework, which defines the triggers for and conduct of debt financing instrument holder meetings and their expected outcome. The framework contains clauses for investor protection for issuance and disclosure documentation related to those debt financing instruments issued in the CIBM that are (to be) registered with NAFMII. The latest rules on meetings of debt financing instrument holders were published by NAFMII in December 2019 and take effect in July 2020.

NAFMII also stipulates in its rules and guidelines that Panda bond (nonresident) issuers shall specify, in their registration and offering documents of their debt financing instruments (to be) registered with NAFMII, the relevant arrangements for debt financing instrument holder meetings and related practices.

Due to the underlying nature of NCD as a money market instrument, there are no provisions in regulations for NCD holder meetings. Market feedback confirmed that no NCD holder meeting has been held in the CIBM since the market's inception. Other than their short tenors, this is also attributed to the fact that NCD issuers are deposit-taking financial institutions with a high credit rating and that issuers have to file their planned issuances with the PBOC on an annual basis prior to any issuance.

1.   Appointment of a Convener

In the Rules and Procedures for Meeting of Debt Financing Instrument Holders of Non-Financial Enterprises in the Inter-Bank Bond Market (revised), published on 27 December 2019 and effective 1 July 2020, NAFMII emphasized the role of a convener (召集人) of the debt financing instrument holder meeting. The role of convener had been introduced in the earlier version of the rules issued in 2013. The issuer will need to name the convener in the issuance documentation.

The convener is expected to be the lead underwriter, which ensures continuity as the respective tasks of the convener were previously also typically carried out by the lead underwriter, under a less formalized arrangement.

The convener is responsible for (i) organizing meetings of debt financing instrument holders to request and collect the views of holders of debt financing instruments on important matters, (ii) carrying out duties relating to information disclosure and the creation of documents for that purpose, and (iii) retaining all relevant documents for the relevant periods.

2.   Triggers of Debt Financing Instrument Holder Meeting

The revised Rules and Procedures for Meeting of Debt Financing Instrument Holders of Non-Financial Enterprises in the Inter-Bank Bond Market (银行间债券市场非金融企业债务融资工具持有人会议规程 (修订稿)), effective 1 July 2020, contain a number of prescriptions for the triggers of a debt financing instrument holders meeting during the lifecycle of a debt financing instrument; the relevant provisions can be found in Article 9.[81]

Accordingly, the convener shall convene a meeting of the debt financing instrument holders (持有人会议) if one of the following circumstances arises:

i.   the principal or interest of the debt financing instruments or other domestic and foreign bonds issued by the issuer fails to be paid in full and on time as agreed;

ii.   the issuer intends to transfer the debt financing instrument to pay off the obligation;

iii.   the issuer intends to change the credit enhancement arrangement of the debt financing instrument or the credit enhancement arrangement, and the institution providing credit enhancement services has a major adverse change in solvency;

iv.   the issuer intends to reduce capital, merge, separate, or dissolve, file for bankruptcy, be ordered to stop production and suspend business, be suspended, or have the license revoked or suspended;

v.   the issuer may, for example, reduce its net assets by more than 10% of the last audited net assets or exceed the net assets of the latest period within 24 months as a result of a proposed asset sale, transfer, nonreimbursable transfer, debt relief, correction of accounting errors, accounting policies (except for changes in requirements such as laws, administrative regulations, or national uniform accounting systems) or changes in accounting estimates, or the net assets of the issuer, or in the event of a significant adverse effect on the sustained and sound operation;

vi.   the issuer has a situation that could result in the loss of actual control over an important subsidiary;

vii.   the issuer intends to carry out a major asset reorganization;

viii.   proposed dismissal or change of bond trustee, or change of bond trustee agreement terms involving rights and obligations of the debt financing instrument holders;

ix.   a written proposal is made by the debt financing instrument holders holding more than 30% of the balance of the debt financing instrument, individually or collectively, for the same period;

x.   the circumstances in which the meeting of the holders shall be held as agreed in the issuance document; and

xi.   other circumstances as prescribed by laws, regulations, and relevant self-regulation rules shall be decided by the meeting of the debt financing instrument holders.

Pursuant to the NAFMII Rules for Information Disclosure on Debt Financing Instruments of Non-Financial Enterprises in the Inter-Bank Bond Market (银行间债券市场非金融企业债务融资工具信息披露规则), effective on 18 December 2017, the issuer of a debt financing instrument will need to disclose during the lifetime of that instrument any material event that may affect its solvency; this includes, but may not be limited to, the reasons given above leading to a debt financing instrument holder meeting.[82]

---

[81] See http://www.nafmii.org.cn/ggtz/gg/201912/t20191227_78733.html.
[82] See http://www.nafmii.org.cn/zlgz/201712/t20171212_66667.html.

3.   Attendance by the Bond Trustee

Pursuant to the Guidelines for Bond Trustee Business of Non-Financial Enterprise Debt Financing Instruments in the Inter-Bank Bond Market (for Trial Implementation), effective 1 July 2020, the bond trustee appointed to a debt financing instrument is required to attend any meeting of debt financing instrument holders or to remain informed about such proceedings.

S.   Bond Trustee or Trustee

A dedicated bond trustee (受托管理人) concept in the CIBM did not exist until the end of 2019, although NAFMII had previously prescribed a number of investor protection roles commonly attributed to a trustee in other markets.[83]

At the same time, regulations set by the PBOC and NAFMII include provisions for the issuer of debt financing instruments in the CIBM, including for nonresident issuers of Panda bonds, to describe specific investor protection mechanisms in their issuance documentation such as the practices for holding meetings of debt financing instrument holders and the corresponding procedures. A general trustee function is also evident in the context of structured instruments such as ABS or ABN.

1.   Introduction of a Bond Trustee

NAFMII published the Guidelines for Bond Trustee Business of Non-Financial Enterprise Debt Financing Instruments in the Inter-Bank Bond Market (for Trial Implementation) (银行间债券市场非金融企业债务融资工具受托管理人业务指引(试行)) and its related supporting notices on the Transitional Arrangements on Recording Matters Related to Bond Trustee Business (过渡期安排的通知/受托管理业务相关备案事项的通知) on 27 December 2019, with an effective date from 1 July 2020; NAFMII indicated that other corresponding notices may be published to further refine the function and related practices by the effective date; the bond trustee, the bond trustee agreement, and related obligations and activities were subsequently described in the Registration Documents and Forms for Non-Financial Enterprises Publicly Offering Debt Financing Instruments, issued by NAFMII in April 2020 and effective from 1 July 2020.

According to the guidelines, effective from 1 July 2020, the issuer shall appoint a bond trustee for the holders of any debt financing instrument issued by a nonfinancial enterprise and sign a bond trustee agreement (受托管理协议) that meets the requirements of the guidelines.[84]

NAFMII administers the bond trustees and may implement mechanisms to evaluate their performance. The following institutions may apply to NAFMII to act as bond trustee:

---

[83] The English term "bond trustee," as suggested in an unofficial translation of the guidelines, is a concept originating from common law. The concept of a bond trustee in a jurisdiction with an original civil law tradition may not represent the concept of the bond trustee as defined in common law jurisdictions. Other markets with a civil law tradition instead use terms such as "bondholder representative." At the same time, English translations of the Chinese term "受托管理人" have been using bond trustee, likely to limit the application of the concept to the bond market. Therefore, this bond market guide is using the English term bond trustee based on the current practice by NAFMII and for consistency.

[84] The Chinese term "受托管理协议" translates into "bond trustee management agreement" or "bond trustee agreement." In view of the fact that the words trustee and management in the same term are potentially ambiguous as management in the capital market is an activity typically defined and regulated separately from trustee activities. As such, the term bond trustee agreement is used in this bond market guide throughout.

   i.   the lead underwriter of the debt financing instrument;

   ii.   a financial asset management company holding a financial license;

   iii.   a trust company with business qualification as an underwriter of debt financing instruments; and

   iv.   a law firm or other professional institutions with experience in debt financing instruments.

Once the relevant institution meets all qualification criteria set out in the guidelines, it may file the application and documents prescribed in the related NAFMII notice.

The applicant will need to establish a dedicated bond trustee team and mechanisms to prevent any conflicts of interest such as a firewall concept or separation of personnel. The guarantor of a bond or the law firm advising the issuer for an issuance are not able to act as the bond trustee for the debt financing instrument. Any residual conflict of interest situation, such as a capital affiliation between the issuer and bond trustee, is to be disclosed in the bond trustee agreement.

The guidelines prescribe fiduciary duties for the bond trustee that include

   i.   managing and safeguarding the legitimate rights and interests of debt financing instrument holders;

   ii.   participating in debt restructuring efforts on behalf of the holders;

   iii.   applying for asset retention, filing a lawsuit, or for arbitration on behalf of the holders;

   iv.   participating in insolvency proceedings on behalf of the holders; and

   v.   other duties as may be prescribed in the bond trustee agreement.

The duties described above include the need to obtain certification of guarantees for a debt financing instrument, if so applicable. The trustee has to report to debt financing instrument holders if any of the above conditions or a change to its duties or the ability to carry out these duties occurs; specific time frames for individual duties may apply.

With the formalization of a bond trustee concept, the change of bond trustee for a debt financing instrument registered with NAFMII has become a reason for the convening of a debt financing instrument holder meeting (see section R for details).

2. Use of a General Trustee

In the context of the issuance and administration of ABS or ABN, the term "trustee" is used in the text of regulations and in documentation. Here, separate from the bond trustee, the term trustee is used to describe the function of an administrator of an ABS and potential issuer of an ABN, with the specific role of collecting cash flows and facilitating the repayment of principal and interest to investors, whether that be in the form of a financial institution as service provider or as a special purpose vehicle.

T.   Bankruptcy and Insolvency Provisions

1. Bankruptcy Provisions

In the PRC, provisions on bankruptcy mainly consist of the prescriptions in the Enterprise Bankruptcy Law (中华人民共和国企业破产法), which came into effect on 1 June 2007; the Company Law; the Securities Law; the Commercial Bank Law; as well as other relevant laws and regulations.[85]

---

[85] Information in part adapted from http://en.wikipedia.org/wiki/Bankruptcy_in_the_People's_Republic_of_China.

According to Article 7 (2) of the Enterprise Bankruptcy Law, a creditor shall be entitled to ask the debtor to declare bankruptcy. If a legal person that is an enterprise cannot repay due debts and its assets are insufficient to pay off all the debt or it apparently lacks solvency, it should resolve its debt in accordance with the prescriptions in the Enterprise Bankruptcy Law. In addition to the provisions of the Enterprise Bankruptcy Law, other relevant provisions exist for, specifically, cases of bankruptcy or insolvency involving financial institutions and are mainly focused on debtor–creditor relationships.

After an enterprise is declared bankrupt in accordance with the Enterprise Bankruptcy Law, its collateral property does not belong to the estate but rather will be used for the repayment of its secured debt, while any remaining amounts will be included in the estate.

2.   Settlement of Assets under Bankruptcy or Insolvency Proceedings

Settlement using available assets from a debtor in bankruptcy or insolvency proceedings will occur in the following order:

    i.   expenses for bankruptcy proceedings include litigation costs involved in a bankruptcy case; expenses for management, realization, and distribution of the debtor's assets; and expenses involved in the administrator's performance of these duties and payment for his remuneration and expenses for the employees recruited;

    ii.   community debts include the debts generated when the bankruptcy custodian or debtor requests the opposite party concerned to perform a contract that is not fulfilled completely by both parties concerned; the debts generated from the custodial management of the debtor's assets; the debts generated from improper gains; the labor cost for the continuance of business operation, social insurance premiums, as well as other debts as incurred therefrom; the debts generated from the damage that occurs during the performance of functions and duties by a bankruptcy custodian or other relevant personnel; and the debts generated from any damage due to the debtor's assets;

    iii.   wages including subsidies for medical treatment and disability, and comfort and compensatory funds as owed by a debtor, the fundamental old-age insurance premiums, fundamental medical insurance premiums that shall have been transferred into the employees' personal accounts, as well as the compensation for the employees as prescribed by relevant laws and administrative regulations;

    iv.   social insurance premiums other than those as prescribed in the aforesaid provisions and tax fees as defaulted by the bankruptcy; and

    v.   common credits of bankruptcy in which the insolvent assets are not enough to meet the requirements for liquidation in the same sequence shall be distributed in accordance with their proportion.

After the global financial crisis and based on lessons learned from the risk of the bankruptcy of large financial institutions, the PRC is developing the Financial Institution Bankruptcy Management Regulations, aiming to find a resolution to the problem of large financial institutions too big to fail.[86]

In general, mechanisms or measures that an issuer can adopt to improve its chances of solvency and exercise risk control include, but are not limited to, the following:

---

[86] ADB. 2012. *ABMF Phase 1 Report: ASEAN+3 Bond Market Guide.* Manila.

    i.   third-party guarantee,

   ii.   insurance,

  iii.   mortgage or pledge assets,

  iv.   limit the issuer's debt and external guarantees,

   v.   restrict foreign investment,

  vi.   limit the sale of mortgage or major assets to a third party, and

 vii.   other measures.

3.   Other Reference Material on Bankruptcy and Insolvency

Further details on the restructuring and insolvency frameworks of Asia-Pacific economies can be found in *The Asia-Pacific Restructuring & Insolvency Guide* and *A Guide to Asia-Pacific Restructuring and Insolvency Procedures.*[87]

U.   Event of Default and Cross-Default

In contrast to the exchange bond market and the region's more mature bond markets, PBOC measures do not contain specific definitions of default or the practices for defining or declaring an event of default, including the time of default.

In the Guidelines for Default and Risk Disposal on Debt Financing Instruments of Non-Financial Enterprises in the Inter-Bank Bond Market (银行间债券市场非金融企业债务融资工具违约及风险处置指南), published by NAFMII on 27 December 2019 and effective from 1 July 2020, "default" refers to an issuer's failure to pay in full the principal or interest of a debt financing instrument as agreed, and includes statutory or agreed reasons such as bankruptcy, or if the debt financing instrument is due for repayment earlier than the maturity date and the issuer is not in a position to pay principal and interest in full and on time.

If a debt financing instrument issuance document or other agreement concluded between the issuer and debt financing instrument holders, or with the bond trustee in future, sets a grace period for payment, the date payable for principal and interest shall be the expiration date of the grace period.

In addition, the NAFMII Rules for Information Disclosure on Debt Financing Instruments of Non-Financial Enterprises in the Inter-Bank Bond Market (银行间债券市场非金融企业债务融资工具信息披露规则) stipulate the default of an enterprise in the event of failure to pay off major debts due (企业发生未能清偿到期重大债务的违约情况) as that, during the life of the debt financing instrument, the enterprise shall promptly disclose to the market when a material event may affect its solvency.

The issuer has to stipulate in the prospectus or other such key disclosure document the circumstances that would lead to a default of the debt financing instrument(s); its liability for breach of contract and covenants; and the way in which potential litigation, arbitration, or other dispute resolution mechanisms are handled after a default of the debt financing instrument has occurred. Usually, a default occurs at the end of the day.

If the issuer commits an actual breach of contract or faces an expected default in the sense of the Contract Law, the parties to the debt financing instrument's legal

---

[87] White & Case LLP. *Asia Pacific Restructuring & Insolvency Guide.*
https://www.whitecase.com/publications/alert/asia-pacific-restructuring-insolvency-guide;
Clifford Chance. 2018. *A Guide to Asia-Pacific Restructuring and Insolvency Procedures.*
https://onlineservices.cliffordchance.com/online/freeDownload.action?key=OBWlbFgNhLNomwBl%2B33Qzd
FhRQAhp8D%2BxrIGReI2crGqLnALtlyZe2I6bUKAO8L%2FFGIGwcvi3Hbp%0D%0A5mt12P8Wnx03DzsaB
GwsIB3EVF8XihbSpJa3xHNE7tFeHpEbaeIf&attachmentsize=30182406.

relationship may still directly claim the breach of contract or bear the liability for breach of contract without having to declare it.

In addition to the case of default on interest or principal by an issuer, an event of default can also occur by a participant in a depository. Such participant default refers to a default either in payment of any sum payable to the depository or a default in the delivery of debt financing instruments to the depository.

An event of participant-versus-investor default is either a client's default in any of the payment obligations due to the clearing participant or a client default in delivery obligations owed to the clearing participant. The clearing participant should recognize and declare an event of default, even if such default is not due to the clearing participant itself. This type of default is often called a technical default, because it is specific to a single transaction (gross settlement) or the result of one or more transactions defaulting as part of a net settlement process, and may not signal a general inability of a participant to meet its obligations to the market at large. If the participant is not an issuer, there are no market consequences beyond the settlement failure.

Covenants, Cross-Default, and Acceleration Clause

The use of a cross-default clause is increasingly common in issuance documentation. An acceleration clause is also becoming more likely to be included in issuance documentation. Banks can offset debts against assets of the same account holder since such an offset of liabilities versus assets is permitted by law.

IV

Bond and Note Transactions and Trading Market Infrastructure

Debt instruments issued in the PRC may be listed and traded on the exchanges and/or traded in the CIBM or other market segments. This chapter details the infrastructure and trading practices of the CIBM.

A. Inter-Bank Bond Market

The CIBM is a regulated OTC market populated by bank and non-bank financial institutions as direct participants, and other investors as indirect participants. The CIBM was established in 1997 and has its origins in the classical interbank market—hence the name—established by the PBOC to conduct open market operation with constituent banks. Over time, the original market was augmented with additional products serving the funding of an increasing number of participants and additional market features to become the CIBM in its current form.

Today, products traded in the CIBM include cash bonds (the term used in the China bond market for outright bond and note trading), pledged repo, outright repo, bond lending, and bond forwards. PFBs, central government bonds (Treasury bonds), local enterprise bonds, and local government bonds are the four most actively traded instrument types in the CIBM. The trading of NCD in the CIBM is significant and also popular with foreign investors as a way to generate extra returns.

The CIBM facilitates two trading modes: bilateral negotiation and click-and-deal (one-click) trading (see also section B in this chapter). A market-maker mechanism was officially introduced in the CIBM in 2001 to improve market liquidity and enhance efficiency. Currently, 24 market makers provide bid–offer quotations for underlying bonds that cover nearly all instrument types and tenors; three of the 24 market makers are subsidiary companies of foreign banks.

Trading is conducted on the CFETS platform (see section B.1 for details); trades may also be concluded between counterparties outside this platform but need to be captured into CFETS on the same day (see section C for details). To access the CIBM, certain types of participants may need to route their orders through specific mechanisms, such as Bloomberg or TradeWeb for Bond Connect, or the CFAE for domestic nonfinancial institutions (see section B.3 for details). Trading intermediaries and other service providers must be members of NAFMII.

The CIBM is regarded by participants as an institutional marketplace. While direct participants are limited to financial institutions, issuers continue to issue debt financing instruments via public offerings that may be on-sold by direct participants to individual or general investors in the commercial banks' counter market (see also Chapter I.A for details). Nonfinancial institutions can trade in the CIBM by placing their orders through the CFAE; their transactions are limited to cash bonds only. All market participants, whether direct or indirect, trade in their own name and need to maintain corresponding trading accounts with CFETS and clearing and/or settlement accounts with either CCDC or SHCH, or both, as the case may be.

Foreign institutional investors using CIBM Direct participate in the market through a bond settlement agent, who executes orders on behalf of the investor and also provides settlement and safekeeping services to the investor. As of November 2019, the PBOC had approved 49 institutions to carry out bond settlement agency business in the CIBM.[88] Of those, 19 institutions had settlement capabilities to service foreign investors. For more information on the role of bond settlement agents or other market participants, please see Chapter III.M.

Foreign investors accessing the CIBM through Bond Connect place orders via their connected trading platform of choice and settle through the depository accounts maintained by the CMU. Most foreign institutional investors are limited to trade cash bonds and engage in bond lending and bond forwards, but not repo transactions (please see section G for more details).

At the time of compilation of this bond market guide, NAFMII listed nearly 6,900 members in the CIBM and CFETS maintained about 30,000 trading accounts for fixed income products. CCDC reported 23,916 domestic institutional participants (participants here representing the number of distinct account names for which settlement is conducted) and 1,095 accounts held by QOII. SHCH reported 23,511 institutional participants (including 1,024 accounts held by QOII), covering all types of financial institutions such as commercial banks, securities companies, and their authorized branches; insurance companies; and different investment vehicles including mutual funds and pension funds. Among these, commercial banks were the most active participants, partially due to the PBOC continuing to conduct its open market operation in the CIBM, for which commercial banks are the primary constituents.

Securities companies with asset management plans that want to engage in the securities asset management business in the CIBM are required to maintain separate bond trading (and corresponding settlement) accounts for each asset management plan, leading to a large number of investment fund participants in the CIBM. At the same time, NCD and other short–term products may be accessed by retail or general investors through money market funds, which are often offered by online payment system providers.

As shown in Figure 4.1, the volume of debt financing instrument trading in the CIBM has grown strongly in recent years. Settlement of trades in the CIBM occurs at CCDC or SHCH, depending on instrument type and where the trading counterparties maintain their depository accounts.

---

[88] The list of bond settlement agents (银行间债券市场结算代理人名单) is available (in Chinese) from the CFETS website at http://www.chinamoney.com.cn/chinese/mtmemrmb/.

Figure 4.1: Debt Instrument Trading Volume in the Inter-Bank Bond Market

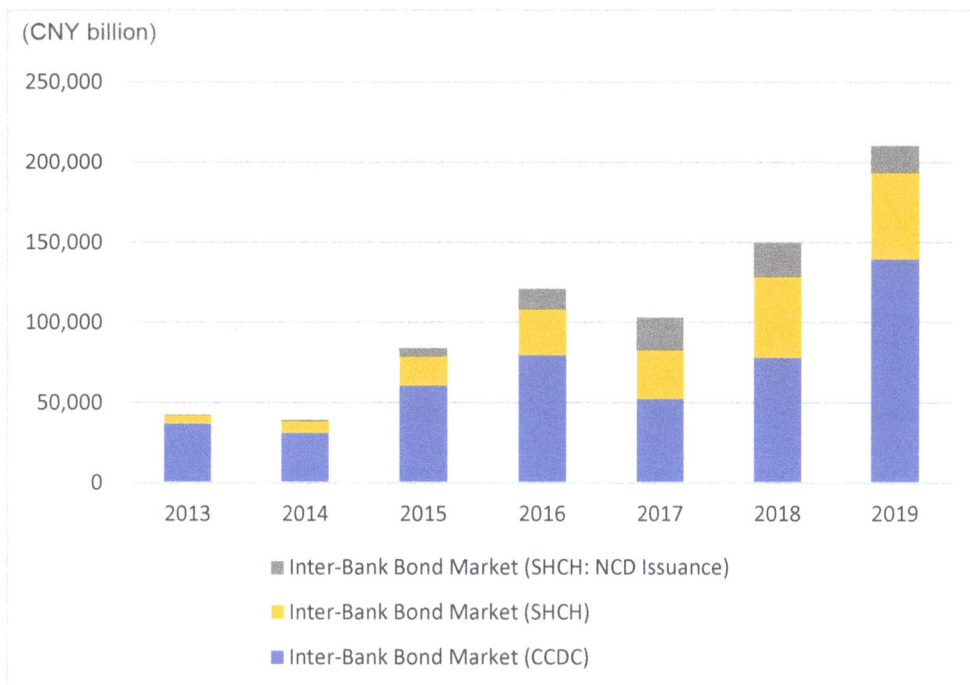

CCDC = China Central Depository & Clearing Co., Ltd; CNY = Chinese renminbi; NCD = negotiable certificates of deposit; SHCH = Shanghai Clearing House.
Sources: *CCDC Bond Market Statistical Analysis Report, 2013–2018; SHCH Yearbook, 2013–2018.*

In addition, SHCH also fulfills a CCP function as the only CCP in the CIBM recognized by the PBOC. The other CCP in the China bond market is CSDC for the exchange bond market.

SHCH's CCP function is not limited by instrument type; for cash bond and repo transactions, if both counterparties are CCP clearing members, the CCP service can be used for any debt instruments deposited with SHCH. At the same time, the use of the CCP for fixed income transaction settlement is not mandatory. Counterparties can opt to use the CCP function at the point of trade in CFETS, or when they instruct SHCH. When using the CCP function, different clearing and settlement fees apply; applicable rules and fee schedules can be found on the SHCH website and are also detailed in Chapter VI.

B.   Trading Platforms

1.   China Foreign Exchange Trading System

CFETS is the common trading platform and liquidity hub of the CIBM. CFETS also fulfills the role as the NIFC and uses Chinamoney as its web handle, which describes its function in the classical interbank market to this day. Both CFETS and NIFC are regulated by the PBOC and treated as one entity.

CFETS and NIFC main functions include (i) providing systems for foreign exchange trading, interbank cash lending, and bond trading; (ii) organizing interbank foreign exchange trading, interbank cash lending, and bond trading; (iii) handling the settlement and clearing of foreign exchange trading; (iv) promoting the clearing of interbank cash lending and bond trading; (v) providing an online commercial paper quotation system; (vi) providing information on the foreign exchange, bond, and money markets; and (vii) engaging in other businesses authorized by the PBOC. However, for the bond market, only CFETS and its functions will be described further.

CFETS has been operating the CIBM trading platform since 1997 and by now has developed into a comprehensive electronic OTC bond trading platform with functions to facilitate and support trading, post-trade services, risk management, and information services. The CFETS platform facilitates activities for all instruments in the CIBM, including cash-bond trading, bond repo, and bond forwards.

On the CFETS platform, the practice of bilateral negotiation is applied to all CIBM products, while one-click trading (点击成交) is only applied to cash bond trading and interest rate derivatives. CFETS provides an interface for members to transfer data from CFETS to their internal systems. Straight-through processing between CFETS and the depositories for the CIBM—CCDC and SHCH—is provided, with transaction data transferred to the respective settlement system automatically. CFETS also provides market information, including quotations and prices, on a real-time basis. The trading platform contains features for post-trade management such as specific modules for post-trade supervision and risk management.

As for the trading method, Treasury bond spot transactions are executed at a clean price, (i.e., transactions are executed at a price quote that excludes accrued interest). Enterprise bond spot transactions are executed at the gross price—also referred to as a dirty price (i.e., transactions are executed at a price quote that includes accrued interest). CFETS trading hours are shown in Table 4; please note the small difference in the afternoon trading session hours for same-day settlement. The trading hours are stated for the Beijing time zone (GMT+8) and apply from Monday to Friday, with the exception of statutory holidays in the PRC.

Table 4: CFETS Trading Platform Hours

For Settlement on	Session	Start Time	End Time
T+0	Morning session	9 a.m.	12 noon
	Afternoon session	1:30 p.m.	4:50 p.m.
T+1	Morning session	9 a.m.	12 noon
	Afternoon session	1:30 p.m.	5 p.m.

Source: China Foreign Exchange Trading System. http://new.chinamoney.com.cn/english/prdbmkcbt/.

Financial institutions can directly trade on the CFETS platform. The participation of other institutions depends on the nature of those participants: nonfinancial institutions must route their orders via CFAE, while foreign institutional investors access the market via a bond settlement agent (in the case of CIBM Direct) or placing their orders via an international trading platform connected to CFETS (for transactions via Bond Connect). However, all trades will be executed on the CFETS platform and trade confirmations are sent back to the platform where the order originated.

At the end of September 2019, CFETS maintained about 30,000 trading accounts on its platform, including for retail investors. Trading accounts contain standard trading and settlement information that allow CFETS to validate which instruments a trading account holder may trade and where the traded instruments should be settled, given that there are multiple depositories potentially covering the same debt financing instruments. As such, foreign institutional investors or those with specific restrictions (e.g., nonfinancial institutions) cannot trade products not available to them under applicable regulations.

As the central trading platform for the CIBM, CFETS formulates and publishes its own trading rules and other rules pertaining to the transactions executed on its platform (see also Chapter II.K) and governs the activities of its trading participants; it is, however, not an SRO and, therefore, is subject to supervision by the PBOC.

2.   Money Brokerage Companies

The systems of currency brokerage companies—or money brokers—are another type of bond trading platform in the CIBM. Money brokers are non-bank financial institutions approved by CBIRC and specialized in the promotion of financial intermediation between financial institutions and foreign exchange transaction and brokerage services through electronic or other means. Money brokers receive a commission for these services.

CBIRC (then CBRC) has been issuing rules and regulations on money brokerage business since August 2005, when it allowed the establishment of joint venture operations of experienced overseas money brokers and eligible domestic broking companies on a trial basis. The Provisional Rules Governing the Money Brokers, 2005 were followed by the Guidance on Money Brokerage and Transactions among Financial Institutions, issued on 30 August 2007, with a view to further regulating the activities of money brokers and dealers, improving their work efficiency, and ensuring orderliness and fairness in the market.[89]

However, the business of money broking companies has not developed as expected due to a weak members' foundation, the difficulty of connecting their technology platforms, and the dominance of the common trading platform at CFETS in the market, among other things.

3.   Beijing Financial Assets Exchange

The Beijing Financial Assets Exchange, also referred to as the China Financial Assets Exchange and abbreviated as CFAE, is a state-owned financial assets transaction platform designated by the MOF as well as a transaction platform designated by NAFMII for the indirect participation of domestic nonfinancial institutions, such as corporates, in the CIBM. CFAE also acts as a feeder mechanism for trading orders for certain instruments in the CIBM, such as Panda bonds and PPN, and offers the function of a centralized book-building platform in the market (see Chapter III.E for a description of this function).

CFAE was established by the Beijing Municipal Government on 30 May 2010 to improve the liquidity of a variety of financial assets. Its business now covers transactions of state-owned assets, credit assets, bonds, trust products, insurance assets, and private equity. CFAE is part of a group of asset transaction venues guided by the China Beijing Equity Exchange (CBEX), a comprehensive equity trading institution approved by the Beijing Municipal Government. CBEX was established in 1994 by the Beijing Municipal Government and is the sole institution for the transfer of ownership of SOEs in the PRC. In turn, CBEX has established a number of separate transaction venues for different asset classes, including the CFAE.

While CFAE may function as a trading venue for a variety of financial asset classes, its main role in the CIBM is focused on routing orders placed by nonfinancial institutional investors, who are unable to directly participate in the CIBM, to the trading platform of

---

[89] This text has been adopted in part from the following CBRC announcement available at http://www.cbrc.gov.cn/EngdocView.do?docID=200709187531B537C9A5E135FF30A98CC6624400.

CFETS for execution. Orders routed via CFAE will be quoted, priced, and executed exclusively via the CFETS platform and trade confirmations will be sent back to the nonfinancial institution via CFAE upon the execution of the order on CFETS. Orders are routed and executed in the name of the actual nonfinancial enterprise placing the order (see flow description in the next paragraph). For that purpose, nonfinancial enterprises wishing to access the CIBM also need to have a trading account on CFETS as well as a depository account at either CCDC or SHCH, or both.

A transaction using order routing via the CFAE would occur in the following manner:

1. Market makers provide anonymous quotes through CFETS to CFAE.
2. A nonfinancial company chooses an anonymous quote for a transaction on CFAE; the transaction type can only be cash bonds.
3. CFAE sends the trading order to CFETS after checking that the nonfinancial company has sufficient holdings of cash or debt instruments.
4. The trade is executed on CFETS through the trading account of the investor.
5. CFETS sends a trade confirmation to CFAE and trade information to the depository.
6. The depository asks both the market maker and nonfinancial company to confirm the trade information.
7. Upon confirmation, the depository settles the trade; any trade or settlement discrepancies will need to be addressed directly by the nonfinancial company.

For the purpose of investments by QOII, all of which to date have been financial institutions, and their activities in the CIBM, the CFAE does not play a direct role. As such, at the time of compilation of this bond market guide, the website of CFAE was only available in Chinese.[90] CBEX maintains an English website.[91]

C.   Trade Reporting

Due to the nature of the CFETS platform, trades executed on the system are automatically captured and disclosed to all participants and available for market monitoring and surveillance. CFETS also publishes information on executed trades on its platform to its constituents and reports trading activities to the PBOC regularly.

In addition, according to a requirement by the PBOC, in the event that bonds are not traded through the trading system of CFETS, both parties should report the trade information for the record to CFETS on the same trading day. If one party or both parties of the transaction instruct a bond settlement agent for trade settlement, then the bond settlement agent should report the trade information to CFETS.

According to prevailing rules and regulations, including the Measures for the Administration of Bond Transactions in the National Inter-Bank Bond Market and the Circular of the People's Bank of China on Issues Concerned in Application to Bond Settlement Agent Business, market makers and settlement agencies shall regularly report their business performance to the PBOC. At present, there is no regulation that requires market makers and settlement agencies to furnish a copy of the report submitted to the PBOC to intermediary platforms or self-regulatory bodies.

---

[90] See https://www.cfae.cn.
[91] See http://www.cbex.cn.

D.   Market Monitoring and Surveillance

The PBOC is responsible for regulating and supervising the OTC bond market overall. Under guidance from the PBOC, NAFMII has formulated a self-regulatory management system for the secondary market and self-regulatory normative documents to strengthen the self-regulatory management of its members when carrying out trading activities. These normative documents include the Working Guidelines for Market Makers of the Inter-Bank Bond Market and the Self-Regulatory Rules for Bond Trading in the Inter-Bank Bond Market.

At the same time, NAFMII is not the regulator for CFETS. CFETS issues its own rules and governs its trading participants under a mandate from the PBOC and conducts market monitoring activities on its participants and their trading activities. CFETS regularly provides trading data to the PBOC for analysis, which may be forwarded by the PBOC to NAFMII for examination.

Under its mandate to improve market transparency in the OTC bond market, CFETS has the primary responsibility to detect and address abnormal transactions. In its market rules, CFETS states its mandate to conduct market surveillance and lists adverse participant behavior that constitutes market rule violations.[92] CFETS may take appropriate disciplinary action(s) against the participant(s) at fault and may report any incident that it deems to have a market impact to the PBOC, as deemed appropriate.

E.   Bond Information Services

To enhance transparency in the bond market, especially with the CIBM being an OTC market, NAFMII, CFETS, SHCH, and CCDC all provide information services on debt financing instruments registered, traded, and cleared and settled in the CIBM, including on initial and continuous disclosure information and market activities. In addition, the PBOC provides general information on government debt instruments used in its open market operation. Some of the bond information services available from institutions in the CIBM are mentioned in the next sections.

Information on debt financing instruments, their features and related disclosure information, trading prices, and other market statistics are available from market makers and other trading participants, as well as from commercial information vendors.

1.   Information on Government Bond Issuances

Treasury bonds are issued and traded in the CIBM, and also listed and traded in the exchange bond market. The issuance of Treasury bonds is the responsibility of the MOF. At the time of compilation of this bond market guide, the official website of the MOF was only available in Chinese.[93] In addition, the English website of the PBOC does not contain information on bond issuances of the state or state-owned agencies and enterprises. However, the English website offers the latest yield information and yield curves for central government bonds; the yield curve is calculated for the PBOC by CCDC.[94] For more information on yields and yield curves, please also see section H.1.

---

[92] China Foreign Exchange Trading System. Rules for Bond Transactions of the National Inter-Bank Market. http://www.chinamoney.com.cn/english/rarrmrrudmrl/20161111/2025.html.
[93] See www.mof.gov.cn.
[94] See http://www.pbc.gov.cn/english/130727/index.html.

2.   China Foreign Exchange Trade System

CFETS discloses market information, particularly pricing-related statistics via the trading system, on a real-time basis to market participants. In addition, CFETS also offers product information on the debt financing instruments traded on its platform and disclosure information including news on new issuances and corporate announcements (Figure 4.2).

Figure 4.2: Example of Disclosure Information on the China Foreign Exchange Trade System Website

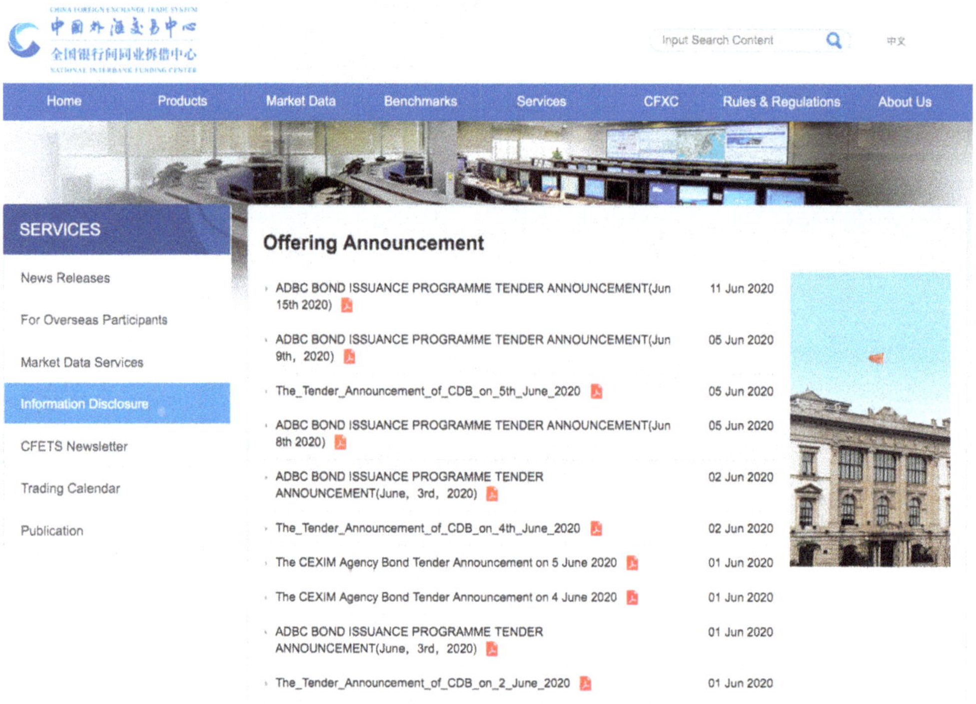

Source: China Foreign Exchange Trade System. Information Disclosure. http://www.chinamoney.com.cn/english/svcidssoan/.

3.   China Central Depository & Clearing Co., Ltd. (ChinaBond)

CCDC publishes extensive bond market information through its very comprehensive website, including information on new issuances, auction and tender results, registration, income payments, as well as market quotations and OTC bilateral prices.[95] CCDC also provides market statistics and calculates debt financing instrument valuations and yield curves under its ChinaBond brand (see Chapter III.K for more details) (Figure 4.3). The website provides access to the Bond Information Disclosure System (in Chinese only) to registered users. The CCDC information services have been in place since 1998.

---

[95] See http://www.chinabond.com.cn/d2s/engindex.html.

Figure 4.3: Debt Securities Information on the CCDC Website

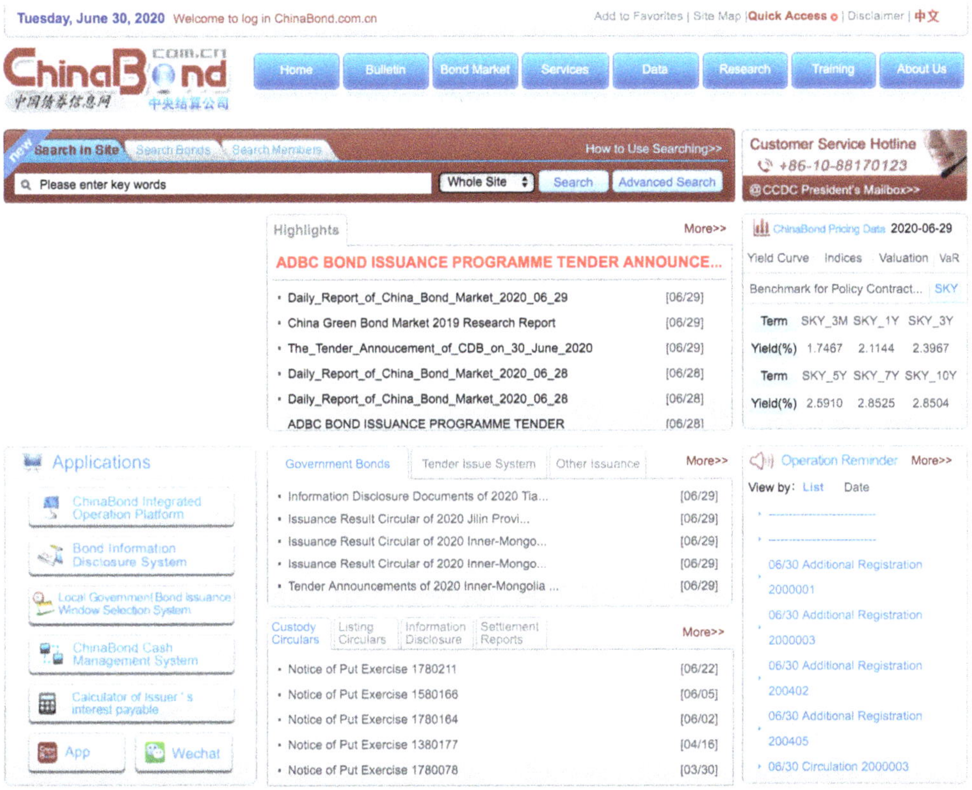

Source: China Central Depository & Clearing Co., Ltd (CCDC). http://www.chinabond.com.cn/d2s/engindex.html.

Under its mandate to further the development of the CIBM, CCDC conducts roadshows and international events to provide information to interested parties in markets outside the PRC. CCDC also holds an annual conference that brings together industry representatives, issuers, and investors on a range of specific topics. In the near future, CCDC intends to launch a dedicated Global Investor Portal, which will aggregate available resources for foreign investors in the CIBM. Already available is an English language e-learning system for interested parties; registration is required but is free of charge.

CCDC periodically publishes issues of *ChinaBond Watch*, which contains macroeconomic data, interest rate, yield and index information and trends, plus updates on the activities of foreign institutional investors and notable recent developments, as well as an annual *CCDC Handbook*, which contains frequently asked questions about the CIBM.

4. People's Bank of China

The PBOC provides information on government bond issuances and other debt instruments issued through the PBOC Bond Issuance System on its website. At the time of compilation of this bond market guide, most of the information was only available via the Chinese version of the website. At the same time, the English version of the website contains general information on instruments and the bond market, announcements on the PBOC's open market operation, and yield curve information (Figure 4.4).

Figure 4.4: The People's Bank of China's Website with Selected Debt Instrument Information in English

Source: People's Bank of China. http://www.pbc.gov.cn/english/130437/index.html.

5.   Shanghai Clearing House Co., Ltd.

SHCH publishes the *Monthly Bulletin on the Shanghai Clearing House Bond Market* on its website. The bulletin is downloadable as a Microsoft Excel workbook and contains a number of spreadsheets with general and specific market statistics on issuances, redemptions, and clearing volumes, with a breakdown for each category by debt financing instrument type (Figure 4.5). The bulletin also contains data on the assets under safekeeping by SHCH by instrument type as well as the holding structure of said instruments by the type of investor.

Figure 4.5: Example of Market Data in Monthly Bulletin on Shanghai Clearing House Bond Market

| | | New | Templates | Open | Save | Print | Cut | Copy | Paste | Format | Undo | Redo | AutoSum | Sort | Filter | For |

Calibri (Body)   12   B   I   U $ %

| ♠ Home | Layout | Tables | Charts | SmartArt | Formulas | Data | Revie |

B17   fx

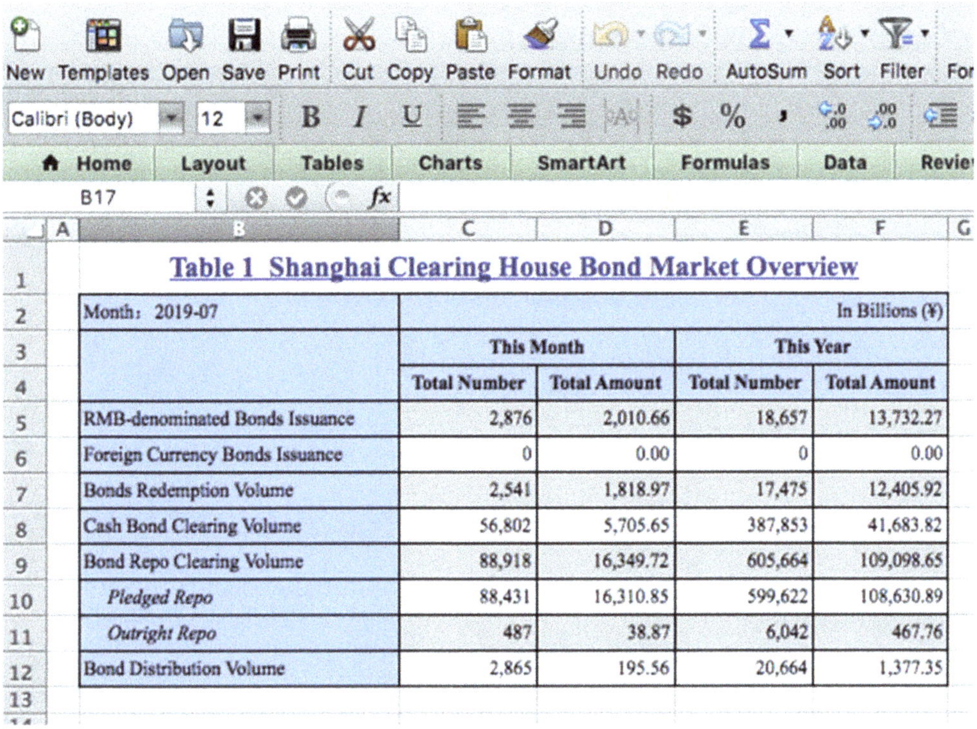

Table 1 Shanghai Clearing House Bond Market Overview

Month: 2019-07				In Billions (¥)
	This Month		This Year	
	Total Number	Total Amount	Total Number	Total Amount
RMB-denominated Bonds Issuance	2,876	2,010.66	18,657	13,732.27
Foreign Currency Bonds Issuance	0	0.00	0	0.00
Bonds Redemption Volume	2,541	1,818.97	17,475	12,405.92
Cash Bond Clearing Volume	56,802	5,705.65	387,853	41,683.82
Bond Repo Clearing Volume	88,918	16,349.72	605,664	109,098.65
Pledged Repo	88,431	16,310.85	599,622	108,630.89
Outright Repo	487	38.87	6,042	467.76
Bond Distribution Volume	2,865	195.56	20,664	1,377.35

Source: Shanghai Clearing House Co., Ltd. Bond Market Overview.
http://english.shclearing.com/data/market/?xyz=0.08571623063476264.

F.   Yields, Yield Curves, and Bond Indexes

Bond yield curves reflect the level of interest rates across different bond tenors in the market and also reflect interest rate differences relative to the credit level of bonds. Bond yield curves are an important pricing reference for deposit and lending, fixed income, and other financial products.

Bond yield curves are available from a number of providers in each segment of the China bond market. For the CIBM, the key information providers are CFETS, CCDC (ChinaBond), and SHCH. The PBOC uses yields and yield curves calculated by CCDC and publishes them on its website and in official publications.

1.   China Foreign Exchange Trade System

CFETS composes intra-day and end-of-day yield curves on six types of benchmark bonds. The intra-day yield curves are the only such benchmarks in the CIBM. Every trading day the first yield curve is published at 9:30 a.m. The curve is updated hourly until the system closes (Figure 4.6).

Figure 4.6: China Foreign Exchange Trade System Closing Yield Curves

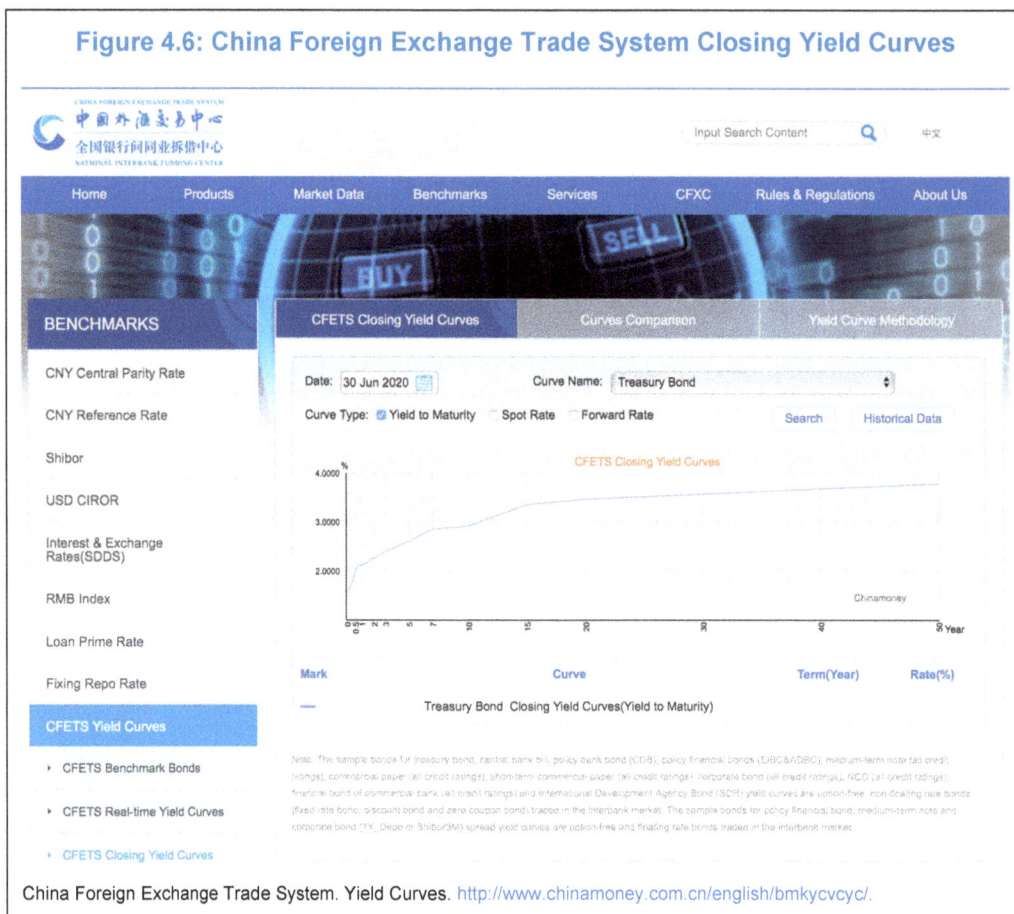

China Foreign Exchange Trade System. Yield Curves. http://www.chinamoney.com.cn/english/bmkycvcyc/.

---

2.   China Central Depository & Clearing Co., Ltd.

CCDC has been providing ChinaBond Yield Curves since 1999. In 2002, the calculation of the ChinaBond Yield Curves was upgraded, following consultations with external experts, using a brand-new modeling method with reference to the particularities of the China bond market. CCDC introduced the Hermite Curve Model, which proved more suitable to the China bond market than those models with an inherent trend as adopted by many other pricing agencies.

ChinaBond Yield Curves are available for many debt financing instrument types, and have generally been recognized by Chinese financial market regulators and participants. ChinaBond Yield Curves are being applied widely, serving the aims of market supervision as well as a pricing benchmark, in the context of internal controls of financial institutions and a performance evaluation of the holdings and market activities of banks, funds, insurance companies, and other market participants (Figure 4.7).

Figure 4.7: ChinaBond Yield Curve Web Page

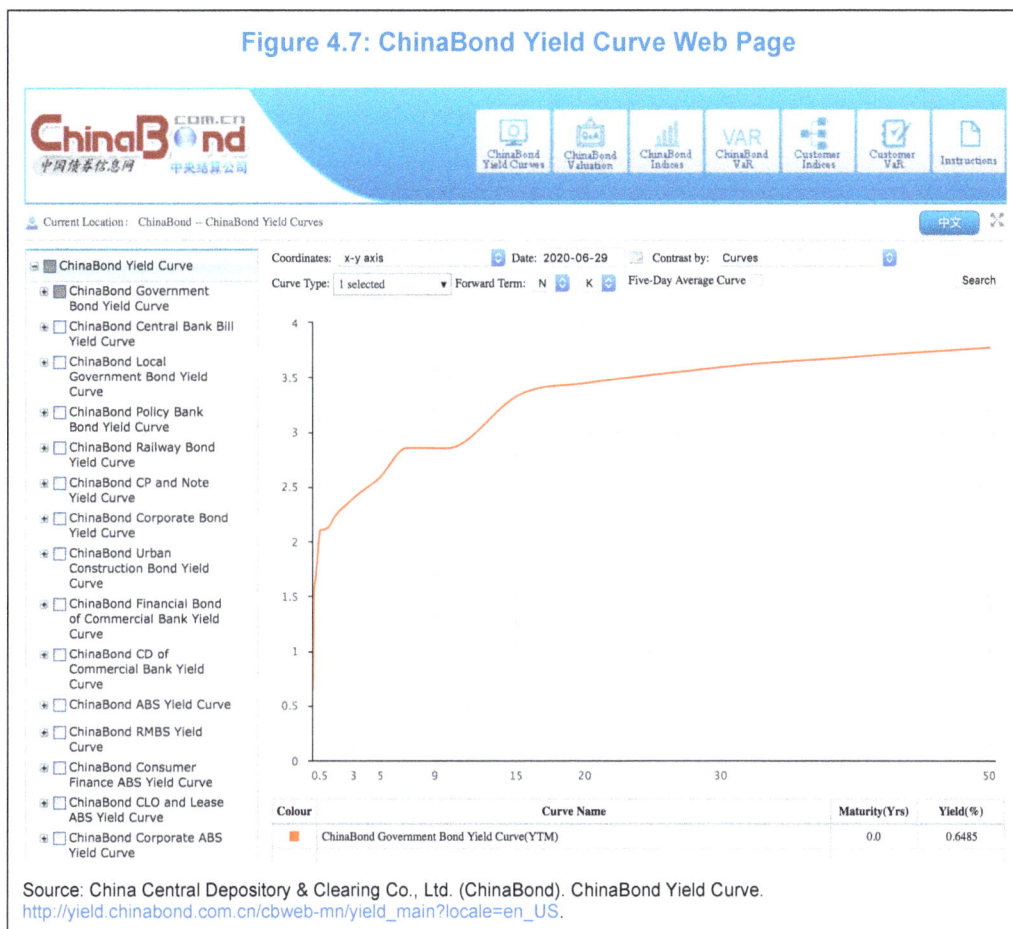

Source: China Central Depository & Clearing Co., Ltd. (ChinaBond). ChinaBond Yield Curve.
http://yield.chinabond.com.cn/cbweb-mn/yield_main?locale=en_US.

ChinaBond price- or index-related products not only include bond yield curves but also bond valuations (see Chapter III.K for more information), bond indexes, and the calculation of value-at-risk metrics. Value-at-risk is an indicator for measuring market risk and forms the basis for risk control and performance assessment.

3.   Shanghai Clearing House Co., Ltd.

SHCH constructs eight categories of yield curves in the CIBM, involving par rate curves, spot rate curves, and forward rates. SHCH adopts the variable roughness penalty method, which is sensitive to interest rate changes and accurately depicts term structure. Yield curves are published daily at about 6 p.m. (Figure 4.8).

Figure 4.8: Shanghai Clearing House Yield Curve Web Page

Source: Shanghai Clearing House. Yield Curve. http://www.shclearing.com/cpgz/zqjqysp/dqsylqx/.

4.   Other Information Sources for Yield Curves

Government bond yields and yield curves, as well as many other pertinent details on the China bond market, are also available from the *AsianBondsOnline* website (Figure 4.9).

Figure 4.9: People's Republic of China's Government Bond Yield Curve on *AsianBondsOnline*

CN = People's Republic of China, CNY = Chinese renminbi, JPY = Japanese yen, LCY = local currency, USD = United States dollar, YTD = year-to-date.
Source: *AsianBondsOnline*. Market at a Glance—People's Republic of China.
https://asianbondsonline.adb.org/economy/?economy=CN.

5.   Bond Indexes in the Inter-Bank Bond Market

For the CIBM, bond indexes are available from CFETS, CCDC (ChinaBond), and SHCH. CCDC calculates a large number of ChinaBond Bond Indices across a number of indicators, including instrument type, tenor, and credit rating. The indexes include green bond and foreign-currency-denominated indexes, and track the activities of foreign institutional investors. CFETS also provides a number of bond indexes for debt instruments traded on its platform, including indexes in cooperation with some of the market participants. SHCH offers the China Credit Bond Index series, which was created in 2016 to track the performance of the Chinese credit bond market.

In addition, professional market data vendors and many market participants may calculate and provide bond indexes for debt instruments traded in the CIBM to their clients and subscribers.

a.   China Foreign Exchange Trade System

CFETS calculates indexes, including for Treasury bonds and PFBs across tenors, and also for debt financing instruments issued by nonfinancial enterprises, including MTN (Figure 4.10).

Figure 4.10: Bond Indexes Provided by CFETS

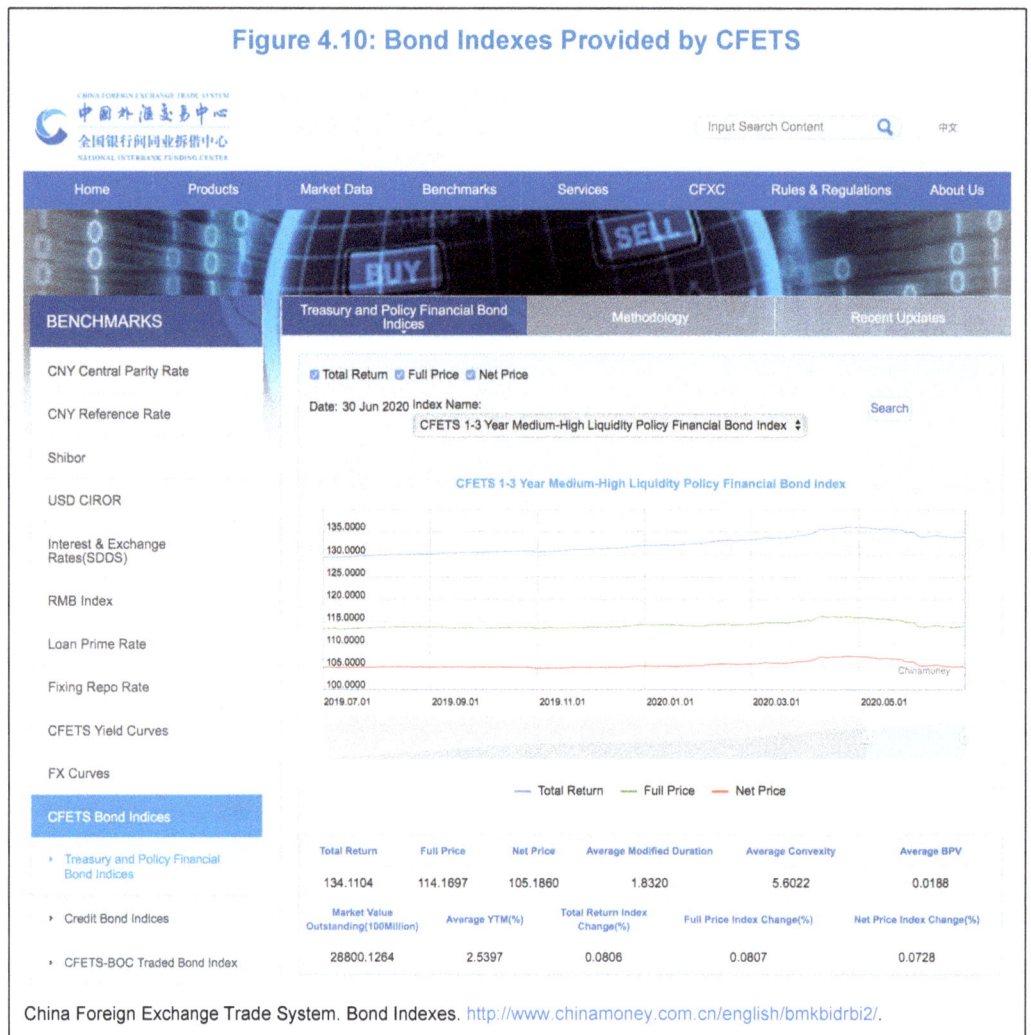

China Foreign Exchange Trade System. Bond Indexes. http://www.chinamoney.com.cn/english/bmkbidrbi2/.

b.   China Central Depository & Clearing Co., Ltd.

CCDC calculates ChinaBond Bond Indices for debt instruments traded in the CIBM as well as for those traded on the exchanges, with the information available from the CCDC website. Every day, CCDC publicly releases 58 indexes and more than 400 subindexes, and calculates position indexes for more than 1,200 accounts. Figure 4.11 illustrates the bond indexes provided, using the example of an iBoxx ChinaBond Government and Policy Banks Bond Index.

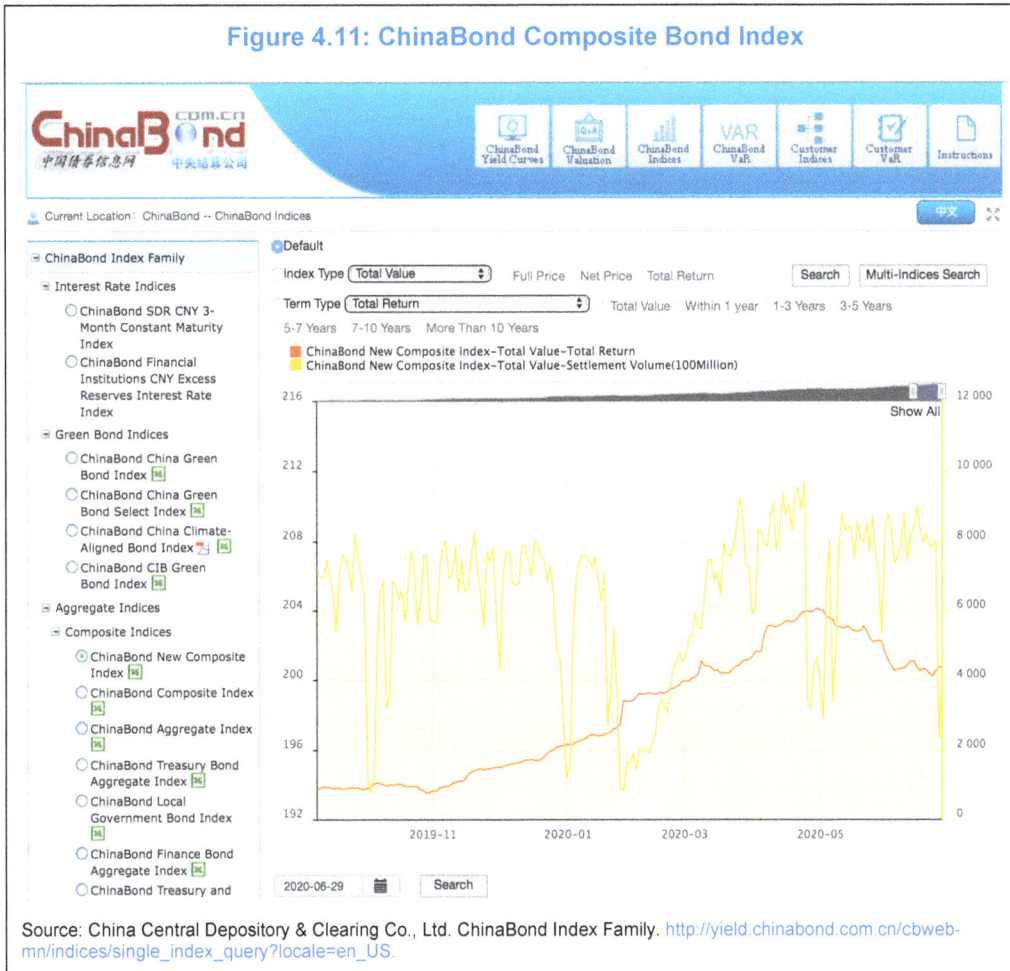

Figure 4.11: ChinaBond Composite Bond Index

Source: China Central Depository & Clearing Co., Ltd. ChinaBond Index Family. http://yield.chinabond.com.cn/cbweb-mn/indices/single_index_query?locale=en_US.

c.   Shanghai Clearing House Co., Ltd.

SHCH provides a comprehensive set of benchmark indexes to track the performance of the Chinese credit bond market. Currently SHCH provides six China Credit Bond Indices, some of which are composite index series designed to track the performance of the broader market, while others are customized to track the performance of certain bond types or investment themes. Each index series includes several indexes differentiated by bond features such as tenor and credit rating. There are 39 indexes in total. SHCH publishes daily index data on SHCH's official website (Figure 4.12).

Figure 4.12: SHCH Bond Index Web Page

Source: Shanghai Clearing House. Bond Indexes. http://www.shclearing.com/cpgz/zqjqysp/zqzs/zshq/.

6.   Inclusion of China Government Securities in Bond Indexes

On 23 March 2018, Bloomberg announced that it would add CNY-denominated government bonds and PFBs to the Bloomberg Barclays Global Aggregate Index once several planned operational enhancements have been implemented by the PBOC and the MOF.

To be considered for inclusion in the Global Aggregate Index, a local currency debt market must be classified as investment grade and its currency must be freely tradable, convertible, hedgeable, and free of capital controls. Ongoing enhancements from the PBOC have resulted in CNY-denominated instruments meeting these absolute index rules.

Following the implementation of a number of market liberalization practices, including a delivery-versus-payment settlement practice and a clarification on tax policies with regard to debt financing instruments, Bloomberg proceeded to phase in these debt financing instruments traded in the CIBM over a 20-month period starting in April 2019.

Once the phase-in process is complete, these debt financing instruments will represent about 6% of the overall index value.[96]

In October 2019, J.P. Morgan announced that high-liquidity CNY-denominated government bonds will be included in its Government Bond Index-Emerging Markets Index (GBI-EM). The inclusion will be phased in over a 10-month period from 28 February 2020, at 1% per month, and eventually represent 10% of the GBI-EM.[97]

G.   Repo Market

There are two repo market segments in the PRC—the inter-bank bond repo market and the stock exchange repo market—each with different structures, characteristics, terminology, and rules.

In the inter-bank bond repo market, transactions are conducted through the OTC method as private one-to-one negotiations between institutional participants, while in the exchange bond market the exchanges not only facilitate transactions, but CSDC also acts as the central counterparty to all repo sellers and repo buyers.

As an illustration, the combined inter-bank bond repo market and exchange repo market turnover was nearly 11 times larger than the CIBM trading turnover (without repo) in 2017. The focus in this bond market guide is on the features of the inter-bank bond repo market.

1.   Inter-Bank Bond Repo Market Overview

The inter-bank repo market is an OTC market, where counterparties conclude transactions based on bilateral negotiation. The PBOC is responsible for the overall market framework and system arrangement. It operates its open market operation through repo and reverse repo transactions in the inter-bank repo market to support market liquidity and stability.

As the self-regulatory body for the CIBM, NAFMII is responsible for conducting supervision and surveillance on daily activities in the CIBM and has long been promoting the development of the OTC bond repo market by establishing rules and regulations. At the beginning of 2013, NAFMII officially released the new version of the Repo Master Agreement, which combines two former master agreements. The changes in the New Master Agreement include the general terms and conditions as well as a special term structure enabling a single agreement structure, thus reducing negotiation costs and the management cost of transaction documentation. A number of core mechanisms were added to the New Master Agreement: the mark-to-market adjustment mechanism, exchange and adjustment, performance assurance mechanism, and the single agreement close-out netting, thereby minimizing systemic risks in the repo market. The New Master Agreement is signed by multiple market members, while the supplementary market agreement is signed bilaterally by the institutions.

CFETS provides the trading platform for the inter-bank repo market and settlement of repo transactions occurs via the counterparties' accounts with CCDC or SHCH, depending on the underlying debt trading instruments. These market infrastructure providers are charged by the PBOC with providing safe and reliable trading and

---

[96] Adopted by ABMF SF1 from a 2018 announcement by Bloomberg Finance L.P. Available at https://www.bloomberg.com/company/announcements/bloomberg-add-china-bloomberg-barclays-global-aggregate-indices/.
[97] As reported in the October 2019 edition of *ChinaBond Watch*.

settlement services to participants, and the keeping and monitoring of transaction data.

Transactions are based on OTC bilateral negotiation between counterparties. Terms and conditions—including tenor, size, collateral, haircut (over collateral), and yield—are negotiated between the two counterparties. Inter-bank repo market participants, therefore, must manage their own credit exposure risk. In the event of a default by either counterparty, the first option would be to negotiate an agreed settlement. If this does not succeed, both counterparties can participate in CCDC-directed arbitration. As a final option, the master agreement gives the inter-bank repo buyer the right to dispose of the collateral to compensate for any losses, including principal, interest, and other related expenses.

2.   Repo Market Size

Inter-bank bond repo dominates the repo market in Chinese renminbi, representing 71% of all repo transactions in the China bond market in 2018 (Figure 4.13). The major product in the inter-bank repo market is the pledged repo, accounting for about 97% of inter-bank repo transactions. The inter-bank repo market also offers an outright repo, but it only amounts to about 3% of transactions.

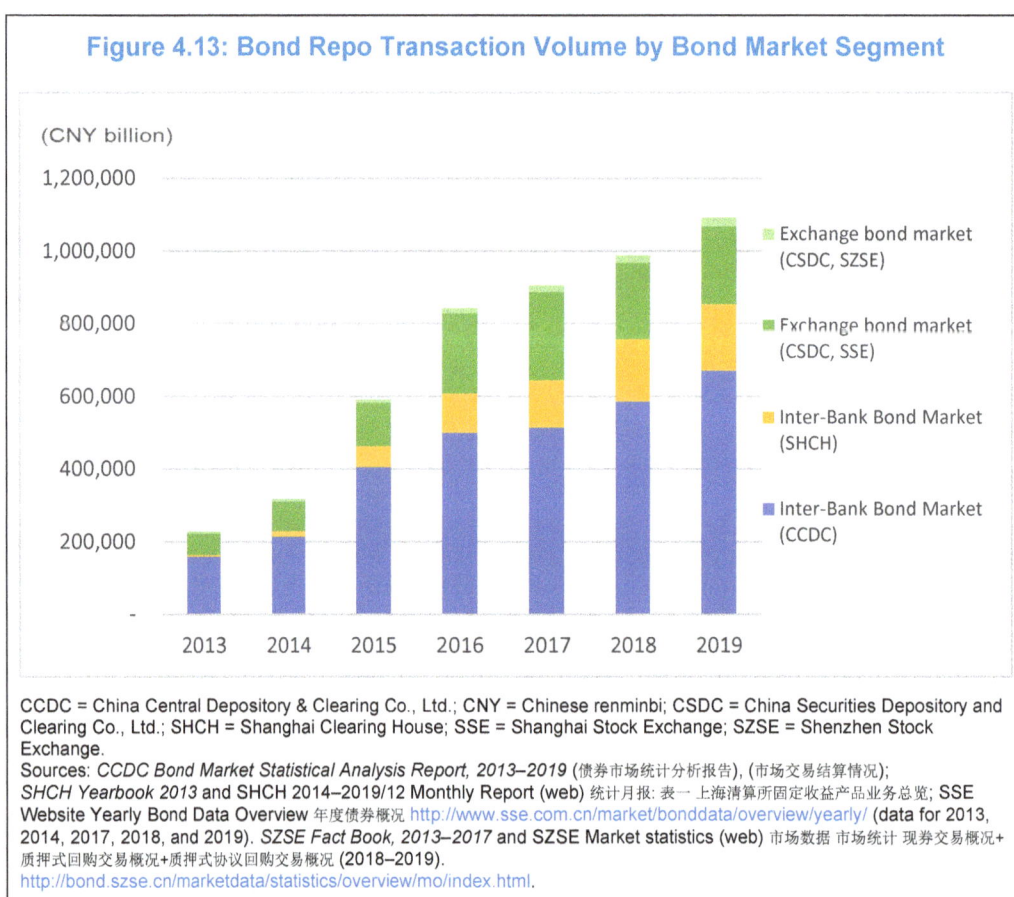

Figure 4.13: Bond Repo Transaction Volume by Bond Market Segment

CCDC = China Central Depository & Clearing Co., Ltd.; CNY = Chinese renminbi; CSDC = China Securities Depository and Clearing Co., Ltd.; SHCH = Shanghai Clearing House; SSE = Shanghai Stock Exchange; SZSE = Shenzhen Stock Exchange.
Sources: *CCDC Bond Market Statistical Analysis Report, 2013–2019* (债券市场统计分析报告), (市场交易结算情况);
SHCH Yearbook 2013 and SHCH 2014–2019/12 Monthly Report (web) 统计月报: 表一 上海清算所固定收益产品业务总览; SSE Website Yearly Bond Data Overview 年度债券概况 http://www.sse.com.cn/market/bonddata/overview/yearly/ (data for 2013, 2014, 2017, 2018, and 2019). *SZSE Fact Book, 2013–2017* and SZSE Market statistics (web) 市场数据 市场统计 现券交易概况+质押式回购交易概况+质押式协议回购交易概况 (2018–2019).
http://bond.szse.cn/marketdata/statistics/overview/mo/index.html.

3.   Acceptance of Standards

To be able to trade repos in the CIBM, participants are required to execute the China Inter-Bank Market Bond Repurchase Master Agreement (中国银行间市场债券回购交易主协议), published by NAFMII on 21 January 2013 and replaced the Pledged Repo Master Agreement and the Outright Transfer Master Agreement.

The Global Master Repurchase Agreement, or the GMRA, which is administered by the International Capital Market Organization and considered the global standard for documentation for repo, is not referenced in the master bond repo agreement published by NAFMII. The CIBM master agreement also differs from the documentation used in the exchange bond repo market.

At the same time, the core mechanisms of the agreements are the same, including document structure and provisions for trade netting and settlement, among others. Key differences include that the NAFMII master agreement is constructed under the law of the PRC and prescribes dispute resolution mechanisms available only in the PRC, and it covers both pledged repo and bilateral repo (also referred to as classic or buy-out repo), while the GMRA only covers the buy-out repo.

4. Specific Repo Practices in the Inter-Bank Bond Market

a. Type of Repo

Repo transactions in the CIBM consist mainly of the so-called "pledged repo," with "outright repo" transactions playing a minor role in terms of total transactions.

A pledged repo refers to a debt financing instrument or bond trade in which at the time the debt financing instrument or bond holder pledges its bonds as collateral in exchange for a cash loan, the two parties agree to return the cash and release the bonds pledged as collateral at the maturity of the repo. In contrast, an outright repo refers to a bond trade in which at the time the bond holder sells its bonds to the buyer, the two parties agree that the seller will buy back the same quantity of the same bonds at a specified price on a predetermined date. One significant distinction between these two repo types is that the collateral pledged in a pledged repo transaction may not be sold or otherwise used during the term.

b. Size and Tenor

Repo terms may be concluded after a period from 1 day to 365 days; standardized repo terms are available in the CFETS trading system for overnight, 7 days, 14 days, 21 days, 1 month, 3 months, 4 months, 6 months, 9 months, and 12 months. Given that banks tend to address their short-term liquidity requirements through transactions via the PBOC's open market operation or with other constituents, overnight, 7-day repo, and 14-day repo are the most active and liquid tenors.

Hence, based on the overnight, 7-day, and 14-day pledged repos, CFETS composes the fixing repo rate, which is now one of the key benchmarks for the financial market in the PRC.

c. Trading Hours

Inter-bank repo market trading hours are the same as for the cash bond market: from 9 a.m. to 12 noon and from 1:30 p.m. to 5 p.m. for settlement on T+1, with a dedicated lunch break. If counterparties wish to settle on the same day, they may only conclude trades until 4:40 p.m. in the afternoon session. No trading is conducted on statutory PRC holidays.

d.   Eligible Debt Securities as Collateral

Collateral, the terms of which are negotiated between the two parties, can include any bonds traded in the CIBM except bonds that will mature before the repo maturity date. The main underlying bonds used as collateral in the inter-bank repo market are government-backed (agency) bonds, such as government bonds, PFBs, and bonds issued by SOEs.

As the inter-bank repo market does not have a margin payment mechanism or collateral mark-to-market, haircuts tend to be higher than for equivalent exchange repo transactions. Collateral registration shall be made with CCDC or SHCH.

e.   Accounting and Tax Treatment

Pledged repo does not constitute the sale and (re-)purchase of the underlying debt financing instruments; hence, no capital gains tax applies since there is no disposal of the underlying assets. Interest paid to the lender for the cash provided against the pledged bonds is considered taxable as income and becomes part of the corporate tax liability of the institution.

f.   Market Participants

About 2,200 bank and non-bank financial institutions are actively involved as participants in inter-bank repo market transactions. They are commercial banks, securities companies, insurance companies, trusts, funds, as well as nonfinancial institutional investors. Commercial banks are the dominant participants. Small banks tend to be collateral providers (repo-sellers) with the aim of seeking funding, and large state-owned commercial banks with excess cash tend to be cash providers (repo-buyers).

To participate in the inter-bank repo market, a CIBM license issued by the PBOC is mandatory. Inter-bank repo market participants must use the China Inter-Bank Market Bond Repurchase Master Agreement prescribed by NAFMII, which details the general terms and conditions that apply to repo counterparties, including their responsibilities and procedures in the event of nonperformance or default.

g.   Market Access and Participation of Foreign Investors

The majority of foreign institutional investors are presently not able to access the inter-bank repo market directly. Under PBOC regulations issued in 2015 and 2016, only foreign central banks, international financial organizations, sovereign wealth funds, and RMB clearing banks and foreign participating banks are allowed to enter into repo transactions in the CIBM.[98] Repo transactions are presently not available for foreign investors accessing the CIBM under the QFII and RQFII concepts.

Please also see Chapter II.N for more information on the QFII and RQFII concepts.

---

[98] Pursuant to PBOC Announcement No. 220 (2015) and PBOC Announcement No. 3 (2016). The latter is available in Chinese only at http://www.pbc.gov.cn/goutongjiaoliu/113456/113469/3070371/index.html.

H.   Securities Lending and Borrowing

At present, bilateral securities lending and borrowing is only operated in the CIBM, and referred to as "bond lending." Bilateral bond lending was launched in 2006. The term bond lending originates from the PBOC Announcement No. 15 (2006), officially titled Tentative Provisions on the Administration of Bond Lending Business in the National Inter-Bank Bond Market, published on 2 November 2006 and effective from 20 November 2006.[99] The provisions refer to bond lending as a transaction where a bond receiver borrows bonds from the bond provider (lender) against a certain quantity of collateral and, at the same time, both parties agree that the bond receiver shall return the borrowed bonds and the bond provider shall return the corresponding collateral on a certain day in the future.

All CIBM participants may participate in bond lending transactions. Plans for bond lending as a market segment include the introduction of a central automatic lending program provided by CDCC and SHCH, which would include collateral management services for the first time.

1.   Trading and Settlement Mechanisms

Market participants may conclude a bond lending transaction bilaterally through the CFETS trading system or via telephone, fax, and other means. CFETS provides quotations, transaction, recording, and information services for bond lending transactions. Where the bond lending transaction is not conducted through the CFETS trading system directly, both counterparties shall record the trade with CFETS before 12 noon on the following business day. CCDC and SHCH are responsible for the settlement of bond lending transactions for instruments deposited with them. Both parties of the bond lending transaction shall send settlement instructions to the respective CSD on the day a bond lending trade is concluded. The lent bonds and the collateral bonds of one transaction could be registered in two different CSDs, which may lead to a cross-CSD bond lending transaction.

2.   Terms and Conditions

The underlying bonds used in bond lending transactions shall be part of the holdings of the bond provider with SHCH or CDCC and should be tradable in the CIBM. The tenor of bond lending and borrowing transactions can be determined by both parties through negotiation, but shall not exceed 365 days. The delivery of bonds upon the closing of the transaction (return leg) should be made with the underlying bonds, but may also be done in cash upon negotiation and with the consent of both counterparties.

If a payment of interest on the underlying bonds occurred during the bond lending period, the bond receiver shall return the interest on the underlying bonds to the bond provider in a timely manner. The bond receiver shall pay fees for the bond lending transaction to the bond provider, with the fees determined through negotiation between the counterparties.

Market participants are required to execute a Master Agreement for RMB Bond Borrowing and Lending Transactions, or a similarly named key document, with their counterparties or their bond settlement agent prior to engaging in bond lending transactions. During the bond lending period, the pledged bonds can be exchanged.

---

[99] The provisions are available in an English translation from the CFETS website at http://new.chinamoney.com.cn/english/rarrmrrudrgl/20061102/899.html.

3.   Size and Tenors

The tenor and terms of bond lending transactions can principally be determined by negotiation between the counterparties, with a maximum tenor of 365 days. At the same time, CFETS offers on its platform bond lending transaction types with 11 standardized terms: 1 day, 7 days, 14 days, 21 days, 1 month, 2 months, 3 months, 4 months, 6 months, 9 months, and 1 year.

4.   Trading Hours

Similar to cash bond and repo trading, bond lending transactions on the CFETS platform may be conducted every working day from 9 a.m. to 12 noon and from 1:30 p.m. to 4:50 p.m. for same-day settlement, and until 5 p.m. for trades to be settled the following business day. There is no trading on statutory holidays in the PRC.

5.   Market Participants

Market participants for bond lending transactions on the CFETS platform are limited to financial institutions. Nonfinancial institutions and selected other types of investors currently may not engage in bond lending transactions.

I.   Debt-Financing-Instrument-Related Derivatives in the Inter-Bank Bond Market

Derivatives related to underlying debt financing instruments in the CIBM may be traded on a dedicated futures exchange or in the OTC derivatives market. The available products include bond futures, bond forwards, interest rate swaps, as well as forward rate agreements. For illustration purposes, this section takes a brief look at bond futures and bond forwards only. Detailed information on all derivative products available in the CIBM is available from the CFETS Derivatives Market web pages.[100]

1.   Exchange Traded Bond Futures on China Financial Futures Exchange

The China Financial Futures Exchange (CFFEX) is a demutualized exchange dedicated to the trading, clearing, and settlement of financial futures, options, and other derivatives. On 8 September 2006, with the approval of the State Council and CSRC, CFFEX was established in Shanghai by the Shanghai Futures Exchange, Zhengzhou Commodity Exchange, Dalian Commodity Exchange, SSE, and SZSE. CFFEX is an exchange-style SRO under the supervision of CSRC.

CFFEX's main functions include organizing and arranging the listing, trading, clearing, settlement, and delivery of financial futures and other derivatives; formulating business rules; conducting self-management; disseminating market-trading information; providing technology, venues, and facility services; and other functions approved by CSRC.[101]

In relation to interest rate futures or other hedging instruments for the fixed-income market, CFFEX currently trades contracts for 2-year, 5-year, and 10-year Treasury bond futures. Figure 4.14 gives an illustration of the contract details, using the example of the 2-year Treasury bond futures contract. The contract employs physical delivery.

---

[100] See http://new.chinamoney.com.cn/english/prddmkfsw/.
[101] This description of activities has been adopted from the CFFEX website.

Transactions in Treasury bond futures are subject to the respective business rules issued by CFFEX, such as the Detailed Trading Rules of China Financial Futures Exchange for 2-Year Treasury Bond Futures Contract (as revised from time to time); the version that was current at the time of the compilation of this bond market guide was adopted on 6 August 2018 and first amended on 28 December 2018.[102]

CFFEX applies a hierarchical member clearing system, with members classified as either clearing members or trading members. Clearing members are further categorized by scope of business into trading clearing members, full-clearing members, or special clearing members. Trading members may conduct futures trading but are not eligible to carry out clearing activities. Members of CFFEX are futures companies with business qualifications for financial futures brokerage services, or other financial institutions that meet the eligibility criteria in the CFFEX Membership Rules.[103] Additional participants are the margin-holding banks with which members deposit the required initial and variable cash margin amounts for their trading positions.

Figure 4.14: Features of a 2-Year Treasury Bond Futures Contract on CFFEX

2-year Treasury Bond Futures	
Underlying Bond	Nominal medium-term and short-term treasury bond with face value of RMB2 million and coupon rate of 3%
Deliverable Bond	Book entry interest-bearing treasury bond with a maximum term to maturity of 5 years and a residual maturity of 1.5-2.25 years upon the first day of the expiry month
Quotation	RMB100 net price
Tick Size	RMB0.005
Contract Months	Three most recent quarterly months (three most recent months in the March, June, September and December quarterly cycle)
Trading Hours	09:15 am - 11:30 am, 01:00 pm - 03:15 pm
Trading Hours on Last Trading Day	09:15 am - 11:30 am
Limit Up/Down	±0.5% of the settlement price on the previous trading day
Minimum Margin Requirement	0.5% of the contract value
Last Trading Day	The second Friday of the expiry month of contract
Last Delivery Day	The third trading day after the last trading day
Delivery Method	Physical delivery
Transaction Code	TS
Exchange	China Financial Futures Exchange

CFFEX = China Financial Futures Exchange; CSI = China Securities Index Co., Ltd.; RMB = Chinese renminbi; SSE = Shanghai Stock Exchange.
Source: CFFEX. 2-Year Treasury Bond Futures. http://www.cffex.com.cn/en_new/2ts.html.

With a series of rules in place—such as evaluating investor suitability, coordinating cross-market regulation, and monitoring abnormal trading activities—CFFEX strives to maintain the orderly functioning of the financial market; safeguard market openness,

---

[102] The CFFEX business rules are available in English at http://www.cffex.com.cn/en_new/ywgz/.
[103] CFFEX. Measures of China Financial Futures Exchange on Membership Management. http://www.cffex.com.cn/en_new/ywgz/20101115/16968.html.

fairness, and impartiality; protect the lawful rights and interests of investors, especially small and medium-sized investors; and prevent systemic risks.

2. Over-the-Counter Derivatives on the China Foreign Exchange Trade System

This section provides a brief overview of bond forwards as an illustration of OTC derivatives traded on CFETS and related to debt financing instruments in the CIBM. A bond forward refers to a transaction where two trading parties agree to sell and buy bonds for a specified price and quantity, and at an agreed date in the future.[104]

a. Size and Tenor

The term of the bond forward—from deal date to settlement date—is agreed in negotiation between the counterparties but may not exceed 365 days. There are no standard deal terms for bond forwards. There is no standard transaction size.

b. Eligible Debt Financing Instruments

Underlying debt financing instruments for forward transactions should be Treasury bonds, central bank bills, and financial bonds for which cash bond transactions are conducted in the CIBM, and other bonds approved by the PBOC.

c. Trading Hours

The CFETS platform trading hours for bond forwards are the same as for cash bond trading, repo, and bond lending transactions, with a morning session from 9 a.m. to 12 noon and an afternoon session from 1:30 p.m. to 4:50 p.m. for same-day settlement, or a 5 p.m. close for transactions to be settled on T+1. No trading occurs on PRC statutory holidays.

d. Market Participants

Financial institutions with market maker or clearing agency business qualifications can conduct bond forward transactions with all other market participants. Other financial institutions can conduct bond forward transactions with all financial institutions, and nonfinancial institutions can only carry out bond forward transactions for hedging purposes with the financial institutions having market maker or clearing agency business qualifications.

---

[104] Information obtained from the CFETS website at http://new.chinamoney.com.cn/english/prddmkbfw/.

Description of the Securities Settlement System

This chapter, as included in the original *ASEAN+3 Bond Market Guide* published in 2012, was discontinued in favor of a more comprehensive and updated description in the Phase 2 Report of ABMF Sub-Forum 2 (SF2), *Information on Transaction Flows and Settlement Infrastructures*, dated 13 June 2014. The SF2 Phase 2 Report contains information on the post-trade features of the bond market in the PRC, its market infrastructure and settlement systems, interest payment and redemption practices, as well as market and message standards (pp. 102–115). In addition, the SF2 Phase 2 Report contains detailed infrastructure and transaction flow diagrams for the bond market in the PRC (pp. 345–383).

The SF2 report is available on a dedicated ADB website, as well as through a number of mirror sites.[105]

---

[105] See http://www.adb.org/publications/asean3-information-transaction-flows-and-settlement-infrastructures.

Fees and Taxation in the Inter-Bank Bond Market

This chapter details the typical costs incurred by issuers and investors in the CIBM, with a particular emphasis on costs associated with bond or note issuance and settlement.

For ease of reference, the descriptions of the types of costs are given in the context of the actions taken by issuers or investors (as explained in this document) and follow the lifecycle of a bond or note in the CIBM.

A. Costs Associated with Bond and Note Issuance

These costs refer to those charges incurred as a result of the issuance of debt financing instruments in the CIBM, as charged by regulatory authorities, market institutions, and market intermediaries. Other costs will or may be incurred by the issuer through services obtained from market intermediates and supporting entities, such as law firms and accounting or audit firms.

The costs for the issuance of Panda bonds in the CIBM are commensurate with the typical costs shown in this chapter. Principally, nonresident issuers do not incur other charges in the market when compared to domestic issuers, with the notable exception being the credit rating process (see also section 5).

1. Approval from the People's Bank of China

Approval from the PBOC for debt financing instrument issuance is required for financial bonds issued by commercial or policy banks, as well as for Panda bonds issued by nonresident financial institutions. Please also see Chapter III.F for descriptions of the respective approval processes.

PBOC approval is mandated by law and does not attract a fee.

2. Registration with the National Association of Financial Market Institutional Investors

As the SRO for the CIBM, NAFMII exercises self-regulatory powers over issuance and market activities in the CIBM and conducts the registration (approval) processes for new issuance of debt financing instruments other than financial bonds and Panda bonds issued by nonresident financial institutions. Please see Chapter III.F for a comprehensive description of the registration process for particular issuer types.

The registration with NAFMII of nonfinancial debt financing instruments by resident and nonresident issuers is mandatory and involves a review and registration (or rejection) process. NAFMII does not levy a fee for this review and registration process.

3.   Underwriter Fee (Mandatory for Public Offerings)

The issuance of debt financing instruments by the private sector in the CIBM requires the use of an underwriter. If the issuer chooses to appoint more than one underwriter, a lead underwriter needs to be appointed. Underwriters for issuances by nonfinancial enterprises will have to be appropriately licensed by NAFMII, while the underwriting of financial bonds does not require a specific license from the PBOC. Please see Chapter III.M for more information on underwriters, as well as other market participants in the context of debt financing instrument issuance.

According to PBOC regulations, the underwriting fee for major underwriters should not be lower than 0.4% of the total bond amount. Typically, the fee may be expected to range between 0.4% and 0.6% of the total bond amount, including the underwriting syndicate fee, if so applicable. As another guide, and depending on the issuance method used, the underwriting fee for Treasury bonds is 0.1% of the total bond amount; for financial bonds, the underwriting fee is 0.15% of the issuance amount.

Ultimately, an underwriter will charge a fee commensurate with the effort and risk of a commitment or agency underwriting service for the debt financing instrument issue of the issuer. The fee is likely to follow established market practice or expectations and may be subject to negotiations between the issuer and (lead) underwriter.

4.   Bond Trustee Fee

Nonfinancial enterprises wanting to issue debt financing instruments in the CIBM are required to appoint a bond trustee effective 1 July 2020. While the role and responsibilities of the bond trustee are prescribed in the underlying NAFMII rules and prescribe the right of the bond trustee to charge fees and recover expenses, no fee guidance had been issued for this service provision at the time of compilation of this bond market guide.

In addition, some of the functions now assumed by the bond trustee had previously been carried out by the lead underwriter and were covered by the overall charges to the issuer. As such, it is likely that market practice will determine the fee level for this new service, which may result in a one-time and/or annual fee.

Please also see Chapter III.S for a description of the bond trustee concept introduced by NAFMII in December 2019.

5.   Initial Rating Fee (Mandatory)

Issuers wishing to issue their debt financing instruments in the CIBM will have to be rated and have their bonds rated by one or more domestic CRA in the case of a public offering. The rating is to be prominently featured in the public offering prospectus of the debt financing instruments to be issued. In turn, Panda bonds (those issued by a foreign entity) will need to be rated by at least one domestic CRA if they are to be publicly offered. In the case of a private placement, a credit rating is not mandatory and credit rating and tracking practices may be subject to the agreement between issuer and investors.

If the issuing company has not been rated for 3 consecutive years, any commercial paper it issues will need to be rated. Please see Chapter III.O for more details on the credit rating requirements in the CIBM.

Rating agencies will charge an initial rating fee commensurate with their expected work to determine such a credit rating. Given that the bond market in the PRC features a number of bond rating agencies, the initial rating fee is likely subject to market practices and commercial considerations. In the case of commercial paper, rating fees in the CIBM are expected to be between 0.01% and 0.02% of the total face value of the commercial paper.

6.   Registration of Debt Financing Instruments at the Central Securities Depositories

Debt financing instruments newly issued in the CIBM will need to be registered and deposited with CCDC or SHCH, depending on the type of instrument. The CSDs will charge the issuer for this initial or issuance registration.

The issuers are expected to pay the initial registration fee within 3 business days of the registration.

a.   China Central Depository & Clearing Co., Ltd.

CCDC charges issuance and registration fees by a certain proportion of the issuance amount from 0.6 basis points to 1.15 basis points, based on the issuance face value and tenor. Table 6.1 provides an overview of the fee distinctions.

Table 6.1: Debt Financing Instrument Registration Fees at CCDC

Tenor of Debt Financing Instrument 债务工具期限	Issuance Amount 发债额	Fee Rate (basis points)	Charging Basis 计费基数	Minimum Charge (CNY) 最低收费额 （万）
Up to 1 year	CNY3 billion (or less)	0.7	Charge by section based on bond face value (cumulative) 按发债面额分段计费 （累加）	5,000
	More than CNY3 billion	0.6		
1 year to 5 years	CNY3 billion (or less)	1.05	Charge by section based on bond face value (cumulative) 按发债面额分段计费 （累加）	10,000
	More than CNY3 billion	1.0		
5 years to 10 years	CNY3 billion (or less)	1.1	Charge by section based on bond face value (cumulative) 按发债面额分段计费 （累加）	15,000
	More than CNY3 billion	1.05		
More than 10 years	CNY3 billion (or less)	1.15	Charge by section based on bond face value (cumulative) 按发债面额分段计费 （累加）	20,000

CCDC = China Central Depository & Clearing Co., Ltd; CNY = Chinese renminbi.
Source: China Central Depository & Clearing Co., Ltd. www.chinabond.com.cn.

b.   Shanghai Clearing House Co., Ltd.

Pursuant to provisions in its issuer service agreement, SHCH charges a fee for the initial or issuance registration of debt financing instruments.

In its Shanghai Clearing House Methods on Charging for Registration and Settlement, issued in 2013, SHCH published the fee levels as shown in

Table 6.2, ranging from 0.3 basis points to 1.15 basis points of the face value and tiered according to the tenor of the debt financing instruments.

Table 6.2: Debt Financing Instrument Registration Fees at SHCH

Product Period	Charging Rate (basis points)		Minimum Fee (CNY)
	The part of issuance amount that is not more than CNY3 billion	The part of issuance amount that is higher than CNY3 billion	
Not more than 90 days	0.3		–
90 days up to 180 days	0.4		–
More than 180 days up to 270 days	0.5		–
More than 270 days up to 1 year	0.7	0.6	5,000
More than 1 year up to 3 years	1.0	0.9	10,000
More than 3 years up to 5 years	1.05	1.0	10,000
More than 5 years up to 10 years	1.1	1.05	15,000
More than 10 years	1.15	1.1	20,000

CNY = Chinese renminbi, SHCH = Shanghai Clearing House.
Source: Shanghai Clearing House Co., Ltd.
http://english.shclearing.com/csd/rules/201705/t20170510_258330.html?xyz=0.5524966347082564.

B.   Ongoing Costs for Issuers of Debt Financing Instruments

Once an issuer has issued debt financing instruments and registered them with the respective CSD, the issuer will incur some recurring costs throughout the lifecycle of the bonds or notes. Costs may include the service provision by a CRA, depending on the type of issuance, or paying agency services by the CSD.

1.   Interest Payment and Redemption Fee (Mandatory)

The CSDs in the China bond market also fulfill the role of a paying agent, carry out the payment of interest to bondholders on behalf of the issuer, and process the redemption of debt financing instruments upon maturity. To defray the costs incurred as a result of this service provision, the CSDs charge an interest payment and redemption fee to issuers during the lifetime of the bond or note.

a.   China Central Depository & Clearing Co., Ltd.

CCDC levies a fee for the provision of interest payment and redemption services through the lifecycle of a bond or note. The fee amounts to 0.05 basis points of the amount of interest payments and the redemption; there are no minimum or maximum amounts.

b. Shanghai Clearing House Co., Ltd.

SHCH charges a service fee for the payment of interest and principal, which is distinguished by the type of instrument. For debt financing instruments with a tenor of not more than 90 days, SHCH charges 0.3 basis points of the issuance amount, and 0.4 basis points for instruments between 90 days and 180 days. Services for those instruments with a tenor longer than 180 days are charged at 0.5 basis points of the issuance amount. No minimum fee applies.

2. (Annual) Credit Rating Fee

Debt financing instruments issued in the CIBM via a public offering will need to be rated upon issuance. In addition, such instruments are required to be monitored by CRAs throughout the tenor of the bond or note; this practice is referred to as rating tracking (跟踪评级).

The review and update of the credit rating by the CRAs results in a fee to the issuer, typically on an annual basis. This rating fee is expected to be subject to negotiation between the CRA and the issuer, and fee scales will follow market practice.

Please also see Chapter III.O for details on credit rating requirements in the CIBM.

C. Costs for Deposit and Withdrawal of Debt Financing Instruments

The CIBM is dematerialized; therefore paper-based certificates are no longer available. As such, there is no concept of a deposit or withdrawal of debt financing instruments by debt financing instrument holders during the tenor of an instrument, and there are no associated fees.

Instead, the CSDs only conduct bond registration and book-entry ownership transfer. The CSDs charge issuers fees for issuance services and charge investors account maintenance fees and settlement fees.

D. Costs for Account Maintenance at the Central Securities Depositories

1. China Central Depository & Clearing Co., Ltd.

CCDC charges its account holders account maintenance fees, either on the basis of the amount of holdings of debt financing instruments in an account, or as a flat fee. The fee method and fee level depend on the type of account holder (Table 6.3).

Table 6.3: CCDC Account Opening and Maintenance Fees

Account Type 账户类型	Charges Subject 收费标的	Fees 收费标准	Payee 收费主体
Type A account holder 甲类账户持有人	Holdings of more than CNY20 billion	CNY24,000 per month per household	CCDC
	Holdings of less than CNY20 billion	CNY12,000 per month per household	CCDC
Type B account holder 乙类账户持有人	Flat fee	CNY2,000 per month	CCDC
Type C account holder 丙类	New account	CNY500 one time per household	CCDC
Type D account holder 丙类账户持有人	Flat fee	CNY100 per month per household	Settlement agent 结算代理人

CCDC = China Central Depository & Clearing Co., Ltd; CNY = Chinese renminbi.
Source: CCDC.

2. Shanghai Clearing House Co., Ltd.

SHCH applies an account maintenance fee, which is charged to the account holder on a monthly basis (for Class A and Class B). The fee level differs depending on the type of account holder (Table 6.4).

Table 6.4: SHCH Account Maintenance Fees

Type of Holder Account	Charging Standard
Bond settlement agent (Class A)	CNY2,500 per month per account
Other direct settlement member (Class B)	CNY1,500 per month per account
Indirect settlement member (Class C)	CNY500 per account, collected when product is established

CNY = Chinese renminbi, SHCH = Shanghai Clearing House.
Source: Shanghai Clearing House Co., Ltd.

E. Costs Associated with Debt Financing Instrument Trading in the Inter-Bank Bond Market

CIBM transactions are carried out through the trading platform of CFETS and via the proprietary systems of money brokerage companies.

1. Transactions via the China Foreign Exchange Trading System

CFETS charges transaction fees to both parties in a transaction, based on the transaction amount. Transaction fee rates differ by product or financing maturity, and range from 0.5 to 2.5 per million, with a ceiling of CNY1,000 per transaction. Details on individual charges are shown in Table 6.5.

Table 6.5: China Foreign Exchange Trading System Transaction Fees for Debt Financing Instruments

Transaction Type	Tenor 交易类别	Fees (ppm) 收费标准（百万分之）
Financing transactions 融资类交易	1 day (including overnight)	0.5
Financing transactions 融资类交易	2 or more days	1.5
Sale transactions 买卖类交易		2.5

ppm = parts per million.
Note: 1 ppm = 0.0001%.
Source: China Foreign Exchange Trade System.

2.   Transactions Using a Money Broker

Money brokers charge a commission to their clients. The commission rate is typically subject to negotiation with each client.

F.   Costs for Settlement of Bond and Note Transactions and Transfers

Trades or transfer transactions in the CIBM are settled through accounts of the market participants or their intermediaries at CCDC or SHCH, typically depending on the type of instrument. The fees charged by the respective CSDs for the settlement of transactions in the CIBM differ by bond type and settlement method.

1.   China Central Depository & Clearing Co., Ltd.

CCDC charges settlement fees to both parties for every transaction. For different bond types and settlement methods, the fees range from CNY100 to CNY200. Table 6.6 contains an overview of the applicable charges.

Table 6.6: Settlement Charges at CCDC

Transaction Type (交易品种)	Settlement Type 结算方式	Charged Object 收费对象	Charge Subject 收费标的	Fee (CNY) 收费标准
Spot transaction 现券	FOP 纯券过户	The two parties of settlement 结算双方	Transaction 笔	100
	DVP			150
Pledged repo 质押式回购		The two parties of settlement 结算双方	Single bond per transaction 单券种 per 笔	120
			More than a single bond per transaction 多券种 per 笔	200
Outright repo 买断式回购		The two parties of settlement 结算双方	Transaction 笔	200
Bond forward 远期交易		The two parties of settlement 结算双方	Transaction 笔	170
Securities lending 证券借贷		The two parties of settlement 结算双方	Transaction 笔	200

CCDC = China Central Depository & Clearing Co., Ltd; CNY = Chinese renminbi; DVP = delivery versus payment; FOP = free of payment.
Source: China Central Depository & Clearing Co., Ltd. www.chinabond.com.cn.

2.   Shanghai Clearing House Co., Ltd.

SHCH charges a settlement transfer fee to both parties for every transaction. Settlement fees range from CNY100 to CNY200 per transaction according to the transaction types and settlement methods (Table 6.7).

SHCH also charges a nontrading transfer fee of CNY200 for each transfer that is not the result of a trade captured on the CFETS platform. The fee is charged to both transferor and transferee. In addition, if an account holder pledges debt financing instruments, the transfer between the bond account of the investor and the pledge account of the investor attracts a pledge transfer fee of CNY100.

If the counterparties settling through SHCH choose to use the CCP function prior to settlement, a different fee schedule applies. Detailed rules for the CCP function and fees can be found on the SHCH website.[106]

---

[106] See http://english.shclearing.com/ccpservices/rules/guidelines/201705/t20170510_258307.html?xyz=0.3852550403147222.

Table 6.7: Settlement Charges at SHCH

Transaction Type	Settlement Method	Charging Object	Charging Base	Charging Standard (CNY)
Cash bond	FOP	Two parties to a settlement	Case	100
	DVP, PAD, DAP			150
Pledged repo	DVP, PAD, DAP	Two parties to a settlement	Single bond type per case	120
			Multiple bond types per case	200
Outright repo	DVP, PAD, DAP	Two parties to a settlement	Case	200
Forward	DVP, PAD, DAP	Two parties to a settlement	Case	170

CNY = Chinese renminbi, DAP = delivery after payment, DVP = delivery versus payment, FOP = free of payment, PAD = payment after delivery, SHCH = Shanghai Clearing House.
Source: Shanghai Clearing House Co., Ltd.
http://english.shclearing.com/csd/rules/201705/t20170510_258330.html?xyz=0.2645883728836979.

3. Cross-Market Transfer Fee

In the event that a participant requests a cross-market transfer between accounts in different market segments, CCDC will charge a so-called cross-market fee.

For example, for Treasury bonds and local government bonds transferred from the CIBM to the exchange market, CCDC charges 0.005% of the bond par value, with a minimum fee of CNY10 and a maximum of CNY10,000 per transfer. Enterprise bonds are exempted from the cross-market transfer fee. This fee is charged to the account holder at CCDC.

G.   Taxation Framework

Tax legislation and policy are developed jointly by the State Administration of Taxation (SAT) and the MOF, with the SAT and its provincial and municipal offices administering taxation policies. Each locality in the PRC has a state tax bureau under the SAT and a local tax bureau under both the SAT and the local government.

Taxation treatment differs for domestic investors and for investments made by QFIIs and RQFIIs, as explained in the following sections.

1.   Tax Treatment for Investments by Qualified Foreign Institutional Investors and Renminbi Qualified Foreign Institutional Investors

According to circulars issued by the SAT and the MOF, as well as other materials, QFII and RQFII investments in central government bonds and local government bonds are exempted from the application of business tax, corporate income tax (CIT), and other relevant taxes.[107]

---

[107] In compiling this information, ABMF SF1 referred to publicly available materials produced by Citibank N.A., BNP Paribas, HSBC, PricewaterhouseCoopers, and others.

Interest income from PFBs and bonds issued by financial institutions is subject to a 10% withholding tax and a 6% value-added tax (VAT). Table 6.8 provides an overview of the taxation treatment for QFIIs and RQFIIs.

Table 6.8: Summary of Tax Treatment for Foreign Investors in the China Bond Market

| Items | Corporate Income Tax (WHT) | | | Value-Added Tax | |
| | Coupon Interest | | | | |
	QFII and RQFII (withheld at source for exchange-traded bonds)	CIBM Direct or Bond Connect (no withholding agent)	Capital Gains	Interest (no withholding agent)	Capital Gains
Government bonds and local government bonds	Exempt		Exempt	Exempt	Exempt
Other nongovernment bonds, including policy bank financial bonds	10%[a]		Exempt	6% (plus applicable surcharge)[a]	Exempt

CIBM = China Inter-Bank Bond Market, QFII = Qualified Foreign Institutional Investor, RQFII = Renminbi Qualified Foreign Institutional Investor, WHT = withholding tax.
[a] The Ministry of Finance and State Administration of Taxation issued a 3-year exemption (from 7 November 2018 to 6 November 2021) from the corporate income tax and value-added tax on interest income derived by foreign investors from their investment in the China bond market. For more details, see
http://www.chinatax.gov.cn/n810219/n810744/n3428471/n3428491/c3913568/content.html.
Sources: BNP Paribas, Citibank N.A., HSBC, PricewaterhouseCoopers, and other publicly available sources.

2.   Summary of Tax Treatment for Domestic Investors

For domestic investors, interest income derived from central government bonds and local government bonds is exempt from CIT and VAT. Capital gains are subject to a 6% VAT.

Table 6.9: Summary of Tax Treatment of Bond Investments by Domestic Institutional Investors

| Items | Corporate Income Tax (WHT) | | Value-Added Tax | |
	Coupon Interest	Capital Gains	Interest	Capital Gains
Government bonds and local government bonds	Not taxed	25%	Not taxed	6%
Government-supported bonds	12.5%	25%	Not taxed	6%
PBOC bills, policy bank financial bonds, commercial bank bonds	25%	25%	Not taxed	6%
Other bonds[a]	25%	25%	6%	6%

PBOC = People's Bank of China, WHT = withholding tax.
[a] The applicable tax rate for bonds issued by railway corporations is 12.5%.
Sources: BNP Paribas, Citibank N.A., HSBC, and other publicly available sources.

Interest income from PFBs and bonds issued by financial institutions is subject to a CIT of 25% and an additional 6% VAT if not held to maturity. Also, capital gains from investment in these instruments is subject to a 6% VAT. Table 6.9 provides an overview of the taxation treatment for domestic institutional investors in the exchange bond market.

3.   Corporate Income Tax

Treasury bonds and local government bonds are not subject to income tax, with the prevailing view and practice in the market that government bonds are specifically exempt from CIT.

4.   Withholding Tax

Interest paid to nonresident investors from debt instruments is subject to a 10% withholding tax (WHT).

According to the Corporate Income Tax Law, which took effect on 1 January 2008, as well as the Implementation Rules issued by the SAT on 23 January 2009, QFIIs and RQFIIs are also subject to a WHT of 10% on their PRC-sourced interest income. At the same time, interest income derived from government bond investments during the holding period is exempt from CIT.

As per market practice, the following entities are responsible for withholding WHT:

i.   bond issuers are required to withhold WHT on interest when the interest is paid or due; and
ii.   custodian agent banks of QFIIs or RQFIIs are also required to withhold a 10% tax on interest from all QFII or RQFII cash accounts, including CNY-denominated and foreign currency accounts.

Under the general tax provisions of the Corporate Income Tax Law, a nonresident enterprise that is not effectively connected with any establishment or place of business in the PRC (refers to tax technical term of permanent establishment) would be subject to a 10% withholding tax on capital gains from listed securities if such a tax were implemented.

On 30 August 2018, the State Committee of the State Council proposed a 3-year exemption from CIT and VAT on interest income derived by foreign investors from their investment in the China bond market. Caishui (财税) No. 108 (2018) announced a 3-year exemption (from 7 November 2018 to 6 November 2021) from CIT and VAT on interest income derived by foreign investors from their investments in the China bond market.

5.   Capital Gains Tax

On 14 November 2014, the MOF, the SAT, and CSRC jointly issued a notice regarding the tax treatment of capital gains for QFIIs and RQFIIs. The notice advised only that QFIIs and RQFIIs will be temporarily exempted from CIT for the capital gains derived from transferring stocks and other equity investments in the PRC, effective 17 November 2014, and they shall pay corporate income tax on the capital gains derived before 17 November 2014.

For securities traded in the exchange bond market (and in the CIBM), capital gains realized from bond sales were theoretically out of the scope for an application of CIT. As further advised by the MOF and the SAT in the PBOC meeting with CIBM bond settlement agents (CCDC and SHCH) on 20 October 2016, the framework for the application of CIT on CIBM capital gains was close to finalization, by which CIT on the capital gains of QFIIs and RQFIIs shall be exempted.

6. Value-Added Tax

On 23 March 2016, the MOF and SAT jointly issued Caishui No. 36, which sets out the detailed implementation rules for the transition from business tax to VAT. From 1 May 2016, VAT replaced the business tax to cover all sectors that used to fall under the business tax regime. For the financial industry, a 6% VAT now applies to nearly all major forms of remuneration derived from financial services.

According to Caishui No. 36 and Caishui No. 70 (released on 30 June 2016), the MOF and the SAT stipulated that

i. interest income from government bonds issued by the MOF and local government bonds is exempted from VAT, and
ii. income derived from securities trading through domestic companies appointed by QFIIs and RQFIIs is exempted from VAT.

According to Caishui No. 36, QFIIs are exempt from VAT with respect to gains derived from the trading of securities investments under the QFII scheme. However, it is uncertain whether RQFIIs can be exempted from VAT with respect to gains derived from the trading of securities investments and whether securities investments also include bond investments.

A 6% VAT will also apply to interest income derived from bond investment by domestic institutional investors, while the deposit interest income derived from cash accounts with commercial banks is beyond its scope.

7. Double Taxation Agreements

The PRC has entered into more than 100 double taxation agreements (DTAs).

If a nonresident investor can apply a DTA and the DTA rate differs, the tax treaty rate should apply. Eligible foreign investors may apply for relief under any relevant tax treaty. Foreign investors are required to submit documents to the SAT and state or local tax authorities for approval or reporting before they can enjoy tax treaty rates on dividends or interest.

RQFIIs who are eligible for a lower tax rate under a DTA can apply for tax-relief-at-source or file a reclaim from the tax bureau at the paying agent's domicile. For an RQFII's deposit interest, the custodian agent bank is willing, through its domicile tax bureau, to help eligible RQFIIs file the application to claim tax treaty benefits.

8. Stamp Duty

Stamp duty is not applicable for transactions in debt financing instruments in the CIBM. The application of stamp duty is limited to the equity market.

9. Transaction Tax

A transaction tax is not applicable in either the CIBM or in other market segments in the PRC.

VII

Market Size and Statistics

The original *ASEAN+3 Bond Market Guide* was published in April 2012 and included several pages of bond market statistics for the PRC, including historical data such as bond holdings, bondholder distribution, outstanding amounts, and trading volumes. Not surprisingly, this data became stale soon after publication.

Since the *ASEAN+3 Bond Market Guide* is most likely to be updated only on a biennial basis, it is not the best channel for the dissemination of market statistics. Hence, a chapter comprising bond market statistics has been discontinued and replaced with a list of recommended sources for detailed, accurate, and current information sources on the China Inter-Bank Bond Market. These sources are listed below in alphabetical order.

- *AsianBondsOnline* (an ASEAN+3 initiative led by ADB)
  https://asianbondsonline.adb.org/economy/?economy=CN.
    - Market-at-a-Glance
    - Data (market size, yields, indicators, ratings, historical data)
    - Market structure and summary
    - News (latest statistics)

- China Central Depository & Clearing Co., Ltd.
  http://www.chinabond.com.cn/Channel/317861.
    - General statistics
    - Indexes, yield curves, valuations
  http://www.chinabond.com.cn/Channel/147253508.
    - Monthly Bulletin of Statistics

- China Foreign Exchange Trade System
  http://new.chinamoney.com.cn/english/mdtrptdbl/.
    - Quotations, prices, yield curves, and indexes

- National Development and Reform Commission
  http://en.ndrc.gov.cn/.
    - General statistics

- People's Bank of China
  http://www.pbc.gov.cn/english/130437/index.html.
    - Yield curves, surveys, and statistics
    - Open market operation announcements

- Shanghai Clearing House
  www.shclearing.com.
    - Statistics

- State Administration of Foreign Exchange
  www.safe.gov.cn/wps/portal/english/Home.

VIII

Presence of an Islamic Bond Market

At present, there is no Islamic bond market in the PRC.

IX

Challenges and Opportunities in the Inter-Bank Bond Market

This chapter discusses some of the real and perceived challenges facing the CIBM, its market institutions, and its participants. This chapter also describes some of the possible mitigating factors or market developments that could address these challenges in an appropriate manner.

The China bond market has been a pioneer in the opening of the capital market in the PRC. Measures such as the launch of Bond Connect, the inclusion of the PRC's government bonds and indexes in global bond market indexes, and the abolition of quotas for the QFII and RQFII schemes have created both opportunities and challenges for the CIBM.

Yet, there is still ample room for further opening of the CIBM, with holdings of overseas investors accounting for only about 3% of the outstanding amount in the CIBM. In addition, available investment channels can be extended. Currently, overseas investors may participate in the CBIM through the QFII and RQFII schemes, or use CIBM Direct or Bond Connect. In the future, more flexible investment channels may be introduced.

A.   Challenges in the Inter-Bank Bond Market

Despite the rapid and successful development of the CIBM, particularly in recent years, there remain a number of challenges for policy bodies and regulatory authorities, market participants, and the bond market as a whole.

The purpose of this section is to state the challenges facing the CIBM and its constituents, together with any remedial action that is being implemented or in the planning stages.

1.   Improving Participation by Foreign Investors

NAFMII recently noted that the ratio of bonds outstanding to GDP in the PRC is far lower than the ratio in Japan, the US, and other developed economies, suggesting the China bond market has tremendous potential for further growth.

Specifically, the holdings of foreign investors in the China bond market accounted for only around 3% of all debt financing instruments outstanding, which is far less than corresponding shares of foreign holdings in Japan, the US, and other developed economies. With the further opening of the China bond market, and given the potentially attractive returns, it should be expected that more international investors will enter the China bond market.

2.   Improving the Investor Protection Mechanisms

NAFMII continues to undertake efforts to further improve the investor protection mechanisms to ensure the smooth operation of the CIBM; a selection of the challenges in this regard that NAFMII is trying to address is given below.

a.   Application of Investor Protection Covenants

NAFMII has been promoting the application of investor protection covenants. In September 2016, NAFMII published examples of investor protection clauses (投资人保护条款范例) for the first time. In April 2019, NAFMII published the Model Investor Protection Clauses (投资人保护条款示范) based on the 2016 version.

The 2019 model clauses provide six categories of investor protection clauses including cross-protection clauses, prior commitment clauses, prior binding clauses, change of control clauses, debt repayment guarantee clauses, and asset collateral clauses. To date, the 2019 model clauses have been for reference by the market only, and market organizations may apply these clauses as they deem necessary. Further development and application of the clauses in market practice among market participants is expected in the near future.[108]

b.   Feasibility of Tender Offer and Exchange Offer

NAFMII has been contemplating the feasibility of a tender offer and exchange offer concept for the CIBM and consulted with market experts.

An exchange offer is a form of tender offer in which bonds or other debt financing instruments are offered as consideration instead of cash. In a bond exchange offer, bondholders may consent to exchange their existing bonds for another class of debt financing instruments, or even equity securities. Companies may seek to exchange their debt financing instruments to extend maturities, reduce debt outstanding, or convert debt into equity.

3.   Building a Benchmark Interest Rate

Feedback from market participants and observers identified the lack of a defined benchmark rate for the China bond market, particularly for the CIBM since significant fundraising is done via shorter-term debt financing instruments. In recent times, the market recognized the significance of the 7-day reverse repo rate applied in the PBOC's open market operation as a key indicator, even a policy rate; this is also because the PBOC has not issued central bank bills regularly since 2016. At the same time, a formal short-term interest rate exists, the Shanghai Interbank Offered Rate (SHIBOR), but it may not be a suitable benchmark for bond issuance.

It is necessary for the policy bodies and regulatory authorities to formulate a strategy for the building of a sustainable benchmark interest rate. This would also improve liquidity in the secondary market, facilitate the innovation process of hedging instruments for interest rate risk (such as futures and options), and make possible the implementation of a monetary policy through direct financing instruments. The Government of the PRC and the PBOC recognize this need and have started to include this goal in the list of initiatives that policy bodies and regulatory authorities are

---

[108] This section is based on an abstract from a 2019 article《投资人保护条款范例》版之解读 from the *China Business Law Journal*《商法》月刊 by Wu Jiejiang 吴杰江, Jingtian & Gongcheng 竞天公诚律师事务所 13 June 2019, with permission from the author. http://www.jingtian.com/Content/2019/08-09/1817561535.html (in English); https://www.vantageasia.com/zh-hans/%E3%80%8A%E6%8A%95%E8%B5%84%E4%BA%BA%E4%BF%9D%E6%8A%A4%E6%9D%A1%E6%AC%BE%E8%8C%83%E4%BE%8B%E3%80%8B2019%E7%89%88%E4%B9%8B%E8%A7%A3%E8%AF%BB/ (in Chinese).

working on; see also Chapter IX.A for information on the new Financial Stability and Development Commission and other relevant developments.

4.   More Financing Opportunities for Small and Medium-Sized Private Enterprises

Presently, the corporate credit fixed-income market is facing the challenge of establishing a submarket that can bring together those issuers with lower credit ratings, such as SMEs, private enterprises that are excluded from the market, and enterprises that rely on higher-cost bank loans to access the fixed-income market to raise money.

Several innovations in relation to SMEs were launched in recent years, including the ability to issue SME collective notes, as well as the initiation and establishment of China Bond Insurance Co., Ltd. So far, these measures have only partially achieved their declared targets.

Companies with a lower credit rating planning to enter the market may face legal restrictions on the investment risks their potential issuances may represent, as stipulated by the regulatory authorities. A more flexible approach would enable the creation of a segment of eligible investment-grade type companies (such as BBB–, which is three levels below the ratings currently accepted by the market) to issue bonds.

Reform measures for both the buy-side and the sell-side are needed, along with innovations to attract appropriate investors. For instance, on 19 September 2018, the PBOC called for financial institutions to improve their service provisions related to the fundraising by private companies. The PBOC now requires financial institutions to treat fairly the private companies and SOEs in their fund- and capital-raising efforts.[109]

5.   Ringfencing of a Professional Investor Market

Traditionally, while participation in the CIBM was considered, typically by its participants, for an institutional investor only market, the absence of a formal professional investor concept and the existence of a number of individual investors among NAFMII's membership provided doubt as to whether the CIBM could indeed be considered a ringfenced professional marketplace like those in many regional bond markets.

The introduction of the concept of DIIs, or private placement investors, in 2011 and the subsequent promulgation of regulations supporting SIIs in 2015, in combination with bond issuance via private placement, have led to a clearly defined issuance method that, for all intents and purposes, represents a closed market place for institutional investors that is comparable to a professional market.

Please also see Chapter III.N for more information on the private placement investor and SII concepts.

6.   Language of Issuance Documentation

Nonresident issuers are already able to issue Panda bonds in either the CIBM or exchange bond market, and recent changes have seen many more nonresident investors access the China bond market, both directly and via other market access concepts, including CIBM Direct and Bond Connect. Common to these parties is the familiarity with English as the typical, common language for issuance documentation

---

[109] Adapted by ABMF SF1 from an article on aastocks.com at https://www.theasset.com/china-today.

and disclosure items in international markets. The increasing participation of nonresident constituents may press for further concessions to use the English language in the context of debt financing instrument issuance and investment.

Policy bodies and regulatory authorities in the PRC have already recognized this demand and introduced the concession that, in the case of Panda bonds offered to private placement investors or DIIs (see Chapter III.N for a description of this investor type) via private placement, nonresident issuers may provide a summary of the issuance documentation and disclosure items in a language other than Chinese, such as in English, in addition to (or instead of) the Chinese language documentation and disclosure.

According to Article 29 of the 2019 NAFMII Guidelines, for debt financing instruments offered by nonresident issuers through private placement, the principal registration and offering documents (private placement agreement for DIIs or private placement offering memorandum for DIIs and SIIs) shall be in Chinese or in English accompanied with a Chinese version. Other documents may be in either Chinese or English as agreed between the issuer and the investors. Information disclosure during the life of such instruments may be made in Chinese or English as agreed between the issuer and the investors. Similar such concessions exist for Panda bond issuers that regularly issue and are subject to continuous disclosure in English in other markets.

7.   Credit Rating Quality

The announcement on the introduction of unified credit rating rules and regulations (see Chapter IX.A.3) has started to address one of the lingering challenges in the China bond market. Until now, the credit ratings given to debt financing instruments issued by enterprises tended to be of very high quality, with a distinct gravitation toward AA and AAA ratings. In a bond market with diversified issuers and instruments, such rating concentration was viewed with concern, and a recent string of defaults has given rise to further doubts.

However, this challenge has been recognized by policy bodies and regulatory authorities in the CIBM and measures taken, such as the proposed uniform credit rating guidelines, together with granting permission to foreign CRAs to enter the bond rating business, are intended to significantly improve the credit rating process and outcome.

On 14 February 2019, in a first-of-its-kind action, NAFMII and the Securities Association of China (the SRO for the exchange market) jointly issued a circular on the fourth quarter of 2018 business operation and compliance of CRAs operating in the China bond market.

8.   Inclusion in Global Bond Indexes

Recently, PRC government bonds have begun to be included in global bond market indexes. Index providers had previously argued that a number of market features would first have to be evident and remaining limitations reduced to make the China bond market and its instruments more comparable to international markets.

However, the recent very rapid developments in the China bond market, particularly in the CIBM, in combination with the significant liberalization of foreign investor access, have changed the perception of the index providers. Please see Chapter IV.F for more information on bond indexes with relevance to the China bond market.

The inclusion in global bond market indexes of PRC government bonds is expected to bring significant additional capital inflows and new investor groups, such as passive (i.e., index-driven) investment funds, into the China bond market.

9.   Straight-Through Processing Limitations under CIBM Direct

Feedback from market participants identified a lack of straight-through processing in the order placing process for investors via CIBM Direct, in particular in comparison to the process prevalent for Bond Connect investors. At present, a trade from a CIBM Direct investor may be placed in Bloomberg (or another trading platform) and requires confirmation on CFETS by the bond settlement agent before trade execution. At the same time, a trade—entered in the same trading platform—placed by a Bond Connect investor will be executed directly in CFETS without further confirmation. For international investors accessing the CIBM through a number of market access channels, this multitude of processes may not be easy to understand and adopt. Market participants have begun to engage the regulatory authorities on this subject.

10.   Separate Registration for Each Investment Fund

At the time of compilation of this bond market guide, the registration of new foreign investors in the CIBM through CIBM Direct was required for every investment fund or vehicle, regardless of whether multiple investment funds are being managed by the same asset manager. The need to provide the same or similar documentation, translated into Chinese, for each investment fund is cost- and time-intensive and represents significant work for both the investing entity and market intermediaries, including the CSDs. Market participants have started a dialogue with the PBOC to address this subject and potentially make the registration process simpler and more efficient.

11.   Repo Transactions Only for Selected Investor Types

Under present regulations, only foreign central banks, international financial organizations, sovereign wealth funds, RMB clearing banks, and foreign participating banks are able to participate in repo transactions in the CIBM. With the majority of repo transactions in the market concluded to achieve additional returns on existing holdings, this opportunity is not available to the majority of QOII accessing the CIBM.

Given that policy bodies and regulatory authorities have signaled a continued liberalization of the China bond and capital market, including the CIBM, this subject may be addressed at the appropriate time.

B.   Opportunities in the Inter-Bank Bond Market

The opportunities described here represent in part the response by policy makers and regulatory authorities to the challenges mentioned earlier, as well as those inherent in recent, announced, or planned market developments in their own right.

1.   Panda Bonds

The increasing issuances of Panda bonds in the China bond market, particularly in the CIBM, is evidence that more issuers and more diversified issuer types are seeing the Panda issuance concept as a viable market access method to raise funds either for domestic use or outside the PRC. The clarification of the Panda bond regulations announced in September 2018 (Interim Measures jointly announced by the MOF and the PBOC) and the subsequent NAFMII Guidelines released in January 2019 (see Chapter X.A.10) might have further led nonresident issuers to consider issuing Panda bonds, as institutional arrangements, including the possibility of issuance documentation and disclosure information in English, continue to be improved.

2. Liberalization of Market Access

The significant changes brought by policy bodies and regulatory authorities to the market access regime for the China bond market in recent years, including the introduction of CIBM Direct and, particularly, Bond Connect, have already resulted in strongly increased investments in the CIBM by nonresidents. Further liberalization measures already announced will amplify the market's attractiveness, and offer opportunities for both investors and domestic service providers.

Please also see Chapter I for a description of the major steps taken in the liberalization of the CIBM and Chapter II.N for more information on the market access avenues available to foreign investors.

3. Inclusion of People's Republic of China Government Bonds into Global Bond Indexes

In 2019, a number of international providers of bond indexes announced the inclusion of PRC government bonds in global bond indexes, with the participation of these bonds phased in over a period of 10–20 months (see Chapter X.A.2 for details).

Investors tracking these global indexes have increased their holdings of PRC government bonds to more closely match their portfolios to these indexes, which is expected to result in significant inflows of additional capital in the next 2 years. The indexes will also provide additional visibility for PRC government bonds to the international investment community.

4. ASEAN+3 Multi-Currency Bond Issuance Framework

The discussion around implementation of AMBIF in the PRC could serve as a conduit for the formal recognition of a professional investor concept and of the CIBM as a professional bond market segment featuring the key market elements that would support issuances under AMBIF. This is likely to significantly increase interest among international institutions—both issuers and investors—to do business in the China bond market.

For a more detailed description of AMBIF, please refer to Chapter X.B.

X

Recent Developments and Future Direction

A. Recent Developments

Recent major developments are considered those that occurred or have been announced in the PRC since the first publication of the *ASEAN+3 Bond Market Guide* in April 2012, with a particular focus on the CIBM.

1. Revision of Rules and Regulations for Registration and Issuance

On 16 April 2020, NAFMII published revisions of a number of rules and regulations related to the registration and issuance of debt financing instruments by nonfinancial enterprises. The revisions included rules for both publicly offered debt financing instruments and provisions related to private placements, specifically PPN. NAFMII's stated purpose of the revisions was to streamline the registration process and to encourage further issuance of debt financing instruments.

NAFMII introduced a further differentiation of issuers through sub-categories and specific disclosure obligations or concessions for each of these sub-categories. NAFMII also included provisions for the use of a bond trustee (see also next section) in the public offering rules. The new rules took effect on 1 July 2020.

The description of the new categories and the related changes and concessions can be found in Chapter II.F.

2. Introduction of a Bond Trustee Concept

On 27 December 2019, NAFMII introduced the concept of a formal "bond trustee" to assume the role of representative of debt financing instrument holders for instruments (to be) registered with NAFMII. The new rules took effect on 1 July 2020.

The new rules, formally called Guidelines for Bond Trustee Business of Non-Financial Enterprise Debt Financing Instruments in the Inter-Bank Bond Market (for Trial Implementation) (银行间债券市场非金融企业债务融资工具受托管理人业务指引(试行)), stipulate that the bond trustee represents the debt financing instrument holders when necessary.

For more details about the designation of bond trustee and their qualifications, as well as provisions for bond trustee activities, please refer to Chapter III.S. The change of a bond trustee or of a bond trustee agreement has also been included as a reason for the calling of a meeting of debt financing instrument holders in corresponding meeting rules and procedures issued by NAFMII in December 2019 and effective in July 2020. Chapter III.R has more details on the reasons and processes around debt financing instrument holder meetings.

3.   State Administration of Foreign Exchange Abolished Qualified Foreign Institutional Investor and Renminbi Qualified Foreign Institutional Investor Quotas

Effective 10 September 2019, SAFE announced the abolition of the investment quotas for the QFII and RQFII schemes for market access into the PRC capital market. With investment allocation and repatriation limitations gradually eliminated in recent years (see also section 6), only the need to apply for a QFII or RQFII license and some administrative actions remain. Please also see Chapter II.N for comprehensive descriptions of the QFII and RQFII market access schemes.

4.   Inclusion of People's Republic of China Government Bonds in International Bond Indexes

In early September 2019, J.P. Morgan announced that it would begin including PRC government bonds in its GBI-EM, eventually comprising a share of 10% of the GBI-EM. The inclusion of PRC government bonds in the BGI-EM commenced on 28 February 2020 and was scheduled to occur over a 10-month period, at a rate of 1% per month, to lessen market impact.

Starting in April 2019, Bloomberg began to include PRC government bonds in its Bloomberg Barclays Global Aggregate Index; the inclusion was to be phased in over a 20-month period and would represent about 6% of the total index value upon completion. At the same time, PRC government bonds also became eligible for inclusion in the Bloomberg Barclays Global Treasury and Emerging Markets Local Currency Government Indexes.[110]

5.   Unified Management of the Credit Rating Business

On 11 September 2018, the PBOC and CSRC announced the creation of unified guidelines for CRAs and their activities in both the CIBM and exchange bond markets in response to findings in a review of CRAs and their work.[111] The guidelines are intended to improve credit rating quality; increase transparency in the credit rating business in the China bond market overall; and unify the admission of CRAs, their supervision and inspection, as well as the actual credit rating process across bond market segments.

In July 2017, the PBOC opened the bond credit rating market to the outside world by permitting the set-up of overseas CRAs and their conducting of credit rating operations in the CIBM, promoting the further liberalization of the CIBM and the healthy development of the credit rating industry in the PRC. In January 2019, the PBOC permitted S&P Global (China) Ratings to register for credit rating services in the CIBM. S&P Global (China) Ratings issued its first bond credit rating in July 2019.[112] In May 2020, Fitch (China) Bohua Credit Ratings Ltd. received PBOC approval and a license from NAFMII to carry out bond rating activities in the CIBM.

For a detailed description of the eligibility and regulation of CRAs, please see Chapter II.O. The actual credit rating requirements for the issuance of debt financing instruments in the CIBM are covered in Chapter III.O.

---

[110] Information adapted from the October 2019 issue of *ChinaBond Watch* and news reports in the public domain.
[111] See Joint Notice No. 14 (2018), Enhance Unified Management of Credit Rating and Facilitate Connectivity of the Bond Market, at http://www.pbc.gov.cn/english/130721/3628161/index.html.
[112] Information adapted from news reports in the public domain.

6.   Introduction of the Financial Stability and Development Commission

In November 2017, the Government of the PRC formally set up the FSDC under the State Council to oversee financial stability and development focusing on the deliberation and coordination of major issues concerning financial stability and related reform and development in the financial and capital markets.

According to a news release by the State Council, the primary purposes of the FSDC are to "strengthen financial regulatory coordination and supplement regulatory shortcomings, strengthen the regulatory role of financial regulatory departments, and ensure the safe and stable development of the Chinese financial sector."[113] Its remit includes structural optimization and improvements to financial markets, financial institutions, and the financial products system.

The FSDC is expected to uphold quality as its chief priority, guide the financial sector's development in coordination with economic and social development, expedite the convenience of financing, reduce costs in the real economy, raise resource allocation efficiency, and ensure that risk is controllable.

In addition, the National People's Congress approved the State Council Organization Reform Plan in March 2018. Under the plan, a restructuring of the financial administration was carried out, including the integration of the CBRC and the CIRC, which led to the new CBIRC with more comprehensive functions. At the same time, the functions of planning legislation and prudential policy making, originally residing with CBRC and CIRC, were transferred to the PBOC.

Traditionally, the functions of financial institution supervision and management were dispersed among the CBRC, CIRC, CSRC, and PBOC. In recent years, obstacles to the development of the domestic financial securities markets have been revealed by the expansion of shadow banking and Internet finance; in particular, the regulatory division of the separate bond markets has been noted as an obstacle. There is an urgent need for more fluid, developmentally comprehensive cooperation among market participants across the traditional industry to address market barriers and a rectification of imbalances with regard to enforcement. The financial supervisory control system under the initiative of the FSDC will use this new environment toward further integration of financial market administration.

7.   One Belt, One Road Bond Issuances

The "One Belt, One Road" initiative, or the Belt and Road Initiative (BRI), is a global development strategy adopted by the Government of the PRC in 2013 that entails infrastructure development and investments in 152 countries and international organizations in Asia, Europe, and elsewhere. BRI-themed, foreign-currency-denominated bonds have been issued since 2015.

In May 2017, the first batch of a China Merchants Port Hong Kong MTN was issued in the Panda bond market, raising CNY2.5 billion and representing the first medium-term Panda bond in the CIBM for projects pursuant to the BRI.

In October 2017, a global provider of modern logistics facilities, Global Logistic Properties (via Iowa China Offshore Holdings [Hong Kong] Limited, GLP's PRC holding company) issued CNY1 billion of Panda bonds in the CIBM to finance construction of properties along BRI routes. GLP became the first international company to issue Panda bonds in both the CIBM and the exchange bond market.

---

[113] State Council, Government of the PRC. 2017. *News Release*. 9 November.
http://english.gov.cn/news/top_news/2017/11/08/content_281475936107760.htm.

In June 2016, Bank of China signed a memorandum of understanding on Panda bond issuance with Poland's Ministry of Finance. In August 2016, the Government of Poland subsequently issued CNY3 billion worth of Panda bonds with a tenor of 3 years.

With its inaugural CNY1.46 billion Panda bond in March 2018, the Philippines became the first ASEAN member to issue Panda bonds. Access to the issuance via Bond Connect resulted in foreign investors representing 87.7% of the allocation, the highest proportion of foreign investors for any Panda bond issuance to date.

8.   Introduction of Bond Connect

On 16 May 2017, the PBOC and the Hong Kong Monetary Authority announced their approval for PRC and Hong Kong, China financial infrastructure institutions to collaborate in establishing mutual bond market access between the PRC and Hong Kong, China under a scheme known as Bond Connect.[114]

Bond Connect is an arrangement that will enable PRC-based and overseas investors to trade, settle, and hold bonds tradable in the China and Hong Kong bond markets through connections between PRC and Hong Kong, China financial infrastructure institutions. The actual connection was established between the CMU of the Hong Kong Monetary Authority with CCDC and SHCH, in the manner that CMU account holders are able to access the CIBM via the CMU by using their preferred electronic trading platforms, such as Bloomberg or TradeWeb, as a conduit to CFETS. For more information on the features of Bond Connect, please refer to Chapter IV.

Bond Connect has been implemented in phases. Trial operation of Northbound Trading commenced on 3 July 2017 as an initial phase so that, for example, overseas investors from Hong Kong, China and other economies and regions can invest in the CIBM through Bond Connect. This aims to provide overseas investors with a new and more convenient channel to invest in the CIBM in addition to existing channels such as the QFII, RQFII, and CIBM Direct schemes.

Bond Connect abides by the relevant laws and regulations of the bond markets of the two jurisdictions. Northbound Trading follows the current policy framework for overseas participation in the CIBM and, at the same time, respects international norms and practices. The scope of eligible investors and products under Northbound Trading are consistent with the scope specified in the relevant notices promulgated by the PBOC. Through cooperation and connections between the financial infrastructure of the two jurisdictions, overseas investors can more conveniently invest in the CIBM, allocate Chinese renminbi assets, and manage associated risks. There is no investment quota for Northbound Trading. A version of Bond Connect that incorporates Southbound Trading may be considered in the future.

9.   Changes in the Qualified Foreign Institutional Investor and Renminbi Qualified Foreign Institutional Investor Schemes

Starting with its inception in 2002, the QFII market access concept resulted in an allocated investment quota of USD111.04 billion through the end of August 2019, before SAFE abolished the quota system in September 2019. In addition, 243 RQFII licenses had been issued through September 2019, amounting to an available quota of CNY1,990 billion, of which CNY691.6 billion had been utilized.

In the past few years, the QFII and RQFII schemes have undergone a significant liberalization in line with the broader efforts of policy bodies and regulatory authorities to liberalize the China bond and capital markets.

---

[114] Information adapted from original press release referenced in NAFMII newsletter dated 19 May 2017.

In 2016, the limitations on QFIIs and RQFIIs to allocate funds to specific instruments and transaction types were removed; in June (RQFII) and September 2018 (QFII), the Government of the PRC announced that the caps and any remaining time limits for the repatriation of capital and interest had also been removed. On 10 September 2019, SAFE announced the abolition of the investment quotas for the QFII and RQFII schemes.

Please also see Chapter II.N for more detailed information on the QFII and RQFII concepts, as well as Chapter I.D for the individual development steps of the QFII and RQFII market access schemes in the context of overall bond market development.

10. China Banking and Insurance Regulatory Commission Issued Guidelines for Commercial Banks to Manage Collateral

In May 2017, CBRC (now CBIRC) issued the Guidelines for Commercial Banks to Manage Collateral (银监会发布《商业银行押品管理指引》). The guidelines, composed of seven chapters with 48 articles, emphasize that commercial banks shall abide by the principles of legitimacy, validity, prudence, and subordination; improve the organizational structure of collateral management; enhance risk management of key aspects such as classification and valuation of collateral, and the rate setting of mortgages or pledges, among others; and regulate such processes as collateral investigation and assessment, pledge or mortgage establishment and duration management, as well as return and disposal of collateral.[115]

The guidelines direct commercial banks to improve their collateral-related systems and rules, as well as the information systems in use, to define job responsibilities, and to regulate the collateral management processes. The guidelines raise clear requirements for the classification and valuation of collateral, concentration management, and stress tests, helping commercial banks strengthen their risk management in relation to raising, valuing, and managing collateral.

11. Launch of CIBM Direct

PBOC Public Notice No. 3, issued on 17 February 2016, paved the way for foreign central banks, foreign currency authorities, sovereign wealth funds, RMB clearing banks in Hong Kong, China and Macau, China, and any foreign institutional investor who was qualified as a QOII to access the CIBM directly to trade cash bonds and other transactions approved by the PBOC, without a ceiling investment amount or restrictions of fund transfer, under the so-called CIBM Direct concept. Please see Chapter I.D.4 for a more detailed description of the CIBM Direct concept.

In the CIBM, QFIIs and RQFIIs (see also Chapter III.N) have been considered and regulated as QOIIs since then.

12. Broadening and Deepening of Panda Bond Issuances

In recent years, the China bond market has seen a significant broadening and deepening of the Panda bond issuance avenue, from initial issuances being made only by multilateral development organizations to present-day corporate and foreign sovereign bond issuances.

In March 2014, German carmaker Daimler AG became the first issuer of a corporate Panda bond in the CIBM. In September 2015, the PBOC eased restrictions on the use of proceeds from Panda bonds to be used within and outside the PRC, and on

---

[115] Information adapted from NAFMII newsletter dated 12 May 2017.

8 September 2018, the PBOC and MOF jointly issued the Interim Measures for Administration of Bond Issuance by Overseas Institutions in the National Inter-Bank Bond Market, which introduced the ability to issue Panda bonds in the CIBM via a public offering or a private placement to DIIs or SIIs, and further defined information disclosure, issuance registration, custody, settlement, as well as CNY-denominated account opening, fund exchange, and investor protection. In 2016, Poland became the first European country to issue Panda bonds in the CIBM, while Hungary issued the first sovereign Panda bond in 2017 for which the subscription and allocation was accessible through Bond Connect.

In January 2019, NAFMII issued the Guidelines on Debt Financing Instruments of Overseas Non-Financial Enterprises (for Trial Implementation), which further clarified details for Panda bond issuance registration and information disclosure by nonresident corporate issuers. Both the interim measures and the NAFMII Guidelines contain concessions for nonresident issuers on the use of English in issuance documentation and disclosure information.

For further information on Panda bonds as the issuance method for nonresident issuers, please see Chapter III.E. In addition, Chapter I.D.5 outlines some of the steps mentioned above in the context of the increased opening of the China bond market overall.

13. First Special-Drawing-Rights-Denominated Bonds in the Inter-Bank Bond Market

In September 2016, the World Bank successfully issued its first tranche of SDR-denominated bonds in the CIBM. The first issuance amounted to SDR500 million with a term of 3 years. The bonds will be payable in Chinese renminbi. Over 50 domestic institutional investors—including banks, securities firms, and insurance companies—as well as foreign monetary authorities and international institutions submitted bids for the bonds, with a bid-to-cover ratio of 2.47. In October 2016, Standard Chartered Bank (Hong Kong) Limited issued SDR100 million worth of 1-year bonds, the first commercial bank to sell SDR-denominated bonds.

The SDR-denominated bond added a new product category to the China bond market, which may be used to diversify the portfolios of domestic and international investors. The issuance also helped broaden the use and acceptance of SDR.

B. Future Direction

1. Further Opening of the People's Republic of China Capital Market (Bond Market)

On 11 April 2018, at the Boao (博鳌) Forum for Asia Annual Conference, President Xi Jinping announced that the PRC would significantly broaden market access, and PBOC Governor Yi Gang announced specific measures and a time frame for the further opening of the financial industry.

The PRC is expected to continue with capital account convertibility reform and deepen the reform of the Chinese renminbi exchange rate formation mechanism. Market participants are expected to be more involved and active in the Chinese renminbi exchange market and the CNY-denominated bond market.

Financial institutions, especially commercial banks, will need to provide better services in Chinese renminbi clearing and settlement, investment and financing, trading, and asset management to facilitate the use of Chinese renminbi in payment, settlement, investment, and as a reserve currency so that the breadth and depth of the Chinese renminbi's internationalization will be enhanced.

The release of the associated PBOC notice improved the institutional arrangements for overseas institutions to issue bonds in the CIBM, aligned the domestic institutional rules with international standards, and helped further the internationalization of the China bond market.

Furthermore, on 30 August 2018, the State Committee of the State Council proposed a 3-year exemption from CIT and VAT on interest income derived by foreign investors from their investment in the China bond market. The MOF and the SAT are expected to issue detailed regulations in due course.

In recognition of the importance of eliminating potential anxiety factors over the medium to long term, it is expected that more permanent tax exemption measures will be put in place to support the development of a stable and sustainable domestic bond market.

2.   Consideration of a China Inter-Bank Bond Market-Wide Trustee Concept

To further strengthen the mechanisms for investor protection in the CIBM, both the PBOC and NAFMII had been considering the implementation of a trustee-like concept for the CIBM, similar to the exchange bond market, which would allow for the consolidation of a number of roles presently performed by different entities in the CIBM. While NAFMII introduced a formal bond trustee concept in December 2019 (effective July 2020) for debt financing instruments (to be) registered with NAFMII, the PBOC may consider implementing a similar concept for all issuances in the CIBM, potentially making allowances for certain types of issuances (e.g., private placements), as is common in other regional markets.

Please see Chapter III.S for more information on the bond trustee concept introduced by NAFMII.

3.   ASEAN+3 Multi-Currency Bond Issuance Framework

The introduction of AMBIF in regional markets in 2015 signaled another potential opportunity for bond issuance activities in markets other than those of the framework's original adopters, which were Hong Kong, China; Japan; Malaysia; the Philippines; Singapore; and Thailand.

Potential issuers have identified the PRC as one of the markets of particular interest, largely due to the size and attractiveness of such a large market but also to support the decentralized funding of domestic business operations in the PRC.

Aimed particularly at the issuance of debt financing instruments and corporate bonds to professional investors in participating markets, AMBIF encourages domestic and regional issuers to take advantage of streamlined issuance approval processes across the region. For additional information on AMBIF, kindly refer to the ADB website.[116]

The key advantage of AMBIF for the PRC lies in the ability of regional issuers (including those from the PRC) to tap multiple markets in addition to their domestic bond market while using the same or similar key disclosure documentation and comparable approval processes. This offers an alternative for corporate issuers to

---

[116] See ADB. 2015. *Implementation of the ASEAN+3 Multi-Currency Bond Issuance Framework: ASEAN+3 Bond Market Forum Sub-Forum 1 Phase 3 Report.* https://www.adb.org/publications/implementation-ambif-asean3-bond-market-forum-sf1-p3.

issue bonds across markets instead of (or in addition to) relying on other forms of funding.

AMBIF prescribes, among other elements, the presence of a professional investors only market segment and the use of documentation in English. The CIBM private placement scheme already contains many of the features necessary for the issuance of AMBIF bonds in the near future.

Notably, the use of issuance documentation and disclosure information in English, possibly in addition to documentation in Chinese, is permitted in principle in the most recent Panda bond regulations (see also Chapter III.G). It has become a subject for adoption in market practice and is under further consideration by the policy bodies and regulatory authorities in the PRC.

Appendix 1
Compliance with International Principles

The Group of Thirty recommendations were originally conceived as the group's Standards on Securities Settlement Systems in 1989, detailing in a first-of-its-kind report nine recommendations for efficient and effective securities markets covering legal, structural, and settlement process areas.

The recommendations were subsequently reviewed and updated in 2001 under the leadership of the Bank for International Settlements and through the efforts of a joint task force of the Committee on Payment and Settlement Systems and the Technical Committee of the International Organization of Securities Commissions.

Compliance with the Group of Thirty recommendations in individual markets is often an integral part in the securities industry participants' and intermediaries' due diligence process.

The China bond market, in fact the capital market at large, only began to open to foreign investors with the introduction of the QFII concept in 2002. As such, policy bodies, regulatory authorities, and market institutions have focused on the more recently introduced benchmarking and monitoring practices in the financial and securities markets.

One critical measure in the securities markets in recent years has been conformity with the Principles of Financial Market Infrastructures (PFMI), jointly introduced in 2012 and also monitored by committees of the Bank of International Settlements and the International Organization of Securities Commissions.[117] The PFMI are international standards for systemically important payment systems, central securities depositories, securities settlement systems, central counterparties, and trade repositories.

According to the third update on the implementation monitoring of the implementation level 1 of the PFMI, published on 28 June 2016, regulators and market infrastructure providers in the PRC had achieved level-1 compliance with the PFMI and were awarded the highest rating, including those in the CIBM.[118]

Level 1 of the implementation monitoring program includes monitoring whether jurisdictions have completed the process of adopting their legislation and other policies that will enable them to implement the PFMI.

---

[117] A portion of the text has been adopted from Bank of International Settlement and International Organization of Securities Commissions. 2012. *Principles of Financial Market Infrastructures.* https://www.iosco.org/library/pubdocs/pdf/IOSCOPD377-PFMI.pdf.
[118] For the full text of the third update report, please see https://www.iosco.org/library/pubdocs/pdf/IOSCOPD534.pdf.

CSRC, as well as the other relevant regulatory authorities in the China bond market and its market institutions, remain committed to adopting international standards and practices.

Appendix 2
Practical References

For easy access to further information about the market features described in this Inter-Bank Bond Market Guide for the People's Republic of China—including information on the policy bodies, regulatory authorities, and securities market-related institutions—interested parties are encouraged to utilize the following links (most web pages are available in English):

AsianBondsOnline (ADB)
https://asianbondsonline.adb.org/economy/?economy=CN.

China Banking and Insurance Regulatory Commission
https://www.cbirc.gov.cn/en/view/pages/index/index.html.

China Central Depository & Clearing Co. Ltd.
http://www.chinabond.com.cn/d2s/eindex.html.

China Foreign Exchange Trade System & National Interbank Funding Center
http://www.chinamoney.com.cn/english/.

Ministry of Finance of the People's Republic of China
www.mof.gov.cn (Chinese only).

National Association of Financial Market Institutional Investors
http://www.nafmii.org.cn/english/.

National Development and Reform Commission of the People's Republic of China
http://en.ndrc.gov.cn.

People's Bank of China
http://www.pbc.gov.cn/english/130437/index.html.

Shanghai Clearing House
http://english.shclearing.com.

State Administration of Foreign Exchange
http://www.safe.gov.cn/wps/portal/english/Home.

Chinalawinfo Co., Ltd.—Peking University online legal information service in English
www.lawinfochina.com.

A list of the applicable laws and regulations with relevance for the CIBM is provided below for easy reference (Table A3). The information given was correct at the time of the completion of this bond market guide and will be updated periodically. Since the CIBM is developing rapidly, interested parties are encouraged to regularly check the links provided elsewhere in this bond market guide for the latest versions.

In the PRC, the terms "Inter-Bank Bond Market," "Inter-bank Bond Market," "Interbank Bond Market," and "national interbank bond market" and similar variations may be used intermittently in the titles and text of regulations and rules, but are considered to have the same meaning. As explained in this bond market guide, the expression "Inter-Bank Bond Market" is used here to differentiate the CIBM from its origins as a typical interbank market and to offer a consistent term.

Table A3: List of Laws and Regulations for the Inter-Bank Bond Market

Legislative Tier	Content or Significant Examples
Laws (key legislation)	• Law of the People's Republic of China on the People's Bank of China • Law of the People's Republic of China on Banking and Supervision • Law of the People's Republic of China on Funds for Investment in Securities • Company Law of the People's Republic of China (中华人民共和国公司法 (2013修正)), 2013 Amendment (effective 28 December 2013)
Administrative regulations	• Measures for the Administration of Listed Corporation Information Disclosure • Interim Measures for Administration of Treasury Bonds of the People's Republic of China implemented since 1997 • Measures for the Administration of Bond Transactions in the National Inter-Bank Bond Market (全国银行间债券市场债券交易管理办法), 2000 • Regulations on the Administration of the Bond Outright Repo in the Inter-Bank Bond Market (全国銀行间债券市场债券回購協議業務管理規定), 2004 • Measures for Administration of Commercial Papers of Securities Companies, 2004 • Measures for the Administration of the Issuance of Financial Bonds in the National Inter-Bank Bond Market, 2005 • Pilot Administrative Measures for the Securitization of Credit Assets (信贷资产证券化试点管理办法), 2005 • Regulations on the Administration of the Forward Transactions of Bonds in the National Inter-Bank Bond Market (在全国銀行间债券市场管理债券遠期交易的规定), 2005 • Provisions for Administrating National Inter-Bank Bond Market Makers, 2007 No.1 • Provisions on the Administration of Market Makers in the National Inter-Bank Bond Market (全国银行间债券市场做市商管理规定), 2007

continued on next page

Table A3 *continued*

	• Administrative Measures for the Disclosure of Information of Listed Companies, 2007 • Administrative Measures for Debt Financing Instruments of Non-Financial Enterprises in the Inter-Bank Bond Market (银行间债券市场非金融企业债务融资工具管理办法), 2008 No.1 PBOC (effective 15 April 2008) • Administrative Measures for the Registration, Depository and Settlement of Bonds in the Inter-Bank Bond Market (银行间债券市场债券登记托管结算管理办法), 2009 No.1 PBOC • Administrative Rules on Forward Bond Transactions in the National Inter-Bank Bond Market • Regulation on Treasury Bonds of the People's Republic of China implemented since 1992 and revised in 2011 • Regulations on the Administration of Enterprise (Corporate) Bonds (企业债券管理条例 (2011修订)), 2011 Revision (effective 8 January 2011) • Opinions of the General Office of the State Council on Further Strengthening the Work of Protection of the Legitimate Rights and Interests of Minority Investors in the Capital Markets (国务院办公厅关于进一步加强资本市场中小投资者合法权益保护工作的意见) (effective 25 December 2013) • Notice of the General Office of the State Council on Further Strengthening Protection of the Lawful Rights of Small Investors in Capital Markets (Title Only) (国务院办公厅关于进一步加强资本市场中小投资者合法权益保护工作的意见 (标题翻译)) (effective 25 December 2013) • Opinions of the State Council on Further Promotion of Healthy Development of Capital Markets (国务院关于进一步促进资本市场健康发展的若干意见) (effective 8 May 2014) • Interim Regulation on Enterprise Information Disclosure (企业信息公示暂行条例) (effective 7 August 2014) • Guidelines for Bidding in Issuance of Enterprise Bonds (Interim) (国家发展和改革委员会财政金融司发布 企业债券招标发行业务指引 (暂行)), implemented since 2014 • Guidelines for Book Building in Issuance of Enterprise Bonds (Interim) (国家发展和改革委员会财政金融司发布企业债券簿记建档发行业务指引 (暂行)), implemented since 2014 • Administrative Measures for the Issuance and Trading of Corporate Bonds (公司债券发行与交易管理办法) (effective 15 January 2015) • Interim Measures for the Administration of Mutual Bond Market Access between Mainland China and Hong Kong SAR (内地与香港债券市场互联互通合作管理暂行办法), 2017 No.1 • Administrative Measures for OTC Business of National Inter-Bank Bond Market, 2016 • Measures for the Administration of Securities Registration and Clearing (证券登记结算管理办法 (2017修改)), 2017 Amendment (effective 7 December 2017) • Interim Measures for the Administration on Bonds Issued by Overseas Issuers on the National Inter-Bank Bond Market (全国银行间债券市场境外机构债券发行管理暂行办法) (effective 8 September 2018)
Departmental rules	• Administrative Measures for the Cross-Market Transfer of Government Bonds (财政部关于印发《国债跨市场转托管业务管理办法》的通知, MOF [2003] 1025号), 2003 • Regulation of the People's Republic of China on Foreign Exchange Administration (中华人民共和国外汇管理条例 (2008修订)), 2008 Revision (effective 5 August 2008) • Notice of the Ministry of Finance, the People's Bank of China, and the China Securities Regulatory Commission on Carrying out the Pilot Program of Pre-issuance of Treasury Bonds (财政部、中国人民银行、中国证券监督管理委员会关于开展国债预发行试点的通知) (effective 13 March 2013)

continued on next page

Table A3 *continued*

	• Notice of the Ministry of Finance, the People's Bank of China and the China Banking Regulatory Commission on Matters concerning the Issue of Local Government Bonds in the Form of Private Placement in 2015 (财政部、中国人民银行、中国银行业监督管理委员会关于2015年采用定向承销方式发行地方政府债券有关事宜的通知) (effective 15 May 2015) • Notice of the General Office of the National Development and Reform Commission and the General Office of the Ministry of Finance on Further Strengthening the Enterprise (Corporate) Bonds' Capacity of Serving the Real Economy and Strictly Preventing Local Debt Risks (国家发展改革委办公厅、财政部办公厅关于进一步增强企业债券服务实体经济能力严格防范地方债务风险的通知) (effective 8 February 2018) Related to Panda Bonds: • Joint Announcement by the PBOC and MOF [2018] No. 16 (中国人民银行 财政部公告〔2018〕第16号) on the Interim Measures for the Administration of Bonds Issued by the Overseas Issuers on the National Inter-Bank Bond Market (全国银行间债券市场境外机构债券发行管理暂行办法), 8 September 2018
Self-regulatory rules, industry provisions, and business rules	Related to Registration and Issuance of Debt Financing Instruments of Non-Financial Enterprises (all by NAFMII): • Rules for the Registration and Issuance of Debt Financing Instruments of Non-Financial Enterprises (非金融企业债务融资工具注册发行规则) in Inter-Bank Bond Market, 2016 version, revised on 6 November 2015 • Rules and Procedures for the Registration of Debt Financing Instruments of Non-Financial Enterprises for Public Offering (银行间债券市场非金融企业债务融资工具注册工作规程), 2020 version, revised on 16 April 2020 (effective 1 July 2020) • System of Registration Documents and Forms for Non-Financial Enterprises Publicly Offering Debt Financing Instruments (非金融企业债务融资工具公开发行注册文件表格体系), 2020 version, revised on 16 April 2020 (effective 1 July 2020) • Rules for Information Disclosure on Debt Financing Instruments of Non-Financial Enterprises in the Inter-Bank Bond Market (银行间债券市场非金融企业债务融资工具信息披露规则), revised on 18 December 2017 Related to Private Placement of Debt Financing Instruments of Non-Financial Enterprises (all by NAFMII): • Rules for Private Placement of Debt Financing Instruments of Non-Financial Enterprises in the Inter-Bank Bond Market (银行间债券市场非金融企业债务融资工具非公开定向发行规则), 29 April 2011 No. 6 　附件1：Private Placement Instruments' Investor Confirmation Letter (Model Sample) (定向工具投资人确认函 (示范样本)) 　附件2：List of Private Placement Instruments Issuance Registration Materials (非公开定向发行注册材料清单) • Registration Documents and Forms for Privately Placed Non-Financial Enterprises Debt Financing Instruments, 2020 version, revised on 16 April 2020 (effective 1 July 2020) • Private Placement Agreement for Debt Financing Instruments, 2020 version, revised on 16 April 2020 (effective 1 July 2020) • Provisions for the Selection of Specialized Institutional Investors of Private Placement Notes (定向债务融资工具专项机构投资人遴选细则), 26 November 2015 • List of the Specialized Institutional Investors of Private Placement Notes (定向债务融资工具专项机构投资人名单), 26 November 2015 　Annex 1: Investor Confirmation Letter for the Directional Tool (sample demo) 　Annex 2: List of Private Placement Registration Materials

continued on next page

Table A3 *continued*

	<ul><li>Guidelines for the Prospectus for Debt Financing Instruments of Non-Financial Enterprises in the Inter-Bank Bond Market (银行间债券市场非金融企业债务融资工具募集说明书指引), 26 December 2012</li><li>Guidelines for the Due Diligence for Debt Financing Instruments of Non-Financial Enterprises in the Inter-Bank Bond Market (银行间债券市场非金融企业债务融资工具尽职调查指引)</li><li>Guidelines on the Issuance Standards of Debt Financing Instruments of Non-Financial Enterprises in the Interbank Market (银行间市场非金融企业债务融资工具发行规范指引)</li><li>Rules for Intermediary Services for Debt Financing Instruments of Non-Financial Enterprises in the Inter-Bank Bond Market (银行间债券市场非金融企业债务融资工具中介服务规则)</li><li>Code of Conduct for Underwriting Staff of Debt Financing Instruments of Non-Financial Enterprises in the Inter-Bank Bond Market (银行间债券市场非金融企业债务融资工具承销人员行为守则)</li><li>Guidelines for Valuation of Debt Financing Instruments of Non-Financial Enterprises in the Inter-Bank Bond Market (Trial) (银行间债券市场非金融企业债务融资工具定价估值工作指引(试行))</li><li>Administrative Rules on Registration Experts of Debt Financing Instruments of Non-Financial Enterprises in the Inter-Bank Bond Market (银行间债券市场非金融企业债务融资工具注册专家管理办法)</li><li>Model Underwriting Agreement for Debt Financing Instruments of Non-Financial Enterprises in the Inter-Bank Bond Market (银行间债券市场非金融企业债务融资工具承销协议文本)</li><li>Model Underwriter Syndicate Agreement for Debt Financing Instruments of Non-Financial Enterprises in the Inter-Bank Bond Market (银行间债券市场非金融企业债务融资工具承销团协议文本)</li><li>Guidelines for Book-Building Issuance of Debt Financing Instruments of Non-Financial Enterprises (非金融企业债务融资工具簿记建档发行规范指引)</li><li>Rules and Procedures for Centralized Book-Building for Debt Financing Instruments of Non-Financial Enterprises (非金融企业债务融资工具集中簿记建档业务操作规程)</li><li>Rules and Procedures for Site Survey relating Debt Financing Instruments of Non-Financial Enterprises in the Inter-Bank Bond Market (银行间债券市场非金融企业债务融资工具现场调查工作规程)</li><li>Market Self-Disciplinary Rules relating to Debt Financing Instruments of Non-Financial Enterprises (非金融企业债务融资工具市场自律处分规则)</li><li>Guidelines on the Issuance of Project Revenue Notes of Non-Financial Enterprises in the Inter-Bank Bond Market (银行间债券市场非金融企业项目收益票据业务指引)</li><li>Guidelines on the Issuance of Commercial Papers of Non-Financial Enterprises in the Inter-Bank Bond Market (银行间债券市场非金融企业短期融资券业务指引), 16 April 2008</li><li>Rules and Procedures for Super Short-Term Commercial Paper Business of Non-Financial Enterprises in the Inter-Bank Bond Market (Trial) (银行间债券市场非金融企业超短期融资券业务规程(试行)), 21 December 2010</li><li>Guidelines on the Issuance of Medium-Term Notes of Non-Financial Enterprises in the Inter-Bank Bond Market (银行间债券市场非金融企业中期票据业务指引)</li><li>Guidelines on the Issuance of Collective Notes of Non-Financial SMEs in the Inter-Bank Bond Market (银行间债券市场中小非金融企业集合票据业务指引)</li><li>Rules for the Pilot Program of Interbank Market Credit Risk Mitigation Instruments (银行间市场信用风险缓释工具试点业务规则)</li><li>Guidelines for the Issuance of Credit Risk Mitigation Agreement (信用风险缓释合约业务指引)</li><li>Guidelines on the Issuance of Credit-Linked Notes (信用联结票据业务指引)</li></ul>

continued on next page

Table A3 *continued*

• Guidelines on Asset-Backed Notes of Non-Financial Enterprises in the Inter-Bank Bond Market (Revised) (银行间债券市场非金融企业资产支持票据指引), 29 August 2017 • Disclosure Guidelines for Asset-Backed Securities Derived from Personal Loans (Trial) (个人消费贷款资产支持证券信息披露指引(试行)) • Model Investor Protection Clauses (投资人保护条款范例) • Information Disclosure Form for Urban Infrastructure Construction Enterprises (城市基础设施建设类企业信息披露表) • Self-Regulatory Rules for Bond Trading in the Inter-Bank Bond Market (银行间债券市场债券交易自律规则) • Master Agreement for Bond Repurchase in China's Interbank Market (中国银行间市场债券回购交易主协议), 2013 Related to Panda Bonds (by NAFMII): • Guidelines on Debt Financing Instruments of Overseas Non-Financial Enterprises (for Trial Implementation) (境外非金融企业债务融资工具业务指引(试行)), 17 January 2019 Related to Default and Risk Disposal/Meeting of Holders/Bond Trustee (by NAFMII): • Guidelines for Default and Risk Disposal on Debt Financing Instruments of Non-Financial Enterprises in the Inter-Bank Bond Market (银行间债券市场非金融企业债务融资工具违约及风险处置指南), 27 December 2019 • Meeting Rules and Procedures for Holders of Debt Financing Instruments of Non-Financial Enterprises in the Inter-Bank Bond Market (revised), (银行间债券市场非金融企业债务融资工具持有人会议规程)(修订稿), 27 December 2019 (effective 1 July 2020) • Guidelines for Bond Trustee Business of Non-Financial Enterprise Debt Financing Instruments in the Inter-Bank Bond Market (for Trial Implementation) (银行间债券市场非金融企业债务融资工具受托管理人业务指引(试行)), 27 December 2019 (effective 1 July 2020)

CIBM = China Inter-Bank Bond Market, CSRC = China Securities Regulatory Commission, MOF = Ministry of Finance, NAFMII = National Association of Financial Market Institutional Investors, OTC = over-the-counter, PBOC = People's Bank of China, SAFE = State Administration of Foreign Exchange, SMEs = small and medium-sized enterprise.
Sources: ASEAN+3 Bond Market Forum Sub-Forum 1 team; China Law Info Co., Ltd. www.lawinfochina.com.

Appendix 4
Glossary of Technical Terms

asset management plan	Term used in the CIBM to describe a collective investment vehicle managed by direct market participants
basic-level enterprise	Term used by NAFMII as categorization of issuers aiming for registration of a debt financing instrument that do not qualify as mature enterprises
Bond Connect	Scheme that allows CMU account holders in Hong Kong, China, to participate in the CIBM through the CMU by using Bloomberg or TradeWeb as a conduit to access trading in CFETS
bond settlement agent	Term used in regulations and rules for a commercial bank that holds a Type A license and is able trade and safekeep debt financing instruments for investors
bond trustee	Formalized concept to assume fiduciary duties in the context of nonfinancial enterprise debt financing instruments
book runner	Party appointed by the issuer to keep track of and ensure a fair book-building process; typically the lead underwriter
business tax	Tax levied on transactions and income derived in financial services prior to 1 May 2016; replaced by a value-added tax
cash bond	Describes the outright trading of debt instruments in contrast to bond forwards or repo transactions
centralized book-building system	Reference to the book-building platform for debt financing instruments mandated by NAFMII and operated by CFAE
CIBM Direct	Defined market access scheme into the CIBM for foreign investors, administered by the PBOC
ChinaBond	English designation for CCDC
Chinamoney	English designation for CFETS
Caishui (财税)	Term often referenced in the public domain with regard to tax administration publications; equivalent to a circular
convener	Appointed by the issuer to call for meetings of debt financing instrument holders; typically the lead underwriter
corporate bond	Debt securities issued under provisions of the Company Law
cross-market transfer	Transfer of debt financing instruments for trading between the market segments of the China bond market
debt financing instrument	Term used in the CIBM for fixed-income instruments not issued under the provisions of the Securities Law

designated institutional investors	Specific investors identified by the issuer and (lead) underwriter for private placement of a debt financing instrument as suitable to market to, offer, and sell said debt financing instrument; equivalent in the CIBM to a professional investor concept
dual-listed	Market term for (enterprise) bonds that are registered in the CIBM and also listed on the exchange market; strictly speaking, there is no listing concept in the CIBM
enterprise	Term used in law and regulations for a company
enterprise bond	Debt financing instruments issued by central government-related agencies, SOEs, or state-owned holding companies affiliated with NDRC
(local) enterprise collective bond	Debt financing instrument issued by a group of local or regional enterprises
financial bond	Term for debt financing instrument issued by a financial institution
free trade zone bonds	Bonds issued in or by an issuer domiciled in one of the designated free trade zones in the PRC
general investors	Term used for retail investors or those that do not fall under the private placement investors in the CIBM
interbank market	Traditional cash funding and lending market between financial institutions and/or the central bank
lead underwriter	Underwriter requiring a separate license from NAFMII to fulfill principal underwriting role, subject to specific eligibility criteria
market maker	Term used to designate government bond auction participants and quotation providers in the CIBM
measures	Term used for administrative regulations of the MOF or the PBOC and other authorities
medium-term notes	Term used in the CIBM specifically for any debt financing instruments issued in tranches with a maturity of more than 1 year
mature enterprise	Term used by NAFMII as categorization of issuers aiming for registration of a debt financing instrument that fulfill certain criteria on size, market recognition, and issuance history
non-bank financial institution	Term used in the CIBM for a company or corporation that is engaging in financial business other than a licensed financial institution, such as leasing
nonfinancial enterprise	Term used in the CIBM for a company or corporation other than a financial institution
nonfinancial enterprise debt financing instrument	Instruments subject to registration with NAFMII
nonpublic placement	Term used to describe what is effectively a private placement in the CIBM
Northbound Trading	Refers to access to the CIBM via Bond Connect by investors with an account at the CMU in Hong Kong, China

offering circular	Key disclosure document in the CIBM for Panda bonds issued via offerings other than private placements; in the CIBM, though not often used as a term, considered equivalent to prospectus
offering memorandum	Issuance and disclosure documentation for all private placements including Private Placement Notes and Panda bonds issued via private placement and targeted at both SIIs and DIIs
Onshore Participating Dealer	Official term for a trading participant in CFETS servicing a nonresident investor accessing the CIBM via Bond Connect
ordinary investors	Alternative term used to describe public (i.e., nonprofessional) investors, including retail investors
outright repo	Repo transaction in which debt securities are sold and bought back
overseas financial institutions	Term used in administrative regulations for issuers of Panda bonds that are nonresident financial institutions
Panda bond	Term used to denote bond issued by nonresident issuers in the CNY-denominated domestic bond market
pledged repo	Repo form where underlying debt financing instruments are lent to the counterparty in return for cash for the term of the trade
policy (bank) financial bond	Debt financial instruments or debt securities issued by the three policy banks
post-registration manager	Market term used for the responsible institution acting as representative of the nonresident issuer of Panda bonds; typically the lead manager or lead underwriter
primary dealer	Term specifically used in the CIBM for financial institutions eligible to participate in PBOC open market operation
private placement	Market term for nonpublic placement, as used in some translations of regulations
private placement agreement	Issuance and disclosure documentation for private placement notes and Panda bonds issued via private placement and only targeted at DIIs
private placement investor	Alternative name for a DII
private placement offering memorandum	Market practice designation for key disclosure document in the CIBM for a private placement of Panda bonds and private placement notes targeted at both SIIs and DIIs
prospectus	Key disclosure document in the CIBM for public offerings (of debt financing instruments by resident issuers); in the CIBM, seen as synonymous with an offering circular
public investors	Synonym for general investors including retail investors; in the absence of an official definition, those that do not fall under the definition of a DII, SII, or institutional investor at large
public offering	Public issuance of debt financing instruments to public investors in the CIBM with full disclosure under the supervision of the PBOC and registration with NAFMII

Qualified Foreign Institutional Investors	Market access scheme for nonresident investors to access the PRC capital market, upon approval from CSRC and SAFE
Qualified Overseas Institutional Investors	Collective term for foreign institutional participants who may directly access the CIBM with approval from the PBOC
registration (with CSD)	Action of depositing a new debt financing instrument into the book-entry system of CCDC or SHCH, by the issuer
registration (with PBOC)	Action of foreign investors wishing to access the CIBM via CIBM Direct; represents submission of registration form without need for approval
Registration Committee	Group of registration professionals at NAFMII who assess the registration application based on a preliminary review (also, the Registration Expert Professional Committee)
registration with NAFMII	Term used for registration of issuance of debt financing instruments of nonfinancial enterprises in the CIBM
Renminbi Qualified Foreign Institutional Investors	Market access scheme for nonresident investors who maintain Chinese renminbi balances to access the PRC capital market, upon approval from CSRC and SAFE
repo	Standard short-form for repurchase agreement
scheme manager	Securities company or asset management firm managing the packaging of ABS, their issuance, and payment flows
short-term notes	Debt securities issued in the exchange bond market only by securities companies (in nature similar to commercial paper)
Southbound Trading	Refers to access for investors in the China bond or capital market to the capital market segments in Hong Kong, China
specialized institutional investors	Specific investors pre-identified by NAFMII as suitable to market to, offer, and sell debt financing instruments issued via private placements; equivalent in the CIBM to a professional investor concept
suggestion letter	Letter from NAFMII indicating incomplete or insufficient registration documents for debt financing instruments
track rating	Refers to the ongoing monitoring (tracking) of the credit rating of an issuer and/or an instrument during its lifecycle by a CRA
underwriter	Institution licensed by NAFMII to carry out underwriting business in the CIBM; specific eligibility criteria apply
value-added tax	Consumption tax levied on transactions and income derived in the financial services from 1 May 2016, replacing the business tax

Source: ASEAN+3 Bond Market Forum Sub-Forum 1 team.

Appendix 5
Chinese Technical Terms
and Their Interpretations

This list of Chinese technical terms and their interpretations for the bond market relative to typical technical terms in English represent the reference framework for ABMF when compiling this bond market guide. The terms and interpretations were discussed with and agreed to by the regulatory bodies and market institutions in the CIBM; they may differ from terms used in other bond market segments in the PRC.

At the same time, for most domestic issuances, there is no English documentation so it is acknowledged that these English terms may rarely appear in practice other than for Panda bonds or where an issuer is a subsidiary or entity of an international corporation. In particular, the Chinese expressions and characters for key disclosure documentation do not have the distinctions typically associated with corresponding documents and terms in international practice. Hence, the list below is compiled to give international readers only a general idea of the use of terminology in market practice in the CIBM.

For the definition of some of the individual terms, please see the glossary section in Appendix 4.

资产支持证券	asset-backed securities
资产支持票据	asset-backed notes
资产证券化	asset securitization
竞价	bidding
大宗交易	block trading
债券违约	bond default
银行间债券市场结算代理人	bond settlement agent
受托管理人	bond trustee
受托管理协议	bond trustee agreement
簿记询价	book-building (process)
违约	breach of contract (in context of event of default)
集合企业债	(local enterprises) collective bond(s)
短期融资券	commercial paper (short-term financing bill[s])
召集人	convener
公司债	corporate bond
信贷资产支持证券	credit asset-backed securities
信贷资产证券化	credit asset securitization
资信评级	credit rating

资信评级机构	credit rating agency
债务融资工具	debt financing instrument(s)
非金融企业债务融资工具持有人会议	debt financing instrument holders meeting or meeting of debt financing instrument holders
非公开定向发行方式发行的债务融资工具	debt financing instrument(s) issued via a private placement method
违约	default
特定机构投资人	designated institutional investor
尽职调查	due diligence
企业债	enterprise bond(s)
集合企业债	enterprise collective bond(s)
金融债	financial bond(s)
绿色债务融资工具	green debt financing instrument(s)
信息披露义务	information disclosure obligations
地方政府债	local government bond
主承销商	lead underwriter
银行间债券市场做市商	market maker
流通市值	market value
重大事项	material event(s)
中期票据	medium-term notes
协议大宗交易	negotiated block trading
协议大宗交易方式	negotiated block trading method
协议交易	negotiated trade
募集说明书	offering circular (for Panda bond offerings other than private placements)
发行文件	offering document or issuance document (prospectus, offering circular, or offering memorandum)
点击成交	one-click trading
普通投资者	ordinary investor
熊猫债	Panda bond
托管面值	par value
收费主体	payee (here receiver of fees)
预审核	preliminary review
债券上市预审核	preliminary review of bond listing
非公开定向债务融资工具	privately placed debt financing instrument(s)
非公开定向发行	private placement
定向发行协议	private placement agreement
定向工具	private placement instrument(s)
定向工具	private placement notes

定向投资人	private placement investor(s)
定向发行协议	private placement offering memorandum (private placements of Panda bonds, and domestic PPN issuances targeted only at DIIs)
定向募集说明书	private placement offering memorandum (for PPN issuances targeted at both SIIs and DIIs)
专业投资者	professional investor
项目收益票据	project income notes
募集说明书	prospectus (for public offerings of debt financing instruments)
公众投资者	public investor
公开发行公司债券	publicly offered corporate bonds
合格投资者中的机构投资者/合格机构投资者	Qualified Institutional Investors
报价	quotation
跟踪评级	rating tracking
注册	registration (for issuance with NAFMII)
登记	registration (for deposit with CCDC or SHCH)
注册办公室	registration office
注册会议	registration committee or registration committee meeting
短期债	short-term notes (similar to commercial paper)
中小企业集合票据	SME collective notes
专项机构投资人	specialized institutional investors
标准化票据	standardized notes
超短期融资券	super short-term commercial paper (super short-term financing bill[s])
(债务工具)期限	tenor
国债	Treasury bond
承销机构	underwriter
承销	underwriting
价值	value

Sources: Compiled by ASEAN+3 Bond Market Forum (ABMF) Sub-Forum 1 team from public domain sources and ABMF contributors.